Consulting on the Inside

An Internal Consultant's

Guide to Living and Working

Inside Organizations

Beverly Scott

ASTD Press is an internationally renowned source of insightful and practical information on workplace learning and performance topics, including training basics, evaluation and return-on-investment (ROI), instructional systems development (ISD), e-learning, leadership, and career development.

Ordering information: Books published by ASTD Press can be purchased by visiting our Website at store.astd.org or by calling 800.628.2783 or 703.683.8100.

Library of Congress Control Number: 99-67866

ISBN-10: 1-56286-131-X
ISBN-13: 978-1-56286-131-5

Printed by Victor Graphics, Inc. Baltimore, MD
www.victorgraphics.com

Contents

"**H**ow can I get access to the senior vice president?"

"What do I do when the boss of my client wants to come to the team off site?"

"I am no longer objective about the direction of the company. Should we part ways?"

"The sponsor of the project expects certain results; unfortunately, they are not the same results that my boss demands. What should I do?"

These questions and more poured forth from the internal consultants who were attending the forum I was leading. As I responded to the questions, I realized that my years of internal consulting experience—largely gained through trial and error—offered perspective and alternatives that would be valuable to new or less experienced internal consultants.

An idea began to crystallize: Develop a book that offers practical advice, tips, and step-by-step guidance for internal consultants—those who live inside their client organizations. Who are these internal consultants? They are often staff members who serve other departments in their organizations with complex expertise that is not easily learned by others, according to Henning's 1997 book, *The Future of Staff Groups*. These professionals are trainers, career-development specialists, employee developers, human performance improvement (HPI) consultants, change management specialists, or OD professionals. Like external consultants, they help their client organizations address problems and improve business results. This book is for them.

Because I wanted to offer a broad scope of advice and wisdom, I turned to other experienced internal consultants. I conducted over 50 interviews with current and former internal consultants whose "inside" experience ranges from a few years to long careers spanning 25 years or more. They define themselves in a variety of ways: OD consultants, HPI specialists, HRD professionals, and change management leaders. They also offer a range of perspectives; some are entry-level novices, some are master consultants who work with senior executives, and others are members of the executive team.

Their wisdom and advice enrich this book. Their stories capture the experience of living inside the organization. Their narratives are, in some cases, detailed descriptions of interventions, and others are tidbits of advice. Some of them generously shared the models and tools that they use in their work. These serve as practical examples of the work and accomplishments of internal consultants.

Most of the internal consultants interviewed for this book were comfortable acknowledging their positions and the companies for which they work. Some did not want to be quoted directly, and others did not identify their companies to protect former colleagues and clients. For these reasons, the reader will find that some quotations are not attributed to a particular person, and, in other places, the internal consultant's position or company affiliation is not identified.

The book is organized into three sections. Section One, "On the Inside," focuses on the challenges and opportunities for internal consultants. Chapter 1 describes the paradox of working at the margins of the organization even though the consultant belongs to the organization and possesses an insider's knowledge of people, culture, and the business. Chapter 2 explores the internal consultant's challenges of navigating the risky shoals of organizational politics and the hierarchy from a middle stance, often through the HR department. Chapter 3 outlines the distinctions between process and expert consultation, describes the need for the internal consultant to provide both types of consulting, and offers guidance in choosing an appropriate role. Chapter 4 identifies the opportunities for internal consultants as their organizations face unpredictable, tumultuous, fast-paced business environments and summarizes ideas and tools to use into the 21st century.

Section 2, "Achieving Success," offers advice to overcome roadblocks from within the organization and from within oneself, as well as what it takes to excel as an internal consultant. Chapter 5 offers suggestions to address successfully the difficulties of working in partnership with external consulting firms or the internal HR function. The chapter also recommends ways to "market" internal consulting services inside the enterprise and suggests means for coping with difficult clients. Chapter 6 provides advice to overcome the hurdles that internal consultants sometimes place in their own paths, such as anxiety and self doubt, lack of confidence in dealing with authority, reluctance to say "no," and heavy workloads with many clients. Chapter 7 discusses the importance of self-knowledge, continued learning, and personal qualities that form the bedrock of successful internal consulting.

Section 3, "The Consulting Process: A Step-by-Step Guide for Internal Consultants," presents an eight-phase consulting process. Chapters 8 through 15 introduce these phases and describe them in detail with checklists, models, and tools to provide a detailed, practical guide for new internal consultants and useful tips for more experienced consultants, as well.

Chapter 16 sums up the challenges and opportunities of living inside the organization. Finally, a section entitled "For Further Reading" lists resources that internal consultants may wish to add to their bookshelves. These publications were not cited in the book but have proven helpful to me over the years.

With the emphasis on HPI and performance consulting and the need for solid advice in managing the pace of change, this book will be relevant to a wide group of professionals. It is my hope that this book—a compilation of experience and advice from many internal consultants—will guide these professionals who provide vital expertise to their organizations as they weather and prosper in today's competitive, global environment.

It is impossible to acknowledge the many individuals who shaped the creation of this book. I appreciate the many colleagues and mentors, who, over the years of my career, guided me, offered insightful feedback, and influenced my consulting practice. In particular, I thank the colleagues and clients with whom I shared challenges, successes, and learning as an internal consultant at Bendix Corporation and at McKesson Corporation. The current and former internal consultants, who shared their wisdom and experience and gave me samples of their tools, models, and interventions, added richness and diverse perspectives for this book. I am deeply grateful for their contributions and their time. Several colleagues reviewed and critiqued my manuscript: Kim Barnes, Jack Loftis, Marilyn Blair, Ashmore, John Dopp, Sandra Florstedt, and Pam Daniels. Their suggestions significantly improved the book. The acquisitions editor for the American Society for Training & Development, Mark Morrow, encouraged me and made valuable recommendations. Most important, I thank my family—Courtney, Darby, and Kim—for putting up with my long days and giving me the emotional support to persevere.

Bev Scott
San Francisco, California

Section One:

On the Inside

Chapter 1

The Life of an Internal Consultant

What Is Internal Consulting?

The term *consultant* often raises images of highly paid business consultants from large firms brought in by senior management to address problems that the organization cannot solve. As a result of their outsider status, consultants are often the targets of some good-natured ribbing. One T-shirt proclaims "I'm not unemployed, I'm a consultant!" (Adams). This joke made the rounds too:

Question: What do you call someone who borrows your watch to tell you what time it is?

Answer: A consultant

Of course, others hold more lofty opinions of consulting:

- A consultant is a person in a position to have influence over an individual, group, or organization but who has no direct power to make changes or implement programs (Block 1981).
- A consultant's job is to focus on the larger system and to help smaller units and individuals take a system perspective (Golembiewski 1978).
- Consultants bring passion for the possible and a strong sense of how to help change occur (Hottle 1990).
- Internal consultants are those who work in one part of an organization to help another part (Meislin 1997).
- "Management consultants must be more than experts in their field. They must serve as effective change agents and share accountability with their clients for the ultimate outcome" (Schaffer 1997).
- Consulting is a process by which an individual or a firm assists a client to achieve a stated outcome. The consultant is a specialist who completes the work needed by the client to achieve desired outcomes (Biech 1999).
- The consultant is in the business of helping others succeed, and, although consultants want to succeed in the process, their success is clearly dependent on others (Bellman 1992).

- Consulting is facilitating change or acting as an agent of change (Beckhard 1997).
- Consulting is disturbing the boundaries by the very act of entering the organization (Nevis 1987).
- The internal consultant is one who enables change (Ray 1997).

Essentially, *a consultant uses expertise, influence, and personal skills to facilitate a client-requested change without formal authority to implement recommended actions.* The change solves a problem, improves performance, increases organizational effectiveness, or helps people and organizations learn. Success as a consultant is based on the ability to leverage expertise with honed consulting skills and self-development.

External and internal consultants share many characteristics. Both types of consultants help their clients address problems and improve business results. Both types of consultants have a passion for the wisdom and expertise they bring to the organization and their ability to galvanize clients into action.

Although it is true that many unemployed professionals do make ends meet through contract work, people who succeed as external consultants focus their energy and vision on the long term. External consultants are brought in because they bring wisdom, objectivity, and expertise to help the organization solve a problem (Nevis 1987). Although external consultants do run the risk of becoming a member of the organization in an emotional sense, they generally are immune to many of the risks involved with being on the payroll, reporting through the management hierarchy, following organizational policies and procedures, and adhering to the organization's cultural norms.

The roles played by external and internal consultants are similar in many ways, but consulting "on the inside" is quite different. One former internal consultant suggests, "The difference is a matter of degree, rather than a black-and-white contrast, but the biggest difference is in having a boss!" Some professionals living inside or employed by the organization do not think of themselves as internal consultants. They are often seen as staff serving other departments in their organization with complex expertise that is not easily learned by others (Henning 1997). These professionals are trainers, career-development specialists, employee developers, performance improvement consultants, change management specialists, or OD professionals.

Internal consultants are valuable assets. They provide vital expertise to help their organizations survive today's competitive, global environment. These professionals bring a variety of positive attributes to the organization:

- skill to analyze and design performance improvement strategies
- expertise to train employees and help them develop needed skills
- knowledge to align the human organization with the business strategy

- objective viewpoint
- deep understanding of the process of change
- strong commitment to learning
- passion about their work
- ability to influence and lead others
- accountability to help solve organizational problems.

Internal-External Differences

External consultants get to go home! They don't live here. The pacing is different for them. External consultants can be involved intensely in sweeping change programs and have the energy to do that. I have to pace myself and choose what requires my high energy because everything can't. I need to think about my schedule so I have the energy for those projects that are most demanding.

Internal consultants have the opportunity to do daily follow-up and to see the end of the project. They can build long-term relationships, and they can establish rapport more easily. They are also around when something falls apart. However, external consultants are more successful at some projects. Executives are more likely to hear an idea from an external consultant even if I, as a middle manager, have already suggested a similar idea. Especially at the senior level, it is easier for the external consultant to give feedback. Senior management likes to hear about the issues that are special to them, and they need someone special from outside the system to deal with them.

**Molly Smith-Olsson, team leader,
organization effectiveness, Blue Shield of California**

Living at the Edge

Without a doubt, the internal consultant is a member of the organization. Yet to be effective, an internal consultant must maintain the same distance, objectivity, and neutrality as the external consultant. This unique role means that although the internal consultant is a member of the organization, he or she must stand

Belong or Be Marginal

I found the organization was a "lifer" organization and believed in one for all, all for one. I was confronted with the conflict between the value of marginality versus the value of belonging.

**Roger G. James, president, Gelinas-James, former internal
consultant with Pacific Gas and Electric Company**

outside the organization—at the margin—to gain a neutral view. The internal consultant is constantly working at the edge, disturbing the boundaries, and serving as a bridge between two worlds that have differing values and norms. Finding this balance is difficult and, according to one former internal, can be a great source of conflict.

What It Means to be an Internal Today

Traditionally our role has been to provide whatever support is need-ed, such as a request for a meeting facilitator. Don't advertise or promote. Be seen but not heard. The shift is that OD is no longer agenda-neutral. We have a stance to take with values and culture and how the business is conducted. We are in a position with a systems perspective to see things around the company and to draw attention to patterns that are emerg-ing. I am also a courageous messenger. Am I a whistle blower or am I simply under contract to do what is best for the organization? If I do blow the whis-tle, is my pay influenced? Organization development is being redefined as an agency of positive change—an area of professional practice that can help in a number of areas, such as large-scale change, executive coaching, first-line development, and a source of objectivity for the system. We are being asked to take a stand.

Michael Lindfield, senior OD consultant, Boeing Company

BEING CONGRUENT BUT MARGINAL

Internal consultants must constantly calibrate their positions in the organization. First, they must be congruent with their clients to be acceptable, build relationships, and increase trust. Then they must shift to a more neutral, outsider stance to bring alternative perspectives, hold up the mirror, or introduce new ideas. On one hand, internal consultants are valued for their knowledge and commitment to the organization. On the other hand, internal consultants must be able to take strong advocacy positions despite established trust and relationships built over the years. The challenge for internal consultants is to stay congruent with their client system and still remain marginal.

A Different Role for the Insider

The psychological contract for an internal is qualitatively differ-ent. If something goes wrong, you are still in the system. There is a different mentality if you are committed to the system for a long time. You grow up with people, see them evolve, and know their history, fears, and struggles. There is a level of personal vulnerability that is dif-

ferent. Your clients are also your friends and colleagues. It feels quite different, and you cannot easily walk away.

**Sue Thompson, Thompson Group,
former internal consultant with Levi Strauss & Company**

Internal consultants do have a difficult role to play. They know their clients, their history, and their sensitivities. Often, these clients are colleagues and friends. These relationships are important assets when internal consultants implement necessary organizational interventions. Yet, these relationships can be the internal consultant's Achilles' heel if confidence or trust is damaged or lost, perhaps through an unintentional comment or a thoughtless act. It is surprising how quickly any indiscretion can move through the grapevine and undermine an internal consultant's reputation. Despite this potential pitfall, the internal consultant can offer a useful, holistic perspective. Internal consultants can create and recognize internal connections and encourage one manager to talk to another to link common activities or build support for change initiatives.

COLLUSION

One of the realities of this work is that these professionals often work for the CEO or other senior managers who want to know the "secrets" held by the internal consultant. It is easy to accept the norms or the myths about what is acceptable to say to a senior executive. Internal consultants collude with their clients when they avoid speaking the truth of what they see and become unwilling to risk challenging organizational norms and confronting a senior manager. Remaining unaligned with either management or line employees is a tricky balancing act, especially if the same CEO or senior manager does not want to hear the "truth" from the

Maintaining Objectivity

Internal Journal

Maintaining objectivity and not aligning with any one group become more challenging the longer you stay internal. You can't afford to align too much with top management or be seen as too connected to the first line. You must represent everyone in the organization in the change process.

**Jim Harley, director, organization development,
Westinghouse Electric Company**

employees' perspective. As Sue Blouch, an experienced internal consultant, says, "There is a risk of getting too confluent with the organization. What makes you good as an internal consultant is being different from the core business. It is important to stay differentiated."

Balancing Act

Managing the political reality almost flies in the face of acting with integrity and not compromising your values. But if you can parlay that balance it will make good business sense as you build relationships and collegiality while not succumbing too much to the need to belong. Collaborating, making a contribution, and feeling valued at the same time you maintain autonomy and accountability is not an easy balance.

Internal Journal

Chrissa B. Merron, senior consultant, Concentrics, former internal consultant in the financial industry

INTEGRITY

Maintaining impeccable standards of integrity and confidentiality is critical for internal consultants when communicating with senior management or frontline employees. Internal consultants who lose their outsider perspective become less effective especially if they are unable to be direct and truthful with their peers or senior members of the organization.

The Importance of Integrity

As an internal consultant you see yourself as a resource to the organization. But it takes quite a bit of personal insight and maturity to . . . not be subsumed and collude with the dynamics of the organization. You are constantly walking a line between making trouble and colluding. Sometimes to do an assignment, you need to create some trouble. You have to be able to confront someone about the source of the problem. It takes self-awareness and ethical, political savvy. You need a strong sense of values, and you need to know what you are willing to fight for.

Internal Journal

Monica McGrath, Resources for Leadership, former internal consultant

Because of this need to bring a fresh and honest perspective to their clients, some have suggested that an internal consultant's "shelf life" is limited to four or five years, especially if the internal works closely with his or her clients. One way to extend the internal consultant's shelf life is to maintain a strong network of external colleagues who can provide alternative perspectives.

Author's Perspective

My own experience as an internal consultant has validated the perspectives outlined here. After spending almost 15 years in one organization, I found that balancing commitment and objectivity is a continuous challenge. I brought a more objective, outside perspective to my clients in the field as a member of corporate staff. Even so, at times they were not sure if I was truly neutral, because, in their eyes, I represented a "corporate" point of view. My standards of integrity and confidentiality led me to clarify my role and let my clients know if I carried "baggage," biases, or opinions. To be able to divulge this personal information required that I be honest with myself, a goal that I did not always achieve. On occasion, when I recognized that I was pushing an agenda, I acknowledged it or went back and cleaned it up. I know in retrospect, however, that there were times when I was unaware of my own position.

My neutral, objective role became even more complicated when I worked with corporate staff departments or when I was mandated to lead a project and carry it throughout the organization. These circumstances heightened the importance of maintaining my standards of integrity regarding my role, my biases, and my charter. To remain marginal over several years and to live within an organization is a real challenge.

Summing Up and Looking Ahead

Although internal and external consultants share many characteristics, life on the inside means internal consultants use their expertise, influence, and personal skills to serve their own organizations. They make a valuable contribution when they are able to balance their commitment and intimate knowledge from inside the organization with an outsider's fresh perspective. It is a tricky balancing act to leverage carefully built relationships and risk giving direct and truthful feedback to a senior manager. High standards of confidentiality and integrity are also critical; a careless comment or momentary indiscretion can quickly destroy what took years to develop. The requirements for success inside the organization seem paradoxical:

- Operate at the margins, yet gain intimate knowledge of the organization.
- Build strong relationships, yet be willing to confront and speak the truth.
- Be congruent with the client organization, but avoid collusion.

Meeting these paradoxical requirements is necessary for a successful career inside the organization. Internal consultants must navigate the political risks that lurk within the organizational hierarchy and establish their competency and credibility by working backstage and performing multiple roles well. The next chapter will continue to explore the challenges confronting internal consultants as they negotiate rocky organizational shoals.

References

Adams, S., creator of the nationally-syndicated "Dilbert" comic strip.
Beckhard, R. (1997). *Agent of Change: My Life, My Practice.* San Francisco: Jossey-Bass.
Bellman, G.M. (1992). *Getting Things Done When You Are Not in Charge* (Fireside Edition). New York: Simon & Schuster.

Biech, E. (1999). *The Business of Consulting*. San Francisco: Jossey-Bass/Pfeiffer.

Block, P. (1981). *Flawless Consulting: A Guide to Getting Your Expertise Used*. San Diego: Pfeiffer & Co.

Golembiewski, R. (1978)."Managing the Tension Between OD Principles and Political Dynamics." In *The Cutting Edge: Current Theory and Practice in Organization Development*, W. Warner Burke, editor. La Jolla, CA: University Associates.

Henning, J.P. (1997). *The Future of Staff Groups*. San Francisco: Berrett-Koehler Publishers.

Hottle, P.M. (1990). "Inside and Outside: Discoveries Along the Way." *OD Practitioner 22*(1), 3.

Meislin, M. (1997). *The Internal Consultant*. Menlo Park, CA: Crisp Publications.

Nevis, E.C. (1987). *Organizational Consulting*. New York: Gardner Press.

Ray, R.G. (1997, July). "Developing Internal Consultants." *Training & Development,* 32.

Schaffer, R.H. (1997). *High Impact Consulting*. San Francisco: Jossey-Bass.

Chapter 2

Navigating the Organization

Navigating the organization's hierarchy is one of the most critical skills for the internal consultant. The position, reporting relationship, and the reputation of the HR function determine the internal consultant's success or failure. Internal consultants must keep a steady hand on the tiller to ensure that they do not capsize or shipwreck because they did not effectively handle these issues while establishing their reputation for competence.

Politics and the Hierarchy

Despite the best efforts of internal consultants to avoid involvement in organizational politics, it is inevitable that they will be judged by how well they juggle their client's demands and the expectations of their bosses and senior management. Being too closely aligned with a senior client or a political faction can undermine overall credibility. The internal consultant's credibility and access to senior clients depend on both the level of the position and the image of the reporting function.

Many organizations place internal consultants in the middle of the organization and provide a reporting hierarchy through the HR department. Although this positioning solves some problems, it may cause others. If the credibility of the HR function is weak, it can hamper the internal consultant's credibility. However, a strong HR function can be an advantage. Human resource managers can identify performance concerns, development needs, or change issues. By forming partnerships with consulting professionals, the HR function can have a more powerful effect throughout the organization. On the other hand, many internal consultants find it very difficult to work with their peers in HR. Human resource managers sometimes envy the internal consultant's access to senior management or covet the power and influence consultants are perceived to have across organizational boundaries.

Reporting Structure

It depends so much on the organization. In one prior organization, calling the president was no big deal, but in another organization I had to go through my boss. It took more maneuvering through gatekeepers. Your position determines at what level you can work and also influences your overall impact. The stature of the person to whom you report is critical to how you can maneuver and manipulate through the hierarchy. It is helpful to have a manager who has credibility and to have access to key stakeholders without having to get permission. I should not have to call my boss and he, in turn, should not have to call someone else's boss just for me to see a senior manager. That puts you in the position of a junior player instead of a consultant.

Bob Browning, director, Global Career Planning and Development, Colgate-Palmolive Company

Boss-Subordinate Relationship

Balancing the boss-subordinate relationship with the ethics of client confidentiality and neutrality presents a unique challenge for the consultant inside the organization. If strong political camps exist within an organization, the internal consultant may be expected to keep the boss apprised of client maneuvers in other camps. Most bosses expect activity reports and need information to evaluate performance. The ethics of client confidentiality conflict with these expectations. The need for client confidentiality is often misunderstood or not appreciated by an internal consultant's manager. In chapter 9 there is a discussion of how the newly employed internal consultant can negotiate expectations with the boss when the internal consultant is first employed.

Negotiating for Confidentiality

As an internal consultant, you have a boss who gives you raises and evaluates you for promotions. Your boss needs to have an understanding of the internal consultant's role and how it differs from the other positions that report to him. I worked through that issue when I was hired. We spent time discussing confidentiality issues and my need for his confidence and respect. He acknowledged that it made sense. But when I said, "There will be things I can't tell you," he said, "How do I evaluate you?" I replied that he would have to evaluate my relationship with him and get data from the outcomes of projects or interventions. When projects involved him, he would be able to see how others perceived me. He accepted that.

Gerald R. Pieters, EverChange Institute, former internal consultant with Signetics Corporation (now Philips Semiconductor)

The pressure of the hierarchy is also felt in the freedom to refuse a client. When clients make outrageous requests or want unrealistic interventions, internal consultants often feel that they cannot decline. One internal consultant reported that she was asked by her boss to help "fix" a problem manager under the guise of team building. Although the internal consultant believed that it was an impossible setting to address the problem and that it was a problem for executive management to resolve, the internal consultant moved ahead with the intervention. The intervention turned into a disaster, and she ultimately recommended that the problem manager be fired for illegal and immoral behavior.

Walking Out Is Not an Option

When you are internal, you can't say "I'm out of here!" even if you have trepidation about a client or concerns about client resistance and organizational politics. Organizational issues are so often great that they interfere with a clean contract. Unless you have a strong foundation and an agreement to have the last word, you may not have a choice—you may have to work with people you don't respect. It is much more difficult for internal consultants.

Peggy J. Beadle, TEC Detroit, former internal consultant with wholesale distribution industry

Internal Consultant Status

Reporting level and reporting status are two of the most challenging structural barriers to consultant effectiveness inside the organization. Whether the internal consultant reports to a midlevel manager in the HR department or a high-status

The Effect of Reporting Relationships

I have to get approval that wouldn't be necessary if I were an external consultant. Before I can present a proposal to my client, I have to go through my chain of command if the project is related to human resources. Whether I can form a partnership or if it is just an approval process depends upon who is involved.

Laura J. Christenson, director of global organization effectiveness for a pharmaceutical/health-care company

manager, the extent of the internal consultant's impact is related directly to the manager's status and reputation. Unfortunately, many companies have a difficult time establishing the level of the reporting relationship. One former internal consultant, Jan M. Schmuckler, says frankly, "Organizations don't know how to level internal consultants."

Positioning is Key

The hierarchy has a big impact on most internal consultants. Ordinarily, internal consultants are not highly placed—at most they are positioned in the upper middle. It is evident that if the powers-that-be . . . are not supportive, it puts tremendous pressure on the consultant not to follow a certain path. It is hard to be successful because of that. There can be a real positive effect if that upper-level person is supportive. Pressure from above can cause you to lose your impartiality and ability to be truly objective.

Kevin B. Wheeler, Global Learning Resources, former internal consultant with Charles Schwab Corporation

In tall hierarchies, in which status is important, the midlevel consultant's access to high-level managers can be severely restricted. In such status-sensitive organizations, senior managers are sensitive to any action that might contradict their superior position. Consultants who come to solve issues with wisdom or objectivity bring a hint of superiority, seemingly elevating the consultant above the client as Nevis (1987) points out in his Gestalt approach to consulting. Such hints of superiority tend to increase the ambivalence of senior managers working with consultants of lower status.

Sharing controversial information or feedback also poses risks for the internal consultant. Senior managers may confuse open and honest feedback with insubordination. It is risky to tell the emperor that he is wearing no clothes. Even when managers directly ask for feedback, they may not really want to hear it, and the power of senior managers over the internal consultant's position can be very threatening.

Reporting to the Senior Level

Many internal consultants and writers (Varney 1977) request and strongly recommend reporting directly to the senior executive. This way, many troubling status issues can be circumvented. In addition, direct reporting provides some important advantages, including

- access to decision makers
- an opportunity to sit at the table and influence strategy
- a chance to really understand the business issues
- a way to keep the focus on critical alignment issues.

Many who report to senior-level managers use their consulting skills but do not define themselves as internal consultants. They are managers and members of the executive team with opportunities to influence and keep the focus on top organizational issues. Those who do define themselves as consultants and do report to high-level managers view the senior-level managers as their primary clients with the benefits of having organization-wide effects on strategic business issues. When it is not possible to report to a senior-level manager, internal consultants will find it helpful to negotiate access and define their roles when consulting to the senior levels of management.

The Consultant's Own Issues

Internal consultants are like everyone else: They are human and they bring their own "psychological baggage" to their jobs. Such baggage is often referred to as the "shadow side" of one's personality. If internal consultants have fears and anxieties about authority figures, then they will find it hard to take controversial positions with senior management (saying no or delivering bad news). If internal consultants find it difficult to form partnerships or work as team players, then they may not be accepted by their peers. Learning to overcome and manage these shadow issues determines the final success of the internal consultant's work.

Supporting Cast Versus Starring Roles

The internal consultant who has low ego needs and is willing to be a partner and a team player will likely survive and find acceptance. Sometimes clients treat exter-

A Matter of Perception

Internal Journal

External consultants immediately have better leverage and are seen as descending from above with wisdom and special counsel. They are trusted because they have experience outside the system and culture of the organization and, therefore, are not seen as part of the problem. When I was an external consultant, I looked for ways to be congruent with the client system so it would not spit me out like an immune system rejecting a foreign object.

If you are an internal consultant working to correct business problems as a part of that system or organization, you are less likely to be rejected. Nevertheless, you can be seen as part of the dysfunction or disease in the system. There are both blessings and curses for internal and external consultants.

**Diane Foster, Diane Foster & Associates,
former internal consultant with Advanced Micro Devices and
California State Automobile Association**

nal consultants as stars, prophets, or gurus who fly in to perform on the center stage. Internal consultants, in contrast, must often work backstage and be part of the supporting cast. An internal consultant who needs time on the pedestal is more likely to alienate peers, colleagues, and other team members.

External Consultants as Experts

> **Internal Journal**
>
> *It is hard to be a prophet in your own land and to be valued in the same way as an external consultant giving advice. When someone is brought in with great fanfare to do something that you can do even better, it is frustrating. They can say the same things and be heard differently because of the "expert mentality" of the organization.*
>
> **Jan M. Schmuckler, Consultation, former internal consultant with high-technology industry**

In general, external consultants enter the organization with credibility and then must work to build relationships. For internal consultants, the converse is true: They begin with relationships and then must work to gain credibility for their consulting competency.

The Perceptual Difference

> **Internal Journal**
>
> *The difference between internal and external consultants is perceptual: Externals are seen as more competent and bringing a higher set of skills or more experience. The organization undervalues what it has internally and thinks it must go outside for the answers—the outsider has more validity . . . Nevertheless, internal consultants are recognized as knowing the business and can be more relevant in applying their expertise and helping the client achieve business results.*
>
> **Helm Lehmann, author, former OD manager, REI**

Multiple Roles of the Internal Consultant

Generally, internal consultants are expected to take diverse consulting roles in an organization, whereas external consultants have the luxury of choosing the focus of their work based on a proven competency. Here are some of the roles that internal consultants (or external consultants) may be expected to take:

- neutral outsider who facilitates resolution of problems or conflicts within a team
- expert who first analyzes the new skills needed and then designs and delivers a training program
- coach who advises executives or managers on the alignment of the culture with the new business strategy
- task-force leader who leads and advocates a change initiative
- performance improvement specialist who identifies and addresses performance gaps

- change management consultant who guides the steering committee through the change process
- initiator or influencer who spurs action to address an organizational problem.

The Eclectic Internal Consultant

The internal consultant is eclectic. You have to have real breadth and scope to know all the things going on in your profession. You need to know a little about a lot. You pair with external consultants for their specialization, but you also need to know exactly what your system needs. This requires a deep understanding of the business. It is not a problem to be an advocate to make something happen. In fact you don't add enough value as an internal consultant if you limit yourself to process interventions. You should use your insider expertise to make recommendations and to advocate a position.

Nedra Weinstein, Catalyst Consulting Team, former internal consultant with communications industry

The client expectation that a trusted internal consultant handle a variety of requests often leads to internal consultants thinking of themselves as a consulting generalist. Internal consultant Elizabeth Schiff considers herself a "Jill-of-all-trades" because she often serves as trainer, facilitator, coach, advocate, and change agent. The expectation that internal consultants perform multiple roles does provide opportunities for learning new skills and competencies. Nevertheless, these multiple roles require that internal consultants be extremely flexible, skilled in a variety of disciplines, and clear with their clients about which role they are performing. Internal consultants must be realistic about their abilities. The word *no* must be part of the internal consultant's vocabulary if a request is beyond his or her capability.

Internal Consultants as Change Agents

Traditionally, internal consultants, especially those who practice OD, see themselves as change agents; their job is to consult and help plan change initiatives. In today's fast-paced environment, internal consultants are often asked to lead the change initiative. This role puts them in an advocacy position of managing change and challenges their neutral status especially among those who disagree or resist the change process.

Internal Consultant as Leader

I am the enabler, supporter, consultant, sounding board, neutral coach, and facilitator. I am often perceived as a leader for an initiative even though I am acting in partnership with someone in the

organization. I am perceived as the initiator of the project, because I am seen as the leader. I try to turn it over to the line person quickly. If I am perceived as driving it too much, I back off. It's a fine line. The critical piece is maintaining neutrality. I try to represent all views and bring them to the table. I want the group to decide collectively. Even when I am in the position of a project leader, I maintain the role as a facilitator.

Mila N. Baker, system director, learning and organization development, Baptist/St. Vincent's Health System

Leadership in a change initiative also aligns an internal consultant with senior management. This alignment is a doubled-edged sword that can help or hurt the internal consultant's credibility. A failed project or the sudden departure of a manager can leave the internal consultant tainted by any residual dissatisfaction with the organization. Nevertheless, accepting an advocacy role offers the internal consultant the opportunity to provide leadership and carry the project forward to a successful conclusion.

Internal Consultant as Advocate

Internal Journal

I tend to advocate. I am an active player, and I provide leadership for interventions. I am not just a process consultant. Typically, I will suggest how the organization can improve by using tools or models to work through the presenting issues. My bias is to be in advocacy roles. I have a different set of skills from others in the organization, and it is my responsibility to use those skills to help my clients achieve business results. I have to influence, lead, direct, and demonstrate relevance to help achieve their goals. If they had that expertise, they wouldn't need me.

Helm Lehmann, author, former OD manager, REI

The opportunities for internal consultants to take leadership roles are more common because of the demands of today's competitive, fast-paced, global business climate. These business demands lead internal consultants to take a much stronger role in advocating new directions, philosophies, or interventions to support business strategies. As one internal consultant suggests, "The senior team members are the organization's drivers, but they need someone to read the map. When they are turning left, we need to be able to say go back and turn right."

Georgia Ireland (Bergman & Morgan 1996) describes the internal consultant's relationship with the organization thus:

Yes, there's a difference when you work in a place for a long time. You become invested in the health of the organization, its viability and success

. . . It is the only organization that matters to you. You are going to stay there, and you have to live with the results of your efforts and the efforts of the external [consultants] who work with you. When you are on the outside, although it may be true that you bond with an organization, you are truly invested in your own business as a consultant.

If you are a successful [external] consultant, you will have a number of customers who are important to you. You are not focused on only one organization in the same way internal consultants are. If you blow it with one customer, it may be upsetting and economically damaging, but the stakes are not as high as for the internal [consultant].

Internal [consultants] have to live more intensively with what they do because their organization is the only organization they are involved with, and the relationships are deeper. When you are on the inside you get to know people over a long period of time; you build relationships; they know who you are, what you can deliver, what your competencies are, and whether they can trust you or not. You live with that day in and day out. If you violate someone's trust or integrity, you lose your credibility . . . External [consultants] may truly not understand what it's like to feel responsible for an organization and to be perceived by your internal business partners as responsible for protecting the integrity and boundaries of the organization.

Summing Up and Looking Ahead

The first two chapters identified some of the paradoxes and the unique challenges that the consultant must navigate living inside the organization. Avoiding the rocky shoals of organizational politics, meeting a boss's expectations without violating client confidentiality, and establishing open and truthful relationships with senior managers requires a deft hand on the tiller. These issues and practical suggestions will be discussed in subsequent chapters.

The internal consultant's life on the inside is characterized by multiple roles. Chapter 3 explores the tension between expert and process roles. The internal consultant's choice of roles depends on his or her characteristics, the client system, relationships with clients, and the organizational context. Playing multiple roles requires flexibility and the ability to change "costumes" frequently.

References

Bergman, L., and N. Morgan. (1996, Winter). "Interview with Georgia Ireland." *Vision/Action* 15(4), 14.

Nevis, E.C. (1987). *Organizational Consulting*. New York: Gardner Press.

Varney, G.II. (1977). *Organization Development for Managers*. Reading, MA: Addison-Wesley.

Chapter 3

The Role Dilemma: Choosing a Costume

Internal consultants face client expectations and demands from their organizations that require them to change roles like actors changing costumes to play their parts. The challenge is to match the costume—the consultant's role—to the part—the client's needs and the organizational setting. In this chapter we will begin by exploring the dilemmas of taking an expert or a process consultation role. The choice of taking the role of an expert or a process consultant should be based upon the consultant's own characteristics and strengths, the needs of the client and the client system, the consultant-client relationship, and the organization situation.

Selecting the Costume: Expert or Process Consultation

Discussions about consulting roles often reflect the tension between process consulting and technical or expert consulting[1] (Marguilles 1978). Technical consultation, or "expert" consulting as Block (1981) calls it, relies on knowledge and expertise of the consultant to solve the client's problem. The expert approach uses data collection and analysis to determine solutions that are recommended to the client. This is the traditional model of business consulting. Process consulting relies more on the intuitive awareness of the consultant who attends to and observes the emotional, nonverbal, perceptual, and spatial aspects of human behavior. Process consultants help the client understand what is happening, identify solutions, and transfer skills to the client to manage the ongoing process. Their focus is on the energy of the client system and a heightened awareness of the dynamics in the group or organization.

The Process Person

Internal Journal

You are the only person in the organization whose job allows you to take responsibility for process. The focus in business is on fast results and is so intense that everyone needs someone who stands up on the balcony and can reflect what is going on. You are helping people see the process versus a set of events.

Marilyn E. Blair, TeamWork,
former internal consultant with 3Com Corporation

Organizations tend to emphasize analytical, logical, and sequential problem-solving processes. Yet process consulting meets an important need in organizations; it raises the awareness of the energy in the organization and lifts hidden feelings to the surface. Organizations need to be task-focused to achieve results, but too often the emotional effects of decisions and buried conflicts are overlooked. Process consulting validates open communication and commitment to a common purpose.

Bringing a Presence

Internal Journal

I was working with two levels of the organization. I had already done team building with the executive level and was focused on the midlevel. I coached the midlevel managers to present what was wrong between the two levels. I encouraged them to take a fun, creative approach. It did not feel like such a risk to them. I coached them on how to give the message about the organizational impact, as well as the impact on them. I coached the top level on what they might hear, how to react, and the need for some decisions. When it came time for the presentation, the executive vice president came in with protective headgear to ward off the message. It made it humorous. The executives said they were nervous, and the midlevel people said they were too. The executives were taken by how well the "mids" had come together. It all worked! I brought a presence that listened and helped them through the hard information. I asked hard questions, gave them courage, and provided a safe place. I encouraged creativity and fun. I brought a presence that was not there before.

Peggy J. Beadle, TEC Detroit,
former internal consultant with wholesale distribution industry

IT TAKES BOTH

Internal consultants are expected to bring more than their presence, process, and observation skills. All internal and external consultants bring their life experience, perspective, wisdom, expertise, and objectivity to the organization. Moreover, they bring technical competence, expertise beyond consulting skills. In the role of coach or teacher, the consultant helps the clients, teams, or organizations to learn more about themselves, their organizational dynamics, and ways to improve their organizational performance. In these roles, the consultant is combining the expert role and the process role. Expertise may lie in such areas as communication, performance technology, group interaction, or organizational behavior. The consultant's effectiveness as a coach or a teacher is measured by several factors:

- ability to model the behaviors that the consultant is teaching or coaching
- observation of the client's behavior and energy
- attunement to the needs of the clients
- facilitative style in promoting learning.

Whatever the internal consultant's technical expertise, it also requires a highly developed sense of limits. Experienced consultants, such as Jeff Cohen, point out that internal consultants should be careful how far out they are willing to climb on a "skinny branch" without a strong base of competence. The deeper the performance intervention, the more critical it is to have deep levels of expertise and

Adding Value

Internal Journal

Ten years ago I was more process-focused—team building and group dynamics, and so forth. Now I am more business-focused. Maybe it's my maturity or maybe it's the field. My goal is to add value to the business. For example, we were bringing together five departments and the operations manager wanted team building. I asked, "What is the business reason for these groups to work together?" The old process and group-dynamics approach can be just an event that is warm and fuzzy, but the question is how much long-term impact does it have? Solving real business problems develops 'neuron' links within the team.

Linda Schomaker, director, corporate human resources, PG&E Corporation

experience. Although internal consultants may be experts on process, participation, strategy, and change, their most valuable expertise is insider knowledge of the organization. The internal consultant is the expert on critical relationships, political skirmishes, historical ghosts, "skeletons in the organizational closet," and a notion of which causes are worth pursuing.

Using Expertise

Internal Journal

The internal consultant cannot afford not to function as an expert in some areas. We have strong opinions about how an organization should be structured, which people should be moved into or out of leadership roles, the process of change, how acquisitions or downsizing should be done. Those are areas about which we know a great deal. To deny the organization an answer is not helpful.

June E. Delano, director, executive and management education, Eastman Kodak Company

DRIVING FORCE

Internal consultants may also be asked to be both the driving force of an initiative and to guide the process. As the driving force, the internal consultant is focused on implementing change. One internal consultant comments, "When I am an advocate and the driving force, employees cannot accept me as a process-communications person." Is it possible to be both a project leader and a process consultant? The answer is that this is a difficult role to take on successfully. When serving as a project leader, the internal consultant is lifted from a neutral process role and becomes identified strongly with the project's success. Eddie Reynolds suggests, "You need to step out of the consulting role and call yourself something else."

To Explore, Not to Advocate

I have never taken offense at being called the psychologist for the organization. I prefer to help people explore the initiative rather than be an advocate. I have talked a vice president or HR staffer out of having me serve as the advocate. Being clear about this issue with your superiors is very important, and it must be continually revisited. It does depend on where you report—if you are in the office of the president, you may have to be in charge of an initiative. I have never been an advocate. I hold to the role of explore-and-discover using a more therapeutic process.

Marilyn E. Blair, TeamWork, former internal consultant with 3Com Corporation

NEED FOR EXPERTISE

Unfortunately, a real need exists for expertise on change leadership and business and organizational alignment. Business conditions may require that internal consultants offer and take critical leadership roles to drive and implement change initiatives. Internal consultants faced with this situation must ensure that the agreement with the sponsor of the project is clear and based on the belief that the internal consultant's job is to help people accept the initiative. With this permission given, internal consultant Michael Crnobna has a license to "go any time and ask questions that others cannot," because he is not wrapped in the content of the initiative. There is no simple answer, and many internal consultants wrestle with this issue of how to perform in both roles and avoid confusing themselves and their clients.

Conflicting Roles

📖 *Part of my responsibility was to roll out a career development ini-*
Internal *tiative, which I had reviewed but not designed. Supporting the ini-*
Journal *tiative roll-out is hardly a neutral stance. It is being the advance*
person and the warm-up act, not being a consultant. The company has
grown rapidly through acquisition. The feedback from the annual survey
indicated that the employees didn't know the career path and how to get pro-
moted. The initiative was an attempt to answer those questions. I was put in
the position of saying, "Here is your new role and how to make it work." We
were expected to train everyone and advocate the use of the program. The
people in my group did not see it as a fit. They saw it as a corporate roll-out
and basically ignored the whole thing saying, "Not invented here."

Internal consultant with a large consulting firm

Practical Advice for Choosing a Role

The current environment for internal consultants demands that they be able to provide both process and expert consulting. Some situations require one or the other;
others require a blend. How to make a choice? Champion, Kiel, and McLendon
(1990) offer some good advice about choosing an internal consulting role. They
list four considerations, which are discussed in greater detail in the subsections
that follow. They are

- characteristics of the consultant
- characteristics of the client
- the client-consultant relationship
- the organizational situation.

CHARACTERISTICS OF THE CONSULTANT

Self-awareness is a key characteristic of an internal consultant. The internal consultant who is self-aware can clearly define his or her "work" to exploit fully those
strengths and achieve a sense of purpose.

Internal Consulting: My Work

📖 *As an internal organization and management development consul-*
Internal *tant, I deal with the interfaces of people, processes, structures,*
Journal *and systems. I work with individuals and groups, and I describe*
my work as

- *identifying, surfacing, discussing multifaceted issues that surround*
  change

- *developing effective multicultural workplaces*
- *improving processes for effective intra- and intergroup communication, conflict resolution, and cooperation*
- *developing cross-functional and cross-discipline teams.*

I facilitate ways for people to think about and work with issues of power, responsibility, interdependence, independence, and relationships. I help people find ways to get their work done or accomplish goals in ways that build on individual and collective strengths and skills while addressing existing challenges and obstacles. My practice theory consists of the following:

- *consulting within a relationship—a series of meaningful conversations*
- *partnering and "midwifery" of the Reflection, Action, Course Correction model*
- *believing that all of us talking, understanding, and being involved in what matters will get us the best, most-effective outcome: "It's in every one of us to be wise"*
- *thinking and planning from all levels, perspectives, and experiences*
- *borrowing and integrating methodologies from other disciplines and using those that are applicable or relevant to create a shared context*
- *mirroring and confronting tough or difficult issues; mentioning the unmentionable.*
- *avoiding collusion or co-opting*
- *being practical and realistic by considering time and other pressures of the current situation*
- *considering options, choices, and alternatives in relation to existing situation*
- *realizing that both task and process are important and must be balanced.*

I have relied on a variety of resources for my consulting work in the areas of large systems change, strategic thinking, reorganization, and reinvention of processes and leadership development. I have used books and articles from journals, magazines, and other publications to provide conceptual frameworks, to generate other ways of thinking, . . . and to adapt relevant ideas about alternative ways to work some issue based on the readings.

Perviz Randeria, organization and management development consultant, former internal consultant with city government

Here are some important questions that internal consultants must ask and answer honestly:

- What are my interpersonal strengths?
- What is my consulting competency?
- What is my technical expertise?
- How is my expertise relevant to the client?

To answer this final, extremely important question, it is essential for internal consultants to understand that they are *expected* to know the culture, the organization, and the business. The most successful internal consultants position themselves as business partners to their clients. They are well grounded in at least the following aspects of the business:

- knowledge of how the industry and business of the organization operate
- understanding of how the organization generates revenue
- awareness of the competitive challenges to success
- familiarity with the business's strategy, direction, and philosophy
- grasp of core business processes.

If necessary, internal consultants can expand their knowledge base by taking time to learn by asking questions, visiting the front line of the operations, going on customer calls, and studying the financial records of the organization. Internal consultants who are steeped in their business environment can take the next step in understanding and defining their role.

You Have to Know the Business

Internal Journal

An internal consultant has to have thick skin and be tough. You have to be willing to take a stand based on your convictions. You can't waffle. You need to step out of the middle position and take a stand on what is best for the business, your recommendation, and why it fits. You have to know the business or you can't do that well.

Mila N. Baker, system director, learning and organization development, Baptist/St. Vincent's Health System

CHARACTERISTICS OF THE CLIENT

The first step in determining the internal consultant's role in an intervention is defining who the client is and who will make the final decisions for a project. More than one person might be involved in the decision, or perhaps the person with the most "passion" for the project is not the actual sponsor. Moreover, the client and customers might not be same person or group. These "customers," those impacted by the intervention, are frequently referred to as the "client system." In addition, internal consultants may work with a partner from HR or another collaborative function who provides technical expertise or adds a credibility factor to the project. Satisfying all of these people is usually critical to a project's success. The following definitions show how these terms are used in this book.

- *Client:* The person with whom the consultant partners and works closely on a project. The client is usually the person who provides the leadership and decision making for a project. In some cases, however, there are two levels of clients.
- *Primary and secondary clients:* When a senior manager requests a consultant to work with an individual or a unit reporting directly to him or her, the senior manager is the primary client and the direct-reporting individual becomes the secondary client.
- *Sponsor:* Usually a senior-level manager who is the decision maker for a major intervention but who has delegated day-to-day project planning to someone else who is the "client."
- *Client system:* The members of the unit, department, or organization who will be affected by the consulting intervention.

Who is the Client?

Internal Journal

Earlier in my career, I did not really understand what I was being asked to do or what to look at in the dynamics of this situation, which was wired for failure. This was a major systems change and I didn't notice that it was flawed. I was caught in the middle and didn't have the skills to extricate myself. I was asked by midlevel management to lead a meeting, which was set up so that several hundred shop-floor employees could voice, air grievances, and respond to an invitation to be more engaged in decision making. The first things that came out were "Who are you?" and "Why are you representing management?" The meeting had been called, and I showed up. I didn't work with the people. There were already perceptions in the room about my agenda. I was seen as representing one part of the system for the other. I had not built a relationship or asked the question, "Who is the real client?"

Michael Lindfield, senior OD consultant, Boeing Company

Support. Even with successful client-consultant partnerships, it is still imperative to ensure support at the highest possible level and from all of the levels involved in an intervention. One internal consultant argued that if he gets support from the top and the first line, the middle always comes along. Another emphasized how taking the position of only accepting work that moves the company's business forward significantly changed the projects to which the consulting group agreed. A systems approach also requires looking at what changes are needed throughout the organization to support the performance improvement desired.

Support from the Top

We had the total support of the CEO and his top external consultant who was a great intermediary. We used his leverage to get the top management team to go first. It was incredibly powerful. We rolled it out through the hierarchy. A three-ring concept evolved: Get top management on board, use external consultants with a core of knowledge appropriately, and use internal consultants to give credibility and continuity—they will hold it together. We modeled that process throughout the company over five years.

Kevin B. Wheeler, Global Learning Resources, former internal consultant with Charles Schwab Corporation

Involvement of the Client. Many internal consultants refuse projects if the client is not willing to be involved or participate actively in the project. Internal consultants who make this choice invite the client into a partnership that uses the internal consultant's strengths and expertise to fill a void in the client system. This does not mean, however, that an imbalance or sharp division of responsibility exists between the internal consultant and the client. The internal consultant brings skills or a perspective the client does not have but can learn; the internal consultant is not just a "pair of hands" to do the work. The client, in turn, has the responsibility to learn and to provide leadership for the project.

Taking Too Much Responsibility

It was an intervention with an objective of bringing a customer focus to the back office. But it was not successful because I ended up taking too much of the responsibility. I was the driver, and too much depended on me. I took an advocacy and control role. The ownership rested with me, and I couldn't shift it back to the management team. I would do it differently in retrospect. I would coach the senior manager on his sponsorship role.

Former internal consultant with the life insurance industry

Client's Readiness for Change. What is the client's readiness for change? Ignoring the signals of readiness can be a fatal consulting flaw (Schaffer 1997). Change at the personal or organizational level is an inside out process with success rooted in the changes made by individuals. Is there an openness and willingness to learn and try new behaviors or implement new directions? Perhaps part of the system is ready, but deep pockets of resistance remain in others. The internal consultant should explore with the client and members of the client system to determine the level of readiness for the proposed change.

CLIENT-CONSULTANT RELATIONSHIP

Clients have a personal stake in their own work, and they want to be perceived as competent. An internal consultant who comes in to work on a particular problem can potentially threaten the client's sense of competence. In addition, the change required by the client may be painful or perceived as risky. Such risks are hard to take unless the client trusts that the consultant is committed to the client's success and has the client's best interest at heart. The responsibility to make the relationship work rests with the internal consultant.

Trust is Important

I was working on a huge culture-change project. The organization had no prior performance accountability. The sponsor's credibility was on the line. No one really wanted performance accountability. Her trust in me allowed her to listen and make adjustments that made the project more successful . . . I was able to add extra time because of the trust I had developed. An external would have had a more difficult sell. I calibrated what was needed because of knowledge of the culture that an external might not have been able to do.

**Emily C. Jarosz, Emily and Associates,
former internal consultant with health-care industry**

How the internal consultant is perceived in the organization can impact every potential client relationship. Credibility as an internal consultant is usually built on personal relationships. Separating the internal consultant's friendship from the professional role is also important. Indeed some consultants recommend not socializing or maintaining close friendships with their clients. Others said they just set very clear boundaries. Losing the trust of one client can damage the internal consultant's reputation throughout the whole organization. An internal consultant who is a long-term member of the organization has already earned trust. There is an assumption that "We are in this together," and internal consultants do not have to prove that they are honorable because they have already established a direct relationship and their credibility.

Relationship Credibility

Being an internal consultant helped in a number of ways. The team had confidence in me because they knew of the work I had done in other parts of the organization. As we moved through the project, I had ongoing relationships not only because we met every week but I also had offline conversations with them. I was accessible.

Helm Lehmann, author, former OD manager, REI

Client reticence may indicate fear or a lack of trust. The contracting process can help allay fear or distrust. A description of the consulting process, including assurances of confidentiality and respect for the client and the organization, also addresses the client's reservations.

Feel for the Organization

Internal Journal

Internal consultants must have a sense of timeliness and how hard to push regardless of whether the client is asking directly for something or not. After our downsizing, people were looking for something to hang onto—vision or values. The CEO said no the first time, but I came back a year later and he said yes. I had a sense of what it was time for.

**Sue Thompson, Thompson Group,
former internal consultant with Levi Strauss & Company**

Commitment to the Client's Success. The ultimate success of the internal consultant depends on the client's definition of success. For the internal consultant, searching out the answer to this question begins with respect for the client's work and with the assumption that the client operates with the best of intentions. The internal consultant's job is to help the client be more effective, voice alternative opinions, observe, and offer creative suggestions. However, the final decisions are the client's. Clients who are comfortable and pleased with their decisions are more likely to provide enthusiastic leadership for the intervention.

A successful intervention leads some internal consultants to take a leadership position to ensure successful results in the organization. Other internal consultants take a broader view: They aim for the overall success of the client and the process, not just the success of the specific intervention or initiative. Commitment to the client's success means taking a stand about how the offered expertise will be used. It means willing to be accountable for the results and letting the client be the hero. It means being committed to an authentic, collaborative partnership and pursuing and supporting learning as a goal for both parties—the client and the internal consultant.

Accountability requires an agreement between the consultant and the client. The agreement defines what must be done in the project, by whom, and how the client organization and consultant will work together to achieve results. The consultant must emphasize the requirement that the client use the expertise offered by the internal consultant. If the client pressures the consultant later in the process to do something the internal consultant does not recommend or is uncomfortable doing, the result is often a failed intervention. Failure to use the consultant's advice and expertise negates the partnership and the consultant's accountability for results. Such a stand may be a hard one to take if the internal consultant is new to the organization or if a consulting practice, such as performance consulting, is unfamiliar to the organization.

Partnerships

I had a client with a military background who met the classic stereo-type. I initially didn't want to deal with him. He was very rigid, but he was very smart. He saw in the beginning the incongruence between his style and the organization's culture. He wanted to change. We did a series of team buildings with his groups. He and I struggled together with some hard employee issues. I was able to play the bad guy in confronting their behavior, so that he could be the good guy. I coached him during subsequent sessions so that he could do things for himself. He took more and more opportunities to do that. He got rid of people who were not team-oriented and moved in people who were. He continued to use much of what I introduced to him.

Jim McKnight, OD consultant, California Federal Bank

Client Learning. Commitment to the client's success ensures that the client is able to carry on without support when the project is complete and that the skills and expertise the internal consultant brings are transferred to the client. To avoid client dependency, the internal consultant should take time to help the client develop necessary skills, schedule time to explore human dynamics, and help the client understand the impact of leadership behaviors on those dynamics. Building in ways for the client to understand the impact and interaction of the system on processes or performance is another way to sustain ongoing performance-improvement projects. One internal consultant enthusiastically recommended using councils or guiding coalitions to establish policy, recommend interventions, and assess the outcomes. These councils or coalitions can "outlive the consultant."

Keeping it Going

I was working with a management team at an organization where they had separate functions that didn't talk to each other. We had five or six off-site functions. I used the left-hand column technique, the ladder of inference, and real examples. They began to use systems thinking to understand events, patterns, and structures underneath their issues. They started to facilitate their own meetings. I coached individuals regarding the impact of their own behavior. When I came to monthly staff meetings, I offered observations and suggested how they might apply to daily issues. The man-

agement team had a desire to do something but it was not a crisis. Organizational learning was supported and happened here!

Scott Burton, internal consultant with consumer products industry

Clarified Expectations. Nothing will more quickly destroy a relationship with a client than misunderstood expectations. If the client is resistant and unwilling, the internal consultant may have to proceed more slowly and serve as facilitator, observer, or diagnostician. Once trust is established, the client may be more open to coaching or counseling.

Developing this relationship with clients is perhaps the most critical ingredient to the internal consultant's success. The internal consultant's work cannot be accomplished without strong, trusting, authentic relationships. Such relationships are more important determinants of a successful career than are credentials.

Building Relationships

Fundamentally, my relationship-building as an internal consultant has to have a longer-term focus. External consultants have more options about how much to invest in relationships. We don't have the same options. What I do have going for me is that since I am employed by the company, my client will give me the benefit of the doubt. But, most of my leverage is in doing relationship-building . . . It is also a strategy issue. If there are many areas to the business, I may combine a strategy of breadth in learning the organization and the business and go for depth with a few key relationships.

Jeff Cohen, director, Leadership Development and Market Coordination, Pfizer Pharmaceuticals Group

ORGANIZATIONAL SITUATION

Internal consultants have in-depth knowledge of the organization, the subtleties of politics, and the nuances of cultural norms. Internal consultants have the challenge of being objective observers while experiencing full immersion in the culture. For many senior-level clients, internal consultants need to hold or represent the culture of the organization as the executive moves toward a decision. Internal consultants are expected to know the business and the strategy and should anticipate the organizational challenges of instigating change. A newly hired internal consultant should respect the new organization and appreciate its history. As internal consultant Bob Browning said, "You have to demonstrate that you can cha-cha before they will tango."

Important questions that influence the role of the internal consultant in the organization include the following:

- Are the organizational vision and strategy clear and understood?
- What are the key strategic needs of the organization?
- What are the effects of the current market and the competition on the organization?
- What is the focus of attention?
- What resources are available to support the project or intervention?
- Are other strategic initiatives being driven in the organization and how might they affect the current initiative?
- What are the cultural norms and the mindset that will influence the project?
- What organizational needs are not being met?
- Is the expertise of the internal consultant relevant to the organization's needs?

The Alternatives: Which Costume to Choose

We have discussed various factors—the consultant's characteristics, the client's needs, the quality of the relationship, and the organizational context—that must be considered when choosing a role for the internal consultant. Williamson (1998) identifies six key roles for internal consultants. The roles vary according to how a great an emphasis each places on expertise or process consultation.

- *Committed partner:* serves the client with collaborative orientation
- *Change leader:* offers strong facilitation and organizational influence
- *Business driver:* emphasizes performance management and results
- *Trusted advisor:* serves as a confidant and provides authentic communication
- *Grounded expert:* has specific HRD, OD, performance-improvement, or business-process expertise
- *Insightful observer:* applies systems thinking and rigorous inquiry.

Some internal consultants can play all of these roles; others may be limited to one or two by experience, expertise, or opportunity. Long-term internal consultants find that their roles change over their careers. Figure 3-1 outlines the stages that internal consultants move through during their careers. Many internal consultants begin their careers at the apprentice stage by delivering training, then move to meeting facilitation and team building. Later in their careers, at the coach/mentor and master stages, they serve as advisors to senior management and strategists for corporation-wide change initiatives. Experienced internal consultants point out the value of first being a trainer or a grounded expert and gradually expanding their

Figure 3-1. Stages of a career in internal consulting.

STUDENT—Mastering a body of knowledge

Take basic courses specific to your field, such as
- Group dynamics
- Organization behavior
- Adult learning
- Individual and organization change
- Consulting process
- Systems thinking.

APPRENTICE—Applying basic knowledge

Use opportunities to apply knowledge, receive specific feedback, and develop skills, such as
- Facilitation
- Team development
- Interviewing
- Learning activity design
- Consulting
- Information and data analysis.

PRACTITIONER—Increasing knowledge and skill base

Discover more and better ways of doing things by
- Attending professional meetings, seminars, and conferences
- Reading professional journals and books
- Networking
- Specializing.

COACH AND MENTOR—Assisting others to develop professionally

Use coaching and counseling skills to develop others by
- Serving as role model and mentor
- Writing, presenting, speaking, training to help others learn skills, tools, and concepts.

MASTER—Leaving your mark and your legacy

Achieve peak performance
- Inspiration and model of career success for others
- Leader in your field
- Creator of legacy through writing, speaking, and teaching.

---

role. This allows them to build relationships and establish trust. In addition, this depth of career experience builds role flexibility and pays off later when internal consultants deal with complex issues at the senior-management level. It enables them to take the multiple roles defined by Williamson.

Broader Role, Broader Experience

📖
Internal
Journal

I worked in two organizations—one with a broad consulting char-ter and the other with a narrow charter. The narrow charter defined consultants as meeting facilitators, conducting off-site meetings, team building. I believe the broader role evolving today. It is broader in scope and requires more experience, better education, and more expertise. The consultant serves as general guru and problem solver for management regarding people issues. Typical tasks include putting together career devel-opment plans for these managers, identifying the reasons a group is not per-forming well, mediating conflicts between key individuals, coaching a high-level manager on his or her communication skills. It is a more complex role across a spectrum of issues. You don't necessarily have to be the expert your-self, but you need to know how to leverage both internally and externally. There is also a trend to lead and advocate change. That requires being an advocate of the new philosophy and helping people adopt it. It is difficult to do if you come from a neutral process background. You need to ask yourself if you can honestly embrace the philosophy and be an advocate. If not, go do something else. I think that is a big issue.

**Kevin B. Wheeler, Global Learning Resources,
former internal consultant with Charles Schwab Corporation**

Summing Up and Looking Ahead

Internal consultants perform multiple roles inside the organization. Internal consul-tants can fill the organization's needs for process consulting and technical or expert consulting. The need for expertise in change leadership and business and organiza-tion alignment requires internal consultants to take leadership and advocacy roles. Experience enables the consultant to choose the best match and also provides the flexibility to play multiple roles. Choosing a role depends on

- personal characteristics and experience of the consultant
- involvement, readiness, and characteristics of the client
- quality and strength of the consultant-client relationship
- business environment, strategy, and culture of the organization.

The pace of change in the business environment over the last decade has changed organizations in a radical way. Rapid change will continue to drive busi-ness into the next century. The next chapter will cover the demands on consultants living inside organizations as they career through this turbulent environment.

References

Block, P. (1981). *Flawless Consulting: A Guide to Getting Your Expertise Used.* San Diego: Pfeiffer & Co.

Champion, D., D.H. Kiel, and J.A. McLendon. (1990, February). "Choosing a Consulting Role." *Training & Development,* 68.

Marguilles, N. (1978) "Perspectives on the Marginality of the Consultant's Role." In *The Cutting Edge: Current Theory and Practice in Organization Development,* Burke, W.W., editor. La Jolla, CA: Pfeiffer & Co.

Schaffer, R.H. (1997). *High Impact Consulting.* San Francisco: Jossey-Bass.

Williamson, S. (1998). Brochure. Lexington, MA: Linkage Inc.

Endnote

1. Marguilles refers to the idea developed by Ornstein of the two-sided person—rational and intuitive—as the historical roots of the major consulting roles. The rational side, which others refer to as left-brain, encompasses analytical, verbal, problem-solving, and linear ways of thinking. This approach is reflected in our scientific and industrial development and the learning processes that dominate our educational institutions. The intuitive side, or right brain, emphasizes nonverbal, emotional, holistic, more esoteric, mystical approaches to learning, knowing, and being. Marguilles suggests that the major traditions of consulting come from each side of the person: The rational side supports technical or expert consultation and the intuitive side supports process or facilitative consultation.

Chapter 4

Challenges from Outside: Opportunities for the Internal Consultant

General Electric CEO Jack Welsh is widely quoted as saying that the 1990s have been a "white-knuckle" ride. The next century will, in all likelihood, offer more of the same and perhaps an even more unpredictable ride. Organizational complexity is increasing as strategic alliances, joint ventures, partnerships, and networks are formed to meet the demands of the marketplace. The themes of globalization, rapidly changing technology, a drive for growth, intellectual capital, and constant change (Ulrich 1998) characterize the continuing challenges predicted for the future. Internal consultants can play an important role advising managers and senior executives who are working to meet the demands of the turbulent marketplace. Internal consultants can also have a significant role in helping frightened, anxious employees cope with dizzying changes in corporate leadership, business strategy, reorganization, and downsizing.

Experienced internal consultants who have lived through significant organizational changes, such as mergers or reengineering, become discouraged when senior managers fail to understand how internal consulting groups can help navigate these changes. They complain that internal consultants are excluded in favor of large external consulting firms that guarantee savings and productivity gains by focusing on nonhuman elements of the business. Nevertheless, other internal consultants are in great demand as their organizations navigate major downsizings or large acquisitions.

The Role is Expanding

Internal Journal

We are now being asked what we think earlier in the process. We are not just seen as facilitators, but we have a legitimate place at the table. It is not just because of the merger or the lay-offs but the belief that maybe we can ameliorate the problems if we are involved earlier upstream. We are gaining credibility, and the company is recognizing what we can offer.

Michael Lindfield, senior OD consultant, Boeing Company

Challenges Bring Opportunities

Turmoil in the business world means opportunity for the internal consultant who has expertise in HRD, performance improvement, or OD. For example, in merged organizations employees need guidance and coaching to meet higher performance standards, to adjust to different management styles, and to figure out expectations as cultural norms and traditions change. In downsized organizations in which the "loyalty paradigm" is dead, the "HOBBOs—Hanging On But Bummed Out" survivors (Kaye 1998) need coaching to take charge of managing their own careers. Internal consultants can be an invaluable resource to executives trying to formulate competitive business strategies; they can advise on how to create the single most important competitive advantage—the organizational capability to achieve high performance results.

Entrepreneurial and Growth Businesses

Internal consultants can also be key players as they guide the leaders of entrepreneurial ventures and growth businesses. The challenges include a number of strategies to attract and keep desirable skilled employees:

- weaving a new cultural fabric
- developing management and leadership competencies
- building communication and employee participation systems.

Often entrepreneurs have little skill at leading organizations and do not understand the importance of developing managers and line employees. The internal consultant can emphasize the importance of investing in the skill training and career development opportunities that are important not only for employee retention but also to keep the workforce skills current with rapidly changing technology. Internal consultants can introduce new leaders to basic concepts, such as organizational behavior, culture, HR management practices, and show how these affect the bottom line.

Help People Through Change

Internal Journal

One of the roles of the internal consultant is to help people through the constant world of transition. Changes used to come one at a time, now they are constant. It is almost more change management . . . Clients are more caught up with us in terms of skills, such as facilitation and being well read regarding organizational behavior issues. The role of change agent is still there, though.

Eddie Reynolds, consultant, executive and organization development, former internal consultant with high-technology industry

Work Across Boundaries

Continuing technological improvements make working from almost any location possible. More employees will be expected to use technology to collaborate on projects and work together on daily assignments. Many of these employees will live and work in other countries and time zones around the world. Internal consultants have opportunities to coach managers, teams, and employees for high-performance work across the boundaries of time, language, culture, organization, and expertise without the benefit of face-to-face interaction.

Alignment with the Business Strategy

Traditional training and development programs delivered by internal consultants were created without much concern about the connection to the business strategy. Managers often thought training and consulting interventions were superfluous to the business needs of the organization. Today, organizations demand that consultants be business partners with deliverables, value-added activities, and business results.

Henning (1997) observes that both clients and staff groups "must change if the full measure of the staff's contribution to the business is to be realized." He believes that staff groups are at risk in today's business environment. For

Stay Ahead of the Game

We have to be anchored in the context of where the organization is. There has to be a strategic component—an understanding of the organization's long-term goals. I try to identify gaps and issues for my clients before they see them. They need to know that I am ahead of the game. Managers don't always have time to anticipate the organizational impact. I can do that. There has to be a direct connection between what I do and what is critical in the organization.

Jeff Cohen, director, Leadership Development and Market Coordination, Pfizer Pharmaceuticals Group

HRD and performance-improvement consultants, it means showing a clear connection to the organization's business objectives and strategy. Researchers at the University of Michigan found that HR professionals were most valued and effective if they understood the business (Ulrich & Lake 1990). Successful internal consultants must know the strategy and become business partners with their clients.

Know the Company Strategy

Learn about your business, understand it. That is just as important as knowing human resources or organization development. Act as if human resources should go away. Our objective is for managers to be responsible for the business and the people in it. We are transferring skills to our line managers. It clears up turf issues.

**Cecily Cocco, vice president, change management,
Blue Shield of California**

Internal consultants are now expected to develop more specific, value-added solutions. They are expected to customize tools to address performance issues and to make tangible contributions to unit performance. In this new role, internal consultants are contributing to the effectiveness of the individual units and teams as consultants and coaches while guiding senior managers in the alignment of the human organization with the company vision and the business strategy.

These are roles that cannot be trusted to outsiders. Sue Thompson, a former internal HR/OD director, explains, "As an internal you are reading the whole culture, knowing the business issues, what motivates your client, and what is going on for your client. If there is a problem situation for the CEO and I can give him information about what might be contributing to the issue, I have helped him solve that problem. As internal consultants, timing is a luxury for us. We can time when providing information is most useful."

Therefore, attending business planning and strategy meetings is a critical activity for internal consultants if they are to be business partners with their clients. Internal consultants must know the key business drivers and understand financial data. They must ask the right questions to ensure that every consulting intervention is directly connected to the business connection and drives performance improvement. Moreover, internal consultants must make sure that there is support for their work at all levels of the organization from senior management to frontline employees.

Alignment with Company Goals

The company had 25 major, agreed-upon goals, one or two of which related to people issues. One of them dealt with the glass ceiling. Engineering was my major client. Working closely with the manager of diversity, I wrote a proposal to the vice president of engineering and the director of HR to do a one-day, off-site event for all the women in engineering at all levels (400 women) with the executive team in engineer-

ing (12 men). I worked with a cross-sectional taskforce of women in engineering to plan the day. We addressed meeting logistics, getting a keynote speaker, and setting up mini-workshops with an outside expert, a facilitator, and an executive team member.

The day was a great success but what was most successful were the self-development and empowerment of the taskforce members . . . This experience was a major event in their lives. It also generated enthusiasm in other parts of the company. The downside was that I did not work enough with HR. Although it was backed by the HR director, I didn't work enough with the function. If any group tried to sabotage the event, HR did.

**Jan M. Schmuckler, Consultation,
former internal consultant with high-technology industry**

The Changing Role of Change Agent

Many internal consultants see their traditional role as change agents becoming a role of guiding and consulting on the management of change. As organizations career through major organizational changes, both management leadership and frontline employees need guidance.

Not only do internal consultants bring an understanding of the business issues, but also as experts in performance improvement and OD, they understand the change process. Meeting the demands of changing business requirements is complicated by the human demands of the heart. Employees in the throes of change seek meaning and purpose, opportunities to contribute, a chance to be creative, and a sense of direction—a vision of where the organization is going and a perspective of how they fit in. As a business partner, the internal consultant can help senior managers articulate and communicate purposeful, visionary messages. The internal consultant can also promote opportunities for employees to contribute ideas and provide leadership in the overall planning, design, and implementation of the change initiatives.

A Change Experience

Internal Journal

During our major reengineering effort, the involvement of the internal consulting group was very different in two different parts of the company. Here in the U.S., neither the external consulting firm we used nor management leadership valued the OD expertise. The internal consultants were also very skeptical about the possibility of this level of change and saw the approach as fraught with problems. The best thinking was not brought to bear on this project. The external firm was not familiar with our culture and not wise enough to seek help about the strength and character of our culture. In the international effort with a different external consulting firm, an internal consulting team was charged with a focus on the human implications of change. Each team member had a

*process team to connect with and brought back issues to refine and coordi-
nate with the larger group. There was solid strategizing to help change happen. The external consultants sought us out and valued the internal perspective to help implement this change.*

**Sue Thompson, Thompson Group,
former internal consultant with Levi Strauss & Company**

Ideas to Use in the 21st Century

It is clear that as business enters the 21st century many of the previous business
and organization models will no longer yield a competitive advantage or even sustain current levels of performance. Thought leaders offer new models and advice
to help organizations revamp strategies, discover leadership strategies, and create
global-networked organizations. Some ideas are not new, but current business
demands suggest that they will find application as organizations seek new ways to
achieve high performance, innovate, develop critical competencies, and motivate
employees. The following sections briefly summarize some useful ideas to take
into the 21st century; many of these concepts will be important for the internal
consultant to leverage his or her future work.

MODELS AND STRATEGIES FOR CHANGE

Models of organization change have been in use for some time. One of the first was
Lewin's (1951) model of unfreeze-change-refreeze. Change occurs at such a pace
today that there is little time for either unfreezing or refreezing—one change follows on the heels of the previous change. For this reason, it is imperative that internal consultants identify and use organizational change models to guide senior
clients to manage change and lead the organization through constant turbulence.
Many in the field (Beckhard & Harris 1977; Beckhard & Pritchard 1992; Stroh
1978; Dannemiller 1988) have introduced change frameworks that focus on moving toward a desired future. Offering a vision of the positive helps motivate and
transform energy among members of the organization to create it. The model of
"appreciative inquiry" emphasizes a focus on what is going well, building on success to envision, and creating a positive future (Hammond 1996). Other change
and transformation strategies suggest asking who, why, what, when, and how questions to ensure that all the bases are covered (Ulrich 1998). Change is also an
inside-out process. Successful organization change requires personal change, as
well. Understanding the personal transition process (Bridges 1980) helps internal
consultants guide employees and coach managers. Further discussion about
change and transition strategies is discussed in chapter 13.

LEARNING ORGANIZATIONS

The concept of organizational learning was introduced 25 years ago. It has now become a concept exciting to managers, academicians, and consultants alike. Companies unable to adapt to the rapid pace of change around them disappear while others adapt and thrive. This observation led to the recognition that organizational learning may be the only sustainable business advantage. Senge, a leading thinker and advocate for the learning organizations, suggests that we are witnessing the shift from one age to another (Senge et al. 1999; Senge 1990; Senge et al. 1994). This shift has been identified by many as moving from a machine model of the organization to a more organic model (De Geus 1997), because learning itself is a natural, organic, living process. Internal consultants are needed to develop processes for intentional, shared learning in organizations—a necessity for business survival. Strategies, learning tools, and models for developing the learning organization have increased over the last 10 years. One of the most valuable contributions that the internal consultant can make is to identify and implement with client leaders the strategies and tools to develop a learning organization as a competitive business strategy.

CHAOS AND COMPLEXITY

Chaos-and-complexity theory emerged about 20 years ago from scientific discoveries that the universe and natural phenomena are composed of chaotic, dynamic, complex systems rather than predictable, law-abiding Newtonian structures. Experts have applied these theories to organizations as a new way to understand the complex, dynamic, nonlinear systems that are today's organizations (Wheatley 1992). Although many employees continue to work in the Newtonian, hierarchical structure, they feel the chaotic complexity of change swirling about them. Chaos—"a state where patterns cannot be made nor details understood"—is a familiar experience for many employees working in settings (Titcomb 1998) where change is resisted until it becomes unavoidable, and then it occurs at a rapid, disorienting pace. The paradox is, however, that from within chaos emerges order—repeated patterns that have coherence and can be recognized.

Organization and management practitioners and visionaries, such as Dee Hock (Durrance 1997) and Margaret Wheatley (1997, 1999) suggest this new scientific theory of the universe offers insight for the leadership and organization of work. Internal consultants at the front line of chaotic change in organizations have opportunity to apply these concepts in their organizations. Some initial steps might be to:

- encourage managers to loosen control and allow teams to "self-organize"
- promote a search for alternative or innovative solutions rather than clinging to past practices

- engage the whole system to participate in planning, problem solving, and creating the future
- help develop and communicate shared values and purpose throughout the organization.

KNOWLEDGE MANAGEMENT

At the close of the century, wealth and economic value are increasingly generated from the creation and manipulation of information, knowledge, and ideas than they are from the manufacture of products (Allee 1997). This is what some are calling the "knowledge economy." It is forcing a radical rethinking of the value of the intangible resources in the heads of employees and the management of these workers who take the company assets out the door every night. The internal consultant has many opportunities to apply the strategies of organizational learning and the insights of the new science. The challenge is helping clients create a motivating and dynamic environment that not only promotes shared learning and the creation of knowledge but also meets the needs of a new generation of workers.

SYSTEMS

Brenneman, Keys, and Fulmer (1998) describe two types of managers. Many business enterprises are filled with "event thinkers"—managers who "interpret current developments as inevitable and view corporate life as a series of unrelated events." In contrast are systems thinkers, "people who see current reality in an organization as only one of many possibilities for the long term." Systems thinking encourages a holistic view in which the situation is considered in the context of the larger whole. Managers often only see the symptoms and miss the source of the problem. Internal consultants can help managers make a "shift of the mind" from seeing issues as separate problems to recognizing the inextricably interconnected nature of organizations (Senge 1990). Underlying patterns influencing undesirable outcomes can be identified and actions taken to increase performance.

ADAPTABILITY

The thriving successful company of the 21st century will not be a rigidly structured hierarchy although many still are. The forces challenging this industrial model demand an adaptable structure that is less concerned with status, where temporary and virtual teams self-organize to meet high performance goals. The strategy, leadership style, HR systems, and even the business will change. As Collins and Porras (1990) discovered in their research, enduring, long-term success was dependent on tightly held, core ideology and vision with a willingness to change everything else. Internal consultants have a role in helping maintain that core while they encourage their clients to learn, generate alternatives, stimulate progress, and adapt the organization to the new environmental forces.

HUMAN PERFORMANCE IMPROVEMENT

Human performance improvement (HPI) is a rapidly growing approach to address issues of individual and organization performance. Many training professionals are adopting this approach too, because it focuses on business needs with concrete business outcomes. Performance improvement requires a systemic examination of the barriers and root causes preventing employees from achieving high performance. Solutions generated to overcome these barriers are more than a training program or a motivational meeting. Internal consultants using this approach recommend changes in the organization's processes or systems that enable, support, reinforce, and reward high performance. Examples of HPI-recommended solutions include the following:

- redesigning the process for employees to receive information
- changing reporting structures
- setting up mechanisms for performance reinforcement and positive feedback
- removing reinforcement or rewards for poor performance
- implementing effective performance management cycles
- tying incentives and rewards to improved performance
- providing tools, job aids, or new technology
- upgrading skills.

When internal consultants document the improvement in savings of time or money using HPI, business managers can quickly see the advantages of applying this approach.

Changing Role of the Internal Consultant

Globalization, rapidly changing technology, the drive for growth, the value of intellectual capital, and the constant, rapid forces of change will continue to challenge the organizations internal consultants serve. New ideas and models from organization and management theorists will help organizations meet these challenges. The internal consultant's role in these demanding times is expanding as senior managers need advice and counsel to navigate global turbulence and to align their organizations with business strategies that must be constantly modified to meet competitive pressures. To succeed in the 21st century, the internal consultant must

- Know the business. Tie consulting interventions to real business issues and ensure that they add value.
- Identify performance gaps or issues before managers do. Be ahead of the game.
- Recognize systemic relationships. Be a systems thinker.
- Build strong skills as a coach, teacher, advisor, and strategist.

- Avoid pitfalls and barriers; learn detours. Be persistent in overcoming them.
- Pay attention to the trends; talk about them. Most importantly, make them relevant to the business.
- Develop the ability to work at all levels of the organization and across boundaries.
- Know the financial picture, participate in business meetings, and ask questions.
- Be an educator about change, systems thinking, learning strategies, chaos and complexity.
- Develop personal mastery and be a constant learner.

Summing Up and Looking Ahead

Challenges in the business economy will expand the influence of the internal consultant in the 21st century. The internal consultant will need to use some of the powerful ideas, tools, and theories outlined here. The internal consultant will need to take the initiative to prepare his or her client organization for enduring success and high performance. It will be an unpredictable and chaotic ride. Complex change offers opportunity for creativity and learning; self-organizing will occur, and patterns and order will emerge if only briefly before the next tidal wave of change.

In the next section of the book, chapters 5 and 6 will explore the organizational roadblocks and pitfalls internal consultants can create for themselves and they must overcome if they are to be successful. Chapter 7 discusses a more challenging topic: the self knowledge, awareness, and personal mastery an internal consultant must have to meet the challenges outlined here and achieve an expanded role of influence in the organization of the next century.

References

Allee, V. (1997). *The Knowledge Evolution.* Boston: Butterworth-Heinemann.

Beckhard, R., and R. Harris. (1977). *Organizational Transitions: Managing Complex Change.* Reading, MA: Addison-Wesley.

Beckhard, R., and W. Pritchard. (1992). *Changing the Essence: The Art of Creating and Leading Fundamental Change in Organizations.* San Francisco: Jossey-Bass.

Brenneman, W.B., J.B. Keys, and R.M. Fulmer. (1998, Autumn). "Learning Across a Living Company: The Shell Companies' Experiences." *Organizational Dynamics,* 63–69.

Bridges, W. (1980). *Transitions: Making Sense of Life's Changes.* Cambridge, MA: Perseus Books.

Collins, J.C., and J.I. Porras. (1990). *Built to Last.* New York: HarperCollins.

Dannemiller, K. (1988). "Team Building at a Macro Level or 'Ben Gay' for Arthritic Organizations." In *Team Building: Blueprints for Productivity and Satisfaction,* W.B. Readdy & K. Jamison, editors. Alexandria, VA: National Institute for Applied Behavioral Science; and San Diego: University Associates.

De Geus, A. (1997). *The Living Company*. Boston, MA: Harvard Business School Press.

Durrance, B. (1997, April). "The Evolutionary Vision of Dee Hock: From Chaos to Chaords." *Training & Development*, 25–31.

Hammond, S.A. (1996). *The Thin Book of Appreciative Inquiry*. Plano, TX: Kodiak Consulting.

Henning, J.P. (1997). *The Future of Staff Groups*. San Francisco: Berrett-Koehler Publishers.

Kaye, B. (1998, March). "The Kept-On Workforce." *Training & Development*, 32.

Lewin, K. (1951). *Field Theory in Social Science*. New York: Harper & Row Publishers.

Senge, P.M. (1990). *The Fifth Discipline: The Art and Practice of the Learning Organization*. New York: Doubleday.

Senge, P.M., C. Roberts, R. Ross, and R. Smith. (1999). *The Dance of Change*. New York: Doubleday.

Senge, P.M., R. Ross, B. Smith, C. Roberts, and A. Kleiner. (1994). *The Fifth Discipline Fieldbook*. New York: Doubleday.

Stroh, P. (1987, Autumn). "Purposeful Consulting." *Organizational Dynamics, 16*, 49–67.

Titcomb, R.J. (1998, July). "Chaos and Complexity Theory." *Info-line*. Alexandria, VA: American Society for Training & Development.

Ulrich, D. (1998, Jan.–Feb.). "A New Mandate for Human Resources." *Harvard Business Review,* 124–134.

Ulrich, D., and D. Lake. (1990). *Organizational Capability: Competing from the Inside Out*. New York: Wiley.

Wheatley, M.J. (1992). *Leadership and the New Science*. San Francisco: Berrett-Koehler Publishers.

Wheatley, M. (1997, Summer). "Goodbye, Command and Control." *Leader to Leader,* 21–28.

Wheatley, M. (1999, Winter). "When Complex Systems Fail: New Roles for Leaders." *Leader to Leader,* 28–34.

Section Two:

Achieving Success

Chapter 5

Circumventing the Roadblocks

This chapter identifies the organizational issues that can throw up roadblocks for internal consultants. To achieve success internal consultants must prevent, avoid, or overcome these challenges. One of the most common demands for the internal consultant is to partner with other professionals to provide the expertise and support for project success. This chapter discusses two of the most difficult partnerships: those with external consultants and those with the HR function. Strategies and the experiences of internal consultants for marketing internal consulting services are also listed. Finally, the last section of the chapter explores ways to cope with difficult clients who resist, refuse to "walk the talk," or have problem personalities.

Partnerships with Externals

Partnership is the key to success for internal consultants who work with outside consulting firms on major change projects. This truly is an experience of "being in it together" when the strengths of the internal consultant are recognized and valued along with the expertise of the external firm. Both drive hard for results with a common investment in achieving the desired outcome. Nevertheless, the clear message from current and former internal consultants who were interviewed by the author is that this situation is the exception, not the rule. Such partnerships occur less frequently when the external consulting firm is large, is hired by senior management to design a major strategic, operational, or technological change, or uses an expert methodology. It is more common when the external firm is small, when the consultants are hired by the internal consulting function, or when they bring a respect for the perspective and expertise of internal consultants.

The Missing Internal Link

Most internal consultants recognize that they do not have the specific expertise or positioning needed to drive major strategic changes desired by senior management.

The outside firm brings needed expertise or provides the leadership to guide executives in meeting the future competitive requirements of the company. Nevertheless, senior managers often do not seem to grasp the value and benefit of the ties between the internal consulting group and the existing organization. Such ties are critical to the successful implementation of a major change effort. This oversight means that the internal group might be totally left out of the contracting process without any connection to the project, much less viewed as a partner.

Why Internal Consultants Are Valuable

Internal Journal

There is no way the internal group could have led this major change effort. The external firm brings the long-term view with their feet outside the organization. External firms can help chart the future—how to get there. But success is totally dependent on the internal capacity for information about what is actually happening. The only way to implement is with the involvement and commitment of people in the organization. The role for the internal group is to help people through the transition because they know the system. To leave them out is to bring chaos!

Hillair C. Bell, Berkeley Consulting Group and Morgan Consulting Resources, former internal consultant with Kaiser Permanente

Exceptions occur, however, when the external consulting firm has the wisdom to recognize and value the inside view of the organization and intentionally reaches out to partner with the internal function. When such partnership occurs, the organization reaps huge benefits from the learning transfer of the consulting firm's expertise and from the response of the employees as they are helped through the transition feeling respected and valued. Without such a partnership, the implementation may be such a disaster that the organization becomes dysfunctional and loses employees; workforce morale and productivity require a long time to recover. The final insult is the departing consulting firm leaving "a mess" for the internal function to clean up.

Painful Experiences

Internal Journal

The most challenging and painful experiences I have had were when we were working in partnership with large external consulting groups. I have been through them all. In every case, I have had a negative experience. There never truly is a partnership even though we contracted up front. We did role clarification: "What we need from you is . . ." and "What do you need from us?" Some were not even willing to do that. They did not have the same accountability as we had. And we even charged internally for our services. They practically had a blank check, but the same standards were not being applied to the large external groups.

We were resource-deficient, and I often encouraged management to hire them because it was too big for us to handle ourselves. They would be given lots of attention by higher management who would just lie down and let them roll over them. In almost every case, we were disappointed. Upper management would get disenthralled, and the internal group would have to come in and clean up the mess. I went through four or five of these, always with the same outcome.

Eddie Reynolds, consultant, executive and organization development, former internal consultant with high-technology industry

Barriers to Partnership

Even with potential involvement of the internal function, a wide chasm can divide the perspectives of the outside consulting firm from the internal consulting function. Internal consultants often doubt the viability of large-scale, systemwide changes or disagree with the approach the outside firm is taking. If the internal consultants have been excluded during the contracting process, they may feel resentful and cling to the "old way" as they commiserate with their clients about the looming change.

On the other side of the chasm, some external consulting firms have senior-level, articulate consultants initially present the project using impressive graphic presentations, but then they bring in lower-level, inexperienced consultants to do the actual work. These unpracticed staffers with their newly minted business degrees are bright and enthusiastic but may lack the personal qualities required for success within an organization and may even come across as arrogant. The external project staff may use academic, jargon-laden language rather than understandable, everyday terms. The large firms, which are steeped in a tradition of expertise and are valued by senior management for that expertise, may furnish analysts who have little time or appreciation for the process of helping people through their resistance. In addition, as a client, "you hang your needs on their framework," one consultant observes. "What you get is their approach, a packaged solution, which is not necessarily the best solution." This consultant opines that this approach is not even consulting, because it is not based on designing alternative solutions to meet the needs of the client.

An Expensive Failure

Internal Journal

One of the most senior people felt we needed more understanding about communication issues in the company. He hired an external consultant from Harvard who was well known in the field. I teamed with him and we did taped, structured interviews, analyzed them, and came up with recommendations. It was an expensive three-month process with a very traditional, external consulting arrangement. The results from these formal interviews were broad, general recommendations that were not at a level of detail we could implement. Maybe we learned a few things we didn't know but if he had taken 15 minutes with the HR people, who understood the issues and would have come up with the same results with the detail level, we could have done something. This project may have validated the problem but it was an expensive failure because the vice president resigned.

Kevin B. Wheeler, Global Learning Resources, former internal consultant with Charles Schwab Corporation

Finally the contract itself can present barriers. Sometimes the external firm is unable to see the big picture; it cannot connect its contracted project to the rest of the organization. Perhaps the client has asked the firm to redesign a subsystem with no linkage to other systems. Another problem is that the inexperienced staff may not recognize the limitations of the contract and may step outside the boundary of the project. In other cases the staff make no efforts to connect their work with the rest of the organization. In fact, their view may be "if you guys are so great, why didn't you fix this mess?"

Other internal consultants are critical of what they consider an outdated consulting model, which is methodologically flawed. The top-down expert model tends to rely on a crew of bright, enthusiastic analysts to do the work of the project. They may draw on the client organization's extra human resources who are then managed by the consulting firm. The growing power of the consulting firm in some organizations leaves some organization members with uncertainty about who is really running the place! Many internals see the change management approach of the large consulting firms as weak and ineffective with

- no linkages to the internal consulting function
- overreliance on skills training and communication to manage change
- little effort to transfer learning to the organization.

In fact, some horror stories described projects without any planning for implementation once the new organization or process design was completed.

Dissatisfaction with the Top-Down Model

Internal Journal

There is lots of dissatisfaction with the top-down model in which consultants go in as the experts. Organization-development staff quit doing that kind of consulting 30 years ago. The consultants keep apart and above the system with their observations and recommendations instead of coming in with a participation process for people. Organization development was developed in opposition to this model, which is a flawed practice. It is still used because organizations think they need to change faster and that it will help them do that. But we know the problems that result: no organizational learning, resistance, dissatisfaction, and little real change.

**Chuck Schaefer, Schaefer Associates,
former senior consultant, Chevron Corporation**

There Is Some Good News

Not all the stories related by internal consultants were critical of external firms, however. Large firms are recognized as having the capacity and infrastructure with brilliant, highly trained staffs to plan large-scale change efforts that internal functions are unable to support. If the external firm is open to partnership (or asked by management to partner) and recognizes the internal consulting group's strengths, the result is solid strategic and successful change.

One internal consultant says that external consultants play valuable roles: they communicate tough information, introduce new ideas, and validate internal consultants' recommendations. When a subject matter expert is needed for expertise and credibility or when the internal function cannot handle the load, many internal functions seek external consultants to meet those needs. External consultants are especially valuable when confronting senior levels of management, saying things that would be suicidal for an internal consultant, and "taking the heat." Figure 5-1 summarizes the advice that experienced internal consultants shared to overcome some of the barriers of work with external consultants.

A Successful Partnership

Internal Journal

We worked with a midsized firm. They did everything we did including the steering committee meetings at 6:00 a.m. They provided training, gave up-front issue analysis, talked to the plant people, and took the time to understand the business, the culture, our managers, and the team leaders. They pushed us as much as we pushed them to keep on target with our time frame. They did a good job with up-front planning and foundation building. It was a cooperative effort. The partnership was strong!

**Bud Roth, vice president, human resources, Conseco Services,
former internal consultant with Novartis Consumer Health**

Partnering with Human Resources

The relationship between the internal consulting group and the HR function is frequently problematic regardless of the reporting relationship. Internal consultants

Figure 5-1. Suggestions for successful partnerships with external consultants.

☐ Go after partnership with the external firm. Be specific and come with a proposal that describes expectations and proposed roles. Seek a contract with senior management about the internal-consulting function's involvement in the project, how the two groups will work together, and how information will be shared.

☐ Ensure that management understands the value and expertise of internal consulting. Take a business orientation emphasizing the bottom line and a focus on improving profitability and return-on-investment.

☐ Don't be offended, don't whine about not being included, and don't act out resentment in petty ways.

☐ Recognize that the external consultants become stakeholders in the organization and that they are under the gun to perform too. Help them understand the dynamics of organizational politics.

☐ Help clients understand that they need to play ball and join the team. Help them get close to the consulting firm so they won't be excluded from the decision process.

☐ The internal consultant must be clear about his or her role and competencies before confronting the challenges of large-scale change planned and managed by an external firm. Choosing a role that will best serve both the consultant's own practice and the organization is critical (chapter 3).

☐ Use small firms that specialize in partnership with internal consultants or a sole practitioner who is often a former internal consultant and understands the value of internal-external partnership. They don't have flashy ads and slogans but word-of-mouth will locate them.

☐ For the internal function that is managing the external consulting firm here are some strong suggestions:
   — Define expectations for the external and internal partners in the project.
   — Discuss and determine how conflicts and differences will be resolved.
   — Manage the scope of the project very carefully.
   — Plan frequent communication.

---

describe experiences in which HR sabotaged, challenged, undermined, resisted, and threatened their consulting projects with clients. Yet a strong collaborative partnership with HR is an asset to the internal consultant and is crucial to the achievement of client goals. Serious challenges to project success can be avoided by taking action in advance. Seek to understand the potential conflicts and differences between HR and the internal consulting function and lay a foundation of cooperation and support.

Sources of Conflict

The root of conflicts with HR lies in the traditional role HR is expected to play: maintaining a steady state, minimizing employee problems, and keeping the company out of trouble. In contrast, the internal consultant's role is to facilitate change. This results in misunderstanding and a lack of appreciation of the differences in approach. The internal consultant is more likely to involve the client system in the solution, direct attention to process, and emphasize learning and growth. The HR manager must solve employee problems directly with an expert answer, give direction to a manager to prevent illegal behavior, and emphasize control and conformity to company policies and procedures.

Conflict can stem from the feelings of powerlessness that arise when HR managers are unable to influence senior management regarding critical human issues. When internal consultants have access and influence with senior executives regarding the very issues HR considers to be its turf, it feels like a slap in the face. An internal consultant reporting to a senior executive also potentially contradicts the salary and grade structure, which HR manages for fairness and equity. Internal consultants who negotiate to turn down requests and say no to clients may be seen as picky and arrogant by HR staff who must deal with all the problems and issues and have no "rights" to refuse anyone.

My HR Boss Was Threatened

Internal Journal

I had more problems within the HR system than I ever had with any of my clients. In one case, when my client was an executive, I went to executive staff meetings that my HR boss did not get to attend. He did not understand that it was not a reflection on his power but rather was required to best serve the client. Unless your boss is a strong and centered individual, he or she can feel pretty threatened when the internal consultant has access that they don't.

**Nedra Weinstein, Catalyst Consulting Team,
former internal consultant with communications industry**

Understanding the issues from the perspective of human resources and "getting inside their heads" is a critical first step. Then internal consultants can educate HR regarding their role, charter, work style, rationale, and approach to partnership. Understanding the importance of autonomy, needs for confidentiality, and access to senior levels will help HR appreciate the differences in the roles. Change and workplace learning initiatives inevitably require collaboration, support, and partnership with the HR function. With such a partnership, there is an opportunity to influence and broaden HR managers' consulting skills and

Partnering with HR

. . . I work with HR staff to broaden their view of themselves as consultants so that I can work with them. They have been a broker for me with their clients. They are very aware of the potential conflicts and very good about honoring the boundaries.

Jim McKnight, OD consultant, California Federal Bank

broker the internal consultants' services to the organization. This is especially true because one of the important trends influencing internal consulting services is that HR itself is outsourcing transaction services and moving toward internal consulting.

Allies in HR

I learned through the years. Originally the consulting function was very separate from HR because it didn't have a good reputation in the organization. That changed during the time I was there. The HR function became more of a business partner. That is the way it is today in most organizations, I believe. Always approach HR as a partner . . . My advice is to work through an agreement with HR about how to get clients through them and how to keep HR informed. It is important to follow the decision processes in the organization and honor them. As an internal consultant, you shouldn't circumvent HR processes; you must work with them because of the need for internal relationships.

Eddie Reynolds, consultant, executive and organization development, former internal consultant with high-technology industry

Internal Marketing

Marketing internal-consulting services can be a challenging issue. The culture of the organization may frown on expending time and money. One consultant stated flatly that the chief operating officer hated marketing. Many acknowledged that they do not publicize their success or "market" their function very well. Yet survival and long-term success of internal-consulting functions require positioning the consulting function, identifying the services to be offered, and finding the strategy to best support the needs of the organization. Other actions to "market" the consultant's services are based on successful consulting.

Marketing is Good Consulting

As an internal consultant I did very little marketing to sell my services. Once I started doing work, the work kept coming—more than I could handle. What contributed to that were the reputation I built and my reporting to the president of the product unit. I was the consultant for the whole division, and I worked with the president and those who directly reported to him. I established my reputation first by educating clients regarding the consulting process.

Jan M. Schmuckler, Consultation,
former internal consultantwith high-technology industry

The internal consultant's approach to marketing depends on the culture of the organization, the charter given when the internal consultant entered the organization, and the prior experience of the client system. Consultants can emphasize their own efforts to market within the organization via several mechanisms, which are outlined in the following sections.

ENTRY CHARTER

The charters given to internal consultants as they enter the organization help position and market their services. The charter is initiated during the interview discussion about the consultant's expertise and the organization's needs. In addition, the consultant is positioned automatically by title, grade level, and reporting relationship. One internal consultant, Bob Browning, emphasized the importance of developing a "story" before walking in the door, a story that not only includes these factors, but also assignments, style of operation, relationship with the boss, types of clients, and access to them. As discussed in prior chapters, two factors determine the internal consultant's access to senior management: the level of the consultant's position and the credibility of the consultant's own boss. One consultant failed at executive coaching and development because "I did not align myself with the upper levels and build relationships when I came into the organization. I made a naive assumption that my expertise and education would give me entry. I needed to be more politically savvy."

RELATIONSHIP BUILDING

Building relationships involves a longer-term focus for internal consultants than it does for external consultants. Jeff Cohen, an internal consultant, identifies the need for developing relationships with key leaders who will stand by him during a reorganization or when survival of political challenges requires the leaders' support. Relationship building is balanced with being task-focused, achieving results desired by the client, and adding value. To demonstrate support and build relationships with clients, internal consultants suggest a variety of actions: follow up on discussions by sending articles of interest to the client, stop by executives' offices to discuss business issues, pitch in to help meet a deadline, or even organize a holiday party. The ability to give advice as a consultant comes from trust and respect, which are rooted in the relationship. Sometimes the little things are as important as big interventions. Kevin Wheeler, a former internal consultant, suggests, "Success as an internal comes through a hundred little interactions and rarely through the big ones. Build relationships over time and you can get things done that no external could ever do!"

BECOME A BUSINESS PARTNER

The biggest advantage internal consultants hold over external consultants derives from their intimate knowledge of the business; after all, they live in the organization. Taking time to learn the business as a new hire will pay large dividends in the future. Mila Baker, an internal consultant, dedicated her first three months to meeting and interviewing key people in the organization. Others mentioned taking months listening, talking to people, attending meetings, and working on the front line to learn as much as possible about the business, the strategy, the numbers, and the competition. Reading about the industry and keeping abreast of changes in the competition, government regulation, and customer expectations is crucial. Cecily Cocco, an internal consultant, emphasizes the need for a deep knowledge of the organization and the business to address the issues of alignment. One consultant asks senior executives, "What keeps you up at night?" These approaches help the internal consultant become a business partner.

New internal consultants must overcome the residue left by prior HR professionals who lacked interest in business issues. They must demonstrate to line management that they can add value by integrating hard business issues with soft human concerns to achieve performance results. Today's environment requires such integration for the internal consultant to survive and be successful. "Be a business partner," Scott Burton, an internal consultant, emphasizes. "Be interested in the business. Don't out-account the accountants. But you need knowledge of where the business is going, where it's been, the business basics, and the business drivers. You need to be business-savvy and business-relevant. You can't come off as not caring about business success."

ASSIGNMENT TO A FUNCTION OR BUSINESS UNIT IN THE ORGANIZATION

In some organizations, a consultant is assigned to support or serve a specific unit. This provides opportunity to get to know the business by working a shift on the shop floor, riding along with sales or service representatives, answering customer calls, or just "hanging out." These activities not only develop credibility but also reveal opportunities where the consultant's expertise can add value. In addition, managers in the business may say, "Production is down, maybe you can help us" or "I have an issue I'd like to talk to you about."

CREDENTIALS, COMPETENCE, AND QUICK HITS

Many internal consultants believe that marketing is just a matter of having the credentials and technical competence to know what they are doing. A solid foundation in the theory and rationale behind why actions work is critical according to one successful, high-level senior consultant. A bag of tricks can wear thin pretty quickly for the internal consultant whose client base is limited to the organization. Several consultants mentioned they demonstrated their competence with an early "home run" that established their reputations. Then with the reputation established and with satisfied clients making referrals, internal consultants have little need to "market" because they will have more work than they can handle.

DEVELOP A STRATEGY

Internal consultants have credibility when they come into the organization as a new hire. Clients will give them the benefit of the doubt, and internal consultants can ride on their bosses' coattails. However, to achieve long-term success, internal consultants must develop their own strategies to approach the work. Do not try be a supermarket source for everyone's needs. Develop a strategy that is organization-specific and anchored in the context of the organization's goals. Determine how best to add value. What will give the early credibility that will open doors, build a reputation, give currency to work on sensitive issues?

Developing a Strategy

Internal Journal

During my first three months, I went around talking to people and doing interviews. I asked them who they thought I was and what I might do. I built relationships, got to know them, and learn about the business. I tried to score some hits by focusing on those needs that could bring about quick results and, at the same time, build a strategy. I wanted them to move away from a "crisis-fix-it" approach, such as asking for a class on conflict management. They thought if I just gave them the class that it would solve the problem. I began telling them that we would address the issues but the answer might not be training, that we were here to help identify problems and potential solutions. So when they called about an issue with a request, we used that as an opportunity to talk about what the issue was and what we could do. It wasn't so difficult because we provided them an option. It did take two years for people to realize that you don't just call up and get a training course.

Mila N. Baker, system director, learning and organization development, Baptist/St. Vincent's Health System

In a large organization with many businesses, a strategy of *breadth* to learn the overall business combined with a strategy of *depth* to develop relationships with a few key, well-placed clients might be the best approach. Another alternative is to meet the pent-up needs with a few quick hits to give the consultant early success, while seeking greater understanding of larger needs that might be best met with systemic, long-term interventions. The strategy need not be a rigid, fixed approach, but a strategy will provide focus, guidance, and structure for approaching the work. It can also be a marketing tool. Nedra Weinstein, a former internal consultant, observes, "You have a host of opportunities and choice points for interventions to help the organization that external consultants don't have . . . These are moment-to-moment opportunities to leverage yourself. I influence the organization by how I choose to use those baby opportunities."

CONFIDENTIALITY AND RESPECT

Maintaining confidentiality is critical not only because it is ethical but also because a violation of confidentiality will undo quickly whatever work the internal consultant has done to build his or her reputation and credibility. Every internal consultant has war stories of colleagues who became useless to the organization after a confidence was broken. Holding firm and taking strong stands about sharing confidential information are linchpins in an internal consultant's reputation. Also important is the perception of the respect the consultant holds for the organization, its history, and all levels of employees. Stories of ignoring the administrative staff or disdainful comments about the past will get passed around quickly and sabotage a carefully crafted image.

Relationships Are Currency

Internal Journal

It is imperative to treat people well. If the executive assistant helps you get information, send her an email to thank her. We don't say thank you enough. The executive secretary has an informal network and can be a powerful ally. Relationships are currency. Spend wisely.

Linda Schomaker, director, corporate human resources, PG&E Corporation

PUBLISH SUCCESSFUL OUTCOMES

Although few consultants reported using media to publish project results, many suggested that it was helpful to find ways to inform a new client about successful work in another part of the organization. That may be as simple as suggesting that one client call the other. Others used in-house newsletters or made presentations to key managers at staff meetings. One consultant offered, "I have to publicize what I do. I want to make it easy for my clients to see my contributions. I believe you should market the state you delivered." Although some expressed regret that they did not publicize results, most consultants were busy and successful without using media to publicize or market their services within the organization.

Client Challenges

Internal consultants have fewer opportunities to choose their clients and are expected to work with a wide variety of clients, some of whom may be difficult or problematic. They are often held accountable for outcomes that may depend on other individuals or functions but over whom they have no control. Assignments or projects may be threatening to others who intentionally refuse to cooperate or consciously undermine or sabotage the efforts. Working with difficult people or overcoming turf issues is seldom easy. Here are some suggestions from experienced consultants:

- Seek feedback. Internal consultants need to know how they are being received.
- Know yourself. Internal consultants must know their own vulnerabilities—how they might get hooked by a difficult client or how another function might be competing—to ensure that they don't contribute to the "problem."
- Take time to understand the history and the way in which this project may threaten HR or other functional areas whose support is needed whenever turf issues might block progress.
- Seek to understand what drives difficult clients, and learn about their experience and approach to the world. This understanding can help a consultant appreciate who the client is and find comfortable ways to work with them.
- Engage the client and seek an agreement for feedback and coaching by saying, "I want to learn how I come across, and I will tell you how you come across."
- Remember that oftentimes difficult people are unaware of what they are doing or the problems they create for others. Holding the assumption that people are basically good and want to do the right thing helps consultants to find ways of working with difficult people.
- Use friends and colleagues from a support network outside the organization to ventilate frustrations and annoyances with client behavior.
- Do not rely on internal support for ventilating except with a totally trusted colleague. A consultant's credibility is at risk if the person leaks the confidence or becomes a potential client.

When Clients Fail to Keep Their Agreements

When senior managers are unwilling to provide the project leadership as defined in the original agreement or are unwilling or unable to model the behaviors or values that they have promised to demonstrate from their leadership position, internal consultants are presented with another challenge. Good contracting is a prevention strategy, but most consultants report that despite good contracting, they have been caught in these sensitive situations. To successfully address these issues requires the courage to confront the client, the right timing to discuss the issue, and the willingness to walk away from the organization.

For some, timing is the toughest issue. Getting an appointment, dropping in on an executive, or finding an informal moment when the client is mentally and psychologically ready to hear and absorb the critical feedback can be very difficult.

Consultants with senior-level access say that dealing with these sensitive issues requires persistence and a long-term view. When the issue was not heard the first time, one consultant came back a year later and found an enthusiastic response.

Tolerance for Disappointment

We must have high tolerance for disappointment. When clients can't walk the talk, they let us down. We get hurt. When we ask people to change, we must realize the difficulty of the task. We need to look for incremental improvement . . . Although people want feedback, it is often not the case especially when we confront them about walk-the-talk issues.

Bob Farnquist, Bob Farnquist Consulting Group, former internal consultant with Santa Clara County

Organization and Leadership Changes

Internal consultants are as vulnerable as the employees to the effects of mergers, acquisitions, downsizings, and changes in reporting relationships, and organizational leadership and strategy. As is true for any employee, internal consultants are best served in these situations by being clear about their career goals and their goals in the organization.

You Likely Will Have a Place

If you do a good job in the organization, you will be more likely to have a place when changes occur. I use my antennae to try to find out about changes before they are public and put myself in a position to help. There are times, however, when the organizational change swallows you up and spits you out. When that happens, you need to know what you are about . . . You need to know yourself, your hot buttons, and how you deal with change—self-awareness.

Jeff Cohen, director, Leadership Development and Market Coordination, Pfizer Pharmaceuticals Group

When major organizational changes do occur, here are several approaches identified by experienced consultants:

- Make every effort to educate and influence new management leadership about leading major organization change, understanding cultural differences, the need for vision, values, strategy, and communication. Internal consultant Jim McKnight bemoans, "I struggled to help them understand what works there doesn't work here." Another complains, "Our biggest problem was getting them to articulate common values."

Put it in Writing

Internal Journal

The fourth year into our ten-year change plan, the top person left and because I didn't have a written agreement, I was back to renegotiating the plan with the new person who was not part of our original management council. I think your agreements need to be in writing and to be shared or published in some form so that it becomes an organization plan and not just an agreement between two people.

**Jim Harley, director, organization development,
Westinghouse Electric Company**

- Provide a service to the organization and help managers learn how to lead reorganizations or downsizings in a humane way.

Develop a System

Internal Journal

Our function decided downsizing was not something the company was just going to do once and it will never happen again. We created a center of excellence in our small team. We did exit interviews. We sorted through literature, looked at studies, talked to academicians, and became well grounded and knowledgeable about best practices. We learned what were the important things to sustain morale and human dignity. We knew if we didn't establish ourselves as content experts, no one else would. We developed checklists and an orientation for managers and set up an active consulting practice. This effort completely changed how the company approached downsizing. The company had been spending money on fancy exit packages that were not values, but it did not do the things that were more important and less costly. We made the few critical items easy to implement and very accessible for our managers.

**June E. Delano, director, executive and management education,
Eastman Kodak Company**

- Meet with the initial sponsor and the new sponsor together if the leadership changes in the midst of an intervention or project. The best option is to review the purpose of the project and its intended outcomes, progress, and accomplishments to date. Seek commitment from the sponsors to support the remainder of the project. If that is not possible, meet with the newly appointed leader to build an important relationship and provide the same project review but without the input and support from the initial sponsor. Realize, however, that despite these efforts, the new leader may not be committed to the project.

Paving the Way

📖
Internal Journal
Whenever I heard of a leadership change coming up, I would bro-ker a meeting with the old manager and the new manager to review why the project existed, the intended outcomes, and the potential impact on the organization. The new manager has the opportunity to cancel the project and rescind its funding. I have to respect that. But I want them to be fully informed when they make the decision about the consequences of canceling it. You have to learn to deal with it. Projects do get canceled.

Jim Fuller, Redwood Mountain Consulting, former internal consultant with technology industry

- Set forth a new contract regarding the scope, timeframe, or outcomes when organization or business issues are distracting the leadership and involvement of the clients. Alternatively, suggest that the project be put on hold for a time until the client can provide the needed direction.
- Explore carefully any changes in strategy and direction with clients to ensure that current projects will continue to add value. If not, contract to make the needed changes to do so.
- Educate and renegotiate with a new boss to secure his or her understanding and support of the internal consulting work. With a change in the consultant's own manager, many of the tactics listed here may also apply.
- Build broad support at multiple levels with key managers who will advocate and continue support for major projects if the top sponsor leaves. Use a representative, diagonal-slice team or steering committee to lead and support large projects even if a sponsor or individual members leave.

Despite these efforts, consultants may find themselves in an untenable position and may need to leave the organization. When internal consultants no longer respect the organization's leadership, cannot find support in the organization for their work, or find that the organization's changing culture is conflicting with their personal or professional values, it is time to update the résumé and get into the market. One consultant reports, "With the merger, I knew they didn't have the values that are important to me, so I planned to leave."

Losing Support

📖
Internal Journal
The president was a tremendous fan of OD work and the values of this work. He retired and a new president came in who had no appreciation. My entire base of support eroded. Even though I was three layers down, my boss knew where his bread was buttered, and I lost a lot of clout. I ultimately left the organization.

Chrissa B. Merron, senior consultant, Concentrics, former internal consultant in the financial industry

Resistance

Change is integral to the work of the internal as an OD consultant, a performance improvement specialist, a learning consultant, or a management developer. Hence, one of the most common client issues is the challenge of dealing with resistance.

Webster's Collegiate Dictionary defines resistance as "the act of resisting, opposition, an opposing or retarding force, an underground force engaging in sabotage." Resistance is more subtle and covert than open disagreement or opposition. It is discomfort or reluctance that people experience but are unable or unwilling to express outright. Clients express resistance when they are reluctant to confront the realities of their situation. Resistance shows up in an individual who drags his or her feet during implementation, a group of individuals who protest learning new skills or knowledge, or a team that quietly continues to ignore newly mandated processes or procedures. Resistance is a sign of change and offers potential for learning. Figure 5-2 lists some of the "faces" of resistance.

How Change Is Introduced

In many organizations, the common wisdom is that resistance holds up progress and must be quashed or dismissed. Nevertheless, resistance is often not a response to the change itself but to the way in which the change or idea is introduced. The traditional, top-down coercion to implement a change forces employees to conform without any consideration of their concerns, wishes, or suggestions. A discussion

Figure 5-2. The faces of resistance.

The person who is resisting may be:

- flooding you with detail or unnecessary explanation
- requesting more detail
- expressing confusion
- delaying or canceling meetings
- remaining silent
- offering easy and unexpected compliance
- saying "Nothing is wrong" or "Everything is fine"
- pressing quickly for solutions
- intellectualizing the issue
- attacking, undermining, or sabotaging
- expressing anger
- saying "I'm not surprised"
- finding "rational" reasons why it won't work in this environment, setting, business, and so forth
- finding an approach, methodology, or data that is wrong or inaccurate
- withholding information, data, or documentation
- postponing
- denying
- suggesting that someone else will not support it.

of the real reasons for the proposed approach and opportunity to contribute and participate usually converts the biggest resisters to champions.

Multilevel Sponsorship

Internal Journal

Multilevel sponsorship is key. Many say that if you don't have CEO support, you won't be successful, but you really need more levels of support than that. I ask myself every day what have I done to build sponsorship for this project . . . I worked on a project to identify high-potential, senior managers all over the world and to help them understand their deliverables and identify their development needs. I had sponsorship from the worldwide chief operating officer who opened the door. But, it was successful because I was painstaking in building the sponsorship of other key people—HR, the bosses of these folks, and the target participants themselves.

Jeff Cohen, director, Leadership Development and Market Coordination, Pfizer Pharmaceuticals Group

Paying Attention to Resistance

Clients who resist acting on agreed-upon goals may need opportunity in a safe environment to explore their anxieties and fears. The intervention may be too great a risk. If the internal consultant encounters resistance, an alternative is to return to the agreement and renegotiate the work. One consultant cautions that consultants also need to be prepared to listen to the "persisters" who may sound like resisters. Persisters may have legitimate concerns about a particular strategy or change initiative. Taking time to explore those specific concerns may contribute significantly to the success of the project. Resistance may also be a legitimate cry from employees who are overloaded with "too much, too fast." Resistance is not a roadblock to be overcome but an expression to be understood.

Summing Up and Looking Ahead

Partnerships with members of external consulting firms or with suspicious members of HR will be more successful if the consultant offers mutual benefit for the collaboration and finds a balance between asserting his or her own position and respecting others. In fact, those same skills will help internals cope with client challenges, as well. Success in working with resistance, problem personalities, or new organizational leadership also builds the credibility and reputation, which internal consultants need to market themselves in the organization.

Thus preventing or overcoming the organizational issues that can cause roadblocks for the internal consultant builds credibility for consulting success. Yet, as we will see in the next chapter, internal consultants can throw up their own roadblocks from rising self-doubt and performance anxiety, fear of authority, or an inability to say no. Success on the inside requires learning to minimize those self-imposed roadblocks, as well.

Chapter 6

When Internal Consultants Throw Up Roadblocks of Their Own

Not only do internal consultants face challenges from their clients, but they must face challenges from within themselves. Although these challenges can impede or interfere with the success of their work, internal consultants must handle them on the run because there is little time to hibernate, process their issues, or lick their wounds before plunging on to the next client or project. For most challenges there are no right answers; the characteristics of the consultant, the client, and the organizational context all play roles. Nevertheless, the wisdom gained from the experience of other internal consultants can provide guidance in overcoming these self-imposed roadblocks.

Anxiety and Self Doubt

Anxiety or self-doubt is a natural reaction for most people when they confront situations that challenge their expertise or competence. Although it is impossible to banish self-doubt and anxieties, it is possible to learn how to cope with these feelings so that they do not distract attention from the client. It is important to stay grounded and centered, to trust intuition, and to focus on the client.

Anxiety Rendered Me Less Effective

Internal Journal

Anxiety about dealing with higher-level clients rendered me less creative and effective. Fear is involved. There sits the ticket to your purse strings and your success. If you step out of line with one person, you can lose out. It is such a political environment. I had a falling out with one person who was in charge of a huge part of the workforce. She would never use me again. It is easier to work at higher levels as an external consultant.

Chrissa B. Merron, senior consultant, Concentrics, former internal consultant with financial industry

When this ability to stay focused fails, the consultant is distracted, immobilized, or emotionally vulnerable. Getting past these feelings of anxiety may require taking a break, leaving the room, or rescheduling a client meeting. For example, trying to win an argument with senior executives is risky business. A better strategy is to "buy some time" and return to the discussion after fully understanding the reasons for the argument. Some internal consultants interviewed for this book stressed the importance of relying on a boss, a sponsor, a peer, or a network of other internal or external colleagues to get another perspective to get them past fear and anxiety.

The Imposter Phenomenon

Internal Journal

We have all dealt with the "imposter phenomenon" when we believe that we don't know enough or we don't know what we are doing. It is normal. I have a network outside the organization where I test ideas and elicit reactions to my concerns and issues. You need to have four or five people to test your "read" of the situation. This network is very important. The people can serve as part-time mentors. Some of network associates are in the discipline and some are not. Their spin on the situation helps maintain perspective.

Jeff Cohen, director, Leadership Development and Market Coordination, Pfizer Pharmaceuticals Group

Authority

Whether acknowledged or not, many people resent or fear those in authority. These reactions often stem from childhood responses to a powerful parent or other significant adults. Internal consultants will not be able to bring value to senior-level management if they "see" a patronizing father or demanding mother in the face of a senior executive. A systems perspective helps to take some of the emotional weight out of the authority issue. All of the organized relationships in the structure can be viewed as necessary components of the system; some have more decision-making power and others have more know-how. Senior managers become less intimidating when they are just viewed as parts of the whole, which contribute to the smooth functioning of the system.

In addition to individual reactions to authority, many large, hierarchical corporations deliver some strong messages: Treat highly placed executives with

Speaking the Truth

Internal Journal

Years ago, one of my projects that was not a success had been imposed by a senior manager who said what we need is management training. He told me to go and develop a series of skill-build-

ing training programs. He made attendance at these programs mandatory for every manager in the organization. The programs were top quality, but they didn't lead to any significant change because the effort was not well thought out. There were no behavioral goals or no real vision of what the results should be. This had a lot to do with my unwillingness to challenge the leader's edict.

Jim Harley, director, organization development, Westinghouse Electric Company

deference, avoid delivering bad news, and support or agree with executive ideas and opinions. Nevertheless, executives usually want to know what is really going on in their organizations and expect candid reactions to their ideas. Senior managers surrounded by yes-men miss business-critical information. Internal consultants have a duty to challenge cultural expectations, provide candid, truthful information, and act in the best interest of the organization.

Delivering the Message

Internal Journal

At least twice when I became aware of a critical issue, sexual harassment, for example, I went to the chairman. I said, "You will not hear about this. I am here to tell you. You can do what you want with it." Since I work at senior levels it is clear where my responsibility is. It would be difficult to move outside the organization that holds your charter.

June E. Delano, director, executive and management education, Eastman Kodak Company

The internal consultant who is courageous and authentic can fill a critical need for executive clients. An established relationship characterized by trust and rapport enables many internal consultants to manage the delicate balance of providing support, communicating tough messages, and serving as trusted advisors. Yet senior managers have reputations for rejecting the feedback and even "shooting the messenger." Consultants interviewed for this book commented that internal consultants must always be "willing to walk" and not carry fear of losing their jobs or they will not take these necessary risks.

Confronting the Client

The city manager for police and fire services had decided that the fire department was going to take on an arduous accreditation process. He had done the same thing with a unilateral decision in the police department a few years earlier. Many police-department employees were resentful that accreditation had been pushed on them. He was a command-and-control person. I explained to him that he was about to make the same mistake with the fire department. I reviewed the history of what had happened. I emphasized the need to involve fire-department personnel up front in deciding whether or not to do it. I strongly advised him against a unilateral decision in this case. It was not his preference, and he made that clear, but I was persistent in expressing my opinion.

I had served under this city manager as a police officer and a firefighter. I had a history and a trusting relationship with him, which I now relied on as an internal consultant. To his credit, he backed off and had the courage to agree he needed to approach it in a different way this time. He formed a group of fire-department personnel who explored the issue and then convincingly sold it to the rest of the department. Unlike the previous experience in the police department, he sought buy-in from the employees. Had this advice come from an external consultant, I doubt he would have agreed with the suggestion.

**Michael Crnobrna, organizational development
coordinator, City of Burnsville, Minnesota**

Saying No

The need to be liked and appreciated drives many internal consultants to accept inappropriate projects or more work than they can handle. Taking fun or creative projects may be tempting but that creates the perception of not adding strategic value to the business. Sometimes, internal consultants care strongly about a project or its proposed results and believe that they need to be involved to ensure its success. Internal consultants may feel pressured to accept a project because they feel obligated to do so, or because they believe that the boss, senior management, or a client requires or expects them to. The long-term impact is work overload, failed interventions, or dissatisfied clients. It is a consultant's responsibility to reserve the right to say no.

The Autonomy to Say No

Internal consultants have to always be willing to say no. Many internals are very good about saying no. If the hierarchy applies pressure when a consultant says no, then managers are not accepting or understanding the role of the consultant. Internal consultants need to contract with management so that they are able to say no, whether in regard to their role or the standards of their work. They need autonomy. I have always operated that way and expect people who report to me to operate that way.

**Eddie Reynolds, consultant, executive and organization
development, former internal consultant
with high-technology industry**

Setting the Parameters

Establishing the flexibility and freedom to say no begins when the consultant is hired and negotiates his or her position (see chapter 9). It is imperative that the immediate boss and potential clients understand the circumstances under which the consultant may refuse a request. The results of defining those parameters ensure a more manageable workload, appropriate use of the consultant's services, and delivery of the greatest possible benefit to the client's system. One internal consultant, Jim McKnight, says, "I can't be all things to all people. If I am in over my head, I look for outside support. I have no vanity about my title and that has enabled me to restructure how I work based on what they need and what I am able to deliver."

For many consultants the parameters for their work include

- accepting only those projects for which the consultant's competencies match the client system
- refusing demands for projects that are likely to fail, do not have sufficient support, or misuse the consultant's expertise or credibility
- reserving the right to refuse projects or to use outside resources when the consultant's own time is limited
- maintaining the confidentiality of any client information.

Reframing the Request

Saying no does not have to be harsh or leave the potential client feeling angry or rejected. Many internal consultants emphasized that they found ways to say no that are diplomatic and clever. As Sue Blouch, an internal consultant, suggests, "You need to say 'No, *and* . . . .'" It is important to respond; do not merely ignore the request. The skills of reframing are helpful to explore the alternatives available to meet the client's request. Here are some hints:

- Listen to the client without rejecting the request or making a commitment.
- Separate understanding from agreement.
- Seek to understand the issue from the client's frame. What are the reasons behind the request? How is the client framing the need?
- Avoid asking *why* questions, which often lead to defensiveness.
- Explore desired outcomes—the client's vision of the results he or she seeks.

Now the internal consultant can offer another way to frame the issue and offer alternatives to achieve the desired outcomes: "Oh, you are in California, this manager is in Paris, and you are not getting the information you need. Okay, let's work on that problem." Once the client believes that the internal consultant hears and understands, the client is usually open to explore the alternatives presented by the consultant.

Guidelines for Saying No

Other consultants apply guidelines for accepting or refusing work based on what will support the strategic direction of the business as a whole, the needs of the specific client unit, and what is best for the potential client. This strategy adds the greatest value to the business. But most consultants deem it very important not to alienate a client whose request does not directly support the business strategy. This requires offering alternative resources or reframing the request. Nevertheless, on some occasions, saying no is the last alternative. One former internal consultant with the life insurance industry reports that after he had refused repeatedly to communicate the client's business-unit strategy to the rest of the senior-management team, the client pulled rank and ordered him to do what he was told. In this case, the internal consultant left the organization.

Taking a Stand

Internal Journal

I was using an individual, leadership-assessment instrument with a leadership team in a powerful business unit. I had a very clear contract that specified the positions involved, how the data would be used, the client's responsibilities, my responsibilities, the timeline, and so forth. I was working with internal HR as a partner. As we got back the feedback forms, it was clear we were getting a low rate of return. I went to the manager and asked if he had done the five things that we had agreed he would do. He said, "No, not exactly." He had not done any of it. Although the intervention was positioned as politically correct, he did not want to do it. He didn't want to do the work. He said that I had to do it because of his commitment to top management. I said I can't make it work and refused. The situation became very political. The good news was I had a contract in writing. The internal HR person had a very hard time when I said no. I went to the senior HR person to explain what happened and why I was choosing not to do it. Everyone agreed it was the right thing to do and that this senior executive needed to learn about the consequences of half-baked interventions.

I felt that I had let down those who did fill out the forms, but I still believe it was the right decision. We never did do the work even though the executive said he would. This was an "old-school" manager who had been called to task because he was not managing the culture of the organization well. To take the pressure off he had called me. If you had asked me at the outset about the potential for success, I would have said it was not very good. But high-level people wanted the project, so I waded in. The fact that he didn't hold up his end and I made it an issue contributed to changing the opinion about him. If I had not had lots of credibility, I would have been "creamed." I also would not have done it, if I had alternatives.

**June E. Delano, director, executive and
management education, Eastman Kodak Company**

Juggling Clients and Workload

The internal consultant usually has several clients with several different projects in different parts of the organization or a large or long-term project with a sponsor, several layers of management, and other functional units and employees involved. Regardless, the consultant's task is to keep multiple clients with different needs, agendas, goals, and time schedules happy.

WHO IS THE CLIENT?

Despite the reference to the client as a single person, many projects for internal consultants are complex with many clients who must be supported, involved, and committed. Some internal consultants consider the total organization their client; others believe that their charter is to serve a particular unit or level. What is most important is to know who is making the decisions, who will work closely with you, and who needs to be involved. All of these individuals are clients. They include

- the sponsor who makes the final decisions and approves the budget but is not involved on a day-to-day basis
- the direct client with whom the internal consultant works most closely to plan and implement the project
- the customers, end users, or participants who will attend the planned workshop or off-site event, apply the recommended performance improvement techniques, or learn the new, required skills
- the stakeholders who are functional clients from HR or information systems or other units who will provide technical or resource support, approve the project, or help navigate the client system.

To achieve a project's desired results, consultants must recognize clients' roles, needs, personal investment in the project, and what issues and concerns they bring. In addition the internal consultant must ensure that all of these "clients" are engaged and committed to achieve the desired results by building relationships, obtaining their support, and keeping them informed.

Contracting with Multiple Clients

Internal Journal

In one of my projects, we were identifying the leadership skills needed for the future. I used large-group methods and action research. The outcome was to be the leadership framework and principles for the leadership-development program. I was contracting with the CEO, two vice presidents, my boss, and my peers in HR.

Former internal consultant with high-technology Internet company

DIVIDING THE PROJECT

Schaffer (1997) advocates taking large projects and carving off short-term chunks that will yield measurable results and that are in step with the client's readiness for change. These steps not only generate momentum but also enable the internal consultant to better manage and balance multiple projects, which are pieces of a larger intervention. The consultant's and client's expectations are kept in closer alignment by determining the scope, timeline, accountability, and measurable outcomes for each of these smaller projects separately.

Dividing large projects into smaller pieces offers other advantages, as well. One of the fatal flaws of large consulting projects, according to Schaffer, is ignoring the client system's readiness for change during efforts that aim for big solutions rather than incremental success. To reverse this fatal flaw, he recommends involving employees in smaller projects that will yield quick results and please multiple stakeholders. Seeing results raises the "zest factor" in the organization and helps build enthusiasm and willingness to support the change initiative (Schaffer 1997). Managers sitting on the sidelines are also more easily convinced of the project's merit.

MULTIPLE CLIENTS, DIFFERENT PROJECTS

Internal consultants often have multiple clients who are not involved in the same project and work in different parts of the organization. These projects may collide with each other on the consultant's schedule unless the client's expectations and the consultant's time are managed carefully. Consulting projects have the tendency to grow beyond the initial request. As clients come to trust the internal consultant, they may seek additional help or raise their expectations once they appreciate the possibilities. To manage "scope creep," many consultants treat these expanded requests as additional projects with new agreements, including timelines, responsibilities, scope, and so forth. This may require communicating to clients that they are not the only ones in the consultant's stable of clients. Being diligent in establishing limits helps internal consultants balance their availability with their clients' needs and expectations.

The Wisdom of Experience

To close chapters 5 and 6, current and former internal consultants from a broad spectrum of backgrounds offer sage advice to avoid pitfalls, overcome roadblocks, and navigate personal landmines. Here is a sampling of their collective wisdom:

- *Don't forget the power of networking.* "Go out of your way to make friends with senior managers, operations staff, peers, secretaries, and frontline employees. Seek out strong-opinion influencers—even those who may be angry at the system. Use them as sounding boards, seek their reactions, and ask them what they see as roadblocks. Never compromise their confidentiality or quote them. This will keep you plugged in about what is really going on." (Sue Thompson, Thompson Group, former internal consultant with Levi Strauss & Company)

- *Always get the right sponsorship for an intervention.* "I planned a meeting with an internal consultant from another division. It was fun doing a new design. But there was no sponsorship, no clear charter, no passionate owners. There were two aspiring 'wannabe' leaders. We planned past those who had roles in the past and ignored people who had been on the agenda. We ended up with hurt feelings and overt hostility. If we had clear sponsorship, we would not have made so many mistakes." (Internal consultant with a large consulting firm)

- *Find someone to listen.* "Find someone you trust implicitly to be an employee with whom you can share your frustrations, complain irrationally, and share your consulting wins, as well." (Nedra Weinstein, Catalyst Consulting Team, former internal consultant with communications industry)

- *Don't label it a value conflict.* "If you couch it as a value conflict, it escalates. I want to do the right thing, and I assume the client wants to do the right thing. Maybe we are making assumptions. Let's talk about those. I am very reluctant to say it is a value conflict because the language is loaded." (Jeff Cohen, director, Leadership Development and Market Coordination, Pfizer Pharmaceuticals Group)

- *Use yourself well.* "Remember that even when it gets lonely, you are a presence the system needs. You are filling a gap. It is your reason for being there." (Sue Blouch, CSC, former internal consultant with Taubman Company)

- *Know yourself.* "Know and understand your own limitations." (Jim Harley, director, organization development, Westinghouse Electric Company)

- *Under-promise and over-deliver.* "Stick with your promises. Always return telephone calls to the client as quickly as possible. Meet the dates you set, or do it even sooner and better!" (Former internal consultant with life insurance industry)

- *Don't take it personally.* "If you're not resilient, you don't belong in this profession. There will always be setbacks, disappointments, and failures. Don't take it personally, recover fast, and move on." (Jim Harley, director, organization development, Westinghouse Electric Company)

- *Everything is not a nail.* "You can't have just one method and one tool. If everything isn't a nail, a hammer doesn't work. You need a toolbox. As an external consultant, I have the luxury of saying I am a plumber. As an internal consultant, I am a handyman. I do lots of things to some degree. I need to be broadly skilled. An internal consultant needs knowledge an inch deep and a mile wide. An external consultant needs knowledge a mile deep and an inch wide." (Kevin B. Wheeler, Global Learning Resources, former internal consultant with Charles Schwab Corporation)

- *Your affiliation needs won't be met.* "Be aware that the internal is always an outsider. If you have affiliation needs, they won't be met in the consulting role." (Jan M. Schmuckler, Consultation, former internal consultant with high-technology industry)

- *You need a strong social network.* "Confluence with the client is hard when you live in the organization. It was almost unavoidable for me with bonding experiences in the smoking room. I am a high extrovert with strong social needs that I want to meet. You need to have a strong social network so you don't depend on work for your social needs." (Sue Blouch, CSC, former internal consultant with Taubman Company)

- *Don't let it go to your head.* "There are challenges of dependency when you are a client's first consultant and he or she won't use anyone else . . . It can be very heady to have so much influence and power at the top of the organization . . . You need to remember that influence is a form of control—too much of it and you lose your role as a consultant." (Gerald R. Pieters, EverChange Institute, former internal consultant with Signetics Corporation [now Philips Semiconductor])

- *You can't fight city hall!* "When the CEO says something is going to happen and the vice presidents are in concurrence, it will happen. And you have to figure out how you are going to behave." (Marilyn E. Blair, TeamWork, former internal consultant with 3Com Corporation)

- *Know your costs.* "You need to know what your proposal costs are in both hard and soft numbers. You should also know your own cost and how much you are worth. Sometimes we may fear being seen as too expensive. But it is better to be clear about the value that we add. Be prepared to share your own costs per hour or day and provide a project budget with appropriate external comparisons." (Linda Schomaker, director of corporate human resources, PG&E Corporation)

- *Shut up and listen.* "Sometimes I have to kick myself because I get so passionate about what I am doing. I have to tell myself to shut up. When I ask follow-up questions and listen, people share so much. As an internal consultant with many working relationships, I can go anywhere in the organization, ask a few questions, and the employees will talk to me. This is an advantage for the city manager, since he can't get that information himself. I make it clear to people what I will share and what I will not share, and I am very careful to keep their trust and appropriately honor their confidentiality." (Michael Crnobrna, organizational development coordinator, City of Burnsville, Minnesota)

- *Set priorities on the basis of the business.* "Basically, the role of the internal is to understand the business needs of clients and help them be successful in meeting those needs. Do whatever it takes to make it happen. Prioritize your work on the basis of the business. Shifting to a charge-back process catalyzed my thinking on this. When we decided to run more like a business and focus on four things we could do to help move the business to the future, we asked, 'Will this make a difference to the bottom line?'" (Jan M. Schmuckler, Consultation, former internal consultant with high-technology industry)

- *Have one foot out the door.* "Internal consultants have to keep moving around or we will get sucked in. It is time to leave when you no longer respect the leadership. Internal consultants are always pushing the organization to go further with teams, learning, systems, TQM, and the like. You stop being effective when you get cynical about the company's ability to grow or do things that are new or in development." (Scott Burton, internal consultant with consumer products industry)

- *Keep learning and improve your craft.* "You need to be in a constant state of learning and improving your craft even if you've been a consultant for a while. Our clients don't want to feel like they are drinking from a stagnant pond." (Jim Fuller, Redwood Mountain Consulting, former internal consultant with technology industry)

- *Take time to renew.* "My promise to myself is that I will not walk through the door if I don't want to come to work and have something to give. If I am feeling bad or resentful, those feelings will come with me in my work with my clients. I work on it before I come in. This doesn't mean faking it; it means realigning, calibrating, tuning, processing, and rediscovering the place where I can say this is what I chose to do." (Michael Lindfield, senior OD consultant, Boeing Company)

- *Expand your horizons.* "To be successful you need to be capable of doing lots of things. As an internal consultant, you don't just do one thing. Pay your dues by doing team building, training, management development, process improvement, TQM, information technology, and interpersonal development. You need a variety of assignments. Get involved in a variety of activities, find opportunities to start a function from scratch, take fix-it positions, and scope out all types of jobs." (Jim Harley, director, organization development, Westinghouse Electric Company)

- *Know what is under the water.* "You have got to know that there is more than the tip of the iceberg here. You have to have a lot under the water— competence, values, ethics, and interpersonal skills. The deeper the intervention, the more important is your expertise. You need to know what to do with the information you get." (Jeff Cohen, director, Leadership Development and Market Coordination, Pfizer Pharmaceuticals Group)

- *Give something to get something.* "Remember when building relationships, you have to give something to get something. To get trust and access, you need to give expertise, facilitation, a write-up, a resource, and you must meet their needs." (Tracey Borst, executive director, human resources, AirTouch Communications)

- *Build in diversity.* "Build diversity—not just gender and race diversity but also different disciplines—into every activity. Get people who will fight and have value clashes. You will get more creative solutions with diverse points of view." (Jim Harley, director, organization development, Westinghouse Electric Company)

- *Know when to pick your fights.* "As internal consultants, we have to know when and how to pick our fights. I've done some work in the last decade that I wanted to say 'no thanks' to. These were issues that lacked indicators of success, but someone wanted to try something. It was easier to say yes than to fight it." (June E. Delano, director, executive and management education, Eastman Kodak Company)

- *Find a way to say yes.* "Always say yes. Find a way to avoid saying no and redirect the client's expectations." (Jim McKnight, OD consultant, California Federal Bank)

- *Don't give up.* "Don't give up, keep coming back, and eventually events will come together to support your position." (Cecily A. Cocco, vice president, change management, Blue Shield of California)

- *Hold an external mindset.* "Hold the mindset of the external who is marketing and delivering a service and who must account for 'billable' hours." (Monica McGrath, Resources for Leadership, former internal consultant)

- *Be courageous and practical.* "Bring tools and technologies to help the client see how he or she can achieve business results. Be a courageous advocate leading an intervention. It is my job to advocate." (Helm Lehmann, author, former OD manager, REI)

- *Make a quick hit.* "When you enter an organization, find a way to have a quick hit to establish your currency. A strong culture has a strong immune system and will try to destroy a new person." (Bob Browning, director, Global Career Planning and Development, Colgate-Palmolive Company)

Summing Up and Looking Ahead

Getting past the deep-rooted personality traits that can destroy successful relationships and sabotage projects is not always easy. Finding ways to overcome these self-imposed roadblocks and navigate these personality landmines takes creativity, courage, and persistence. The payoff is personal and professional competence and, of course, a more successful client outcome. Many experienced internal consultants find this challenge a deeply satisfying one. Chapter 7 further explores this pursuit of self-knowledge and its impact on consultant effectiveness.

Reference

Schaffer, R. (1997). *High Impact Consulting.* San Francisco: Jossey-Bass.

Developing Your Best Self

The principal *work* of the internal consultant is building relationships with clients. It is the *work* of establishing the trust and credibility to allow management and employees to share their issues, their concerns, their dreams, and their secrets. The *work* is not in applying skilled expertise, brilliant competence, or unique academic models. It is a skilled craft that requires building trusting relationships across all levels of the organization. Some of the tools that this work requires are competence-based, but other tools are built from the self-knowledge of a lifetime of learning from experience. This chapter discusses the personal values and self-knowledge that are the bedrock of a successful internal consultant.

Building Relationships Will Add Value

One of the most difficult things for an internal is to show a manager that you can add value. Most managers don't believe that we can add value. Relationships with managers need to be personal to enable you to identify the needs of management that you can address. If you don't have the rapport, you won't be successful. The ability of the client to hear your advice comes from trust and respect, which emanate from the relationship.

**Kevin B. Wheeler, Global Learning Resources,
former internal consultant with Charles Schwab Corporation**

Internal
Journal

Stewardship of Internal Consultants

Internal consultants are stewards of the organization in the same sense that Block (1993) described stewardship: a willingness to be accountable without the control of leadership and without the paternalism of caretaking. Stewardship is a choice for service in partnership with clients to build a more meaningful, productive, and

Relationships Are My Work

The work is all in relationships. There is more real work through the relationships you build as an internal, because you are more able to navigate the potholes and work with the executives on their issues.

Internal Journal

Diane Foster, Diane Foster & Associates, former internal consultant with Advanced Micro Devices and California State Automobile Association

empowered workplace. Internal consultants are stewards of the culture of the organization amidst the turmoil of wrenching change. Stewardship requires that internal consultants be accountable for results and be responsible for themselves and what they project onto others.

Accountability as an Internal Consultant

I feel the consequences and ramifications more deeply when I am an internal consultant. An external consultant is not part of the system and not really accountable to anyone for the results (other than for their own reputation). When you are working in one system, your feet are held to the fire by the norms, values, and culture of the organization.

Internal Journal

Chrissa B. Merron, senior consultant, Concentrics, former internal consultant in the financial industry

Palmer (1994) emphasized responsibility in this definition of a leader: "a person who has an unusual degree of power to project on other people his or her shadow or his or her light . . . to create the conditions that can either be as illuminating as heaven or as shadowy as hell." Internal consultants have considerable opportunity to bring light or shadow to their client systems in how they approach their clients. According to Palmer, "A leader must take special responsibility for what's going on inside his or her own self, inside his or her consciousness, lest the act of leadership create more harm than good."

To be stewards, internal consultants must take responsibility for what is going on within themselves in their consciousness. That means looking for ways to project more light than shadow, searching internal monsters, claiming them, and finding ways to tame and integrate them into the psyche. It is only by continuing to face their own internal shadows that consultants can be authentic with their clients. Taking this journey, a spiritual journey, is demonstrating the responsibility in stewardship. A spiritual journey is not a religious journey, although it may be for some. It is the internal exploration to become aware of the person inside with hidden feelings and emotions, power and will, purpose and values. It is also a journey that explores the search for connection and community, for an understanding of how to develop meaningful relationships with others. It is a journey to develop one's best self.

Building Ethical and Credible Relationships

The best advice for internals is to build relationships that are ethical and credible. You come in the door with assumed technical competence. The work for the internal consultant is to build relationships . . . but it is to build ethical relationships . . . You need to see yourself as a resource to the organization. It takes quite a bit of personal insight and maturity to avoid being subsumed and colluding with the dynamics of the organization.

Internal Journal

**Monica McGrath, Resources for Leadership,
former internal consultant**

The job of internal consultants is to make the contact with their clients, build a relationship, and help them take ownership of their responsibility for change. If the consultant does not do this job, there will be no real change in clients, in performance results, or in the organization. Committing to the client's success and making the relationship work require the consultant to focus on the client, not him- or herself. Beckhard (Bergman 1996) said that consultants need to turn themselves off and try to understand the client's music.

To be a steward of the organization and to understand the client's music require that the consultant be present, focused, and balanced. It also requires confidence and comfort with oneself and one's abilities, to be self-aware, and to practice integrity with one's own physical, emotional, and mental energy. It requires the discipline of personal mastery. The rest of this chapter elaborates on these areas, which enable internal consultants to bring their best selves to their work.

Personal Mastery

Senge (1990) introduced the concept of personal mastery as one of the five disciplines for the learning organization. "Personal mastery goes beyond competence and skills, though it is grounded in competence and skills. It goes beyond spiritual unfolding or opening, although it requires spiritual growth. It means approaching one's life as a creative work, living life from a creative, as opposed to a reactive, viewpoint."

The discipline of personal mastery calls for internal consultants to be clear about what is important, what is their vision of who they are, and how they want to be in their lives and work. Personal mastery also requires continuously seeking clarity about what is happening in the present. When something happens with a client or a colleague that is discomforting, the internal consultant needs to seek to understand the negative emotional reaction. Senge (1990) uses the metaphor of a rubber band to describe the tension that exists when one holds a vision with the discomfort of the present reality and pulls toward the desired future. That creative tension helps people learn more about themselves, work through emotional barriers, develop new competence, and overcome negative energy.

Purpose and Mission

Human beings are "meaning-seeking" as Wheatley and Kellner-Rogers (1996) remind us. Finding meaning and purpose in work can bring the internal consultant true joy, satisfaction, and creative results. Block (1993) called it "connecting the heart and the wallet." An internal consultant who finds purposeful work or even a sense of calling will bring his or her creative energy and high levels of performance to the work with clients. Purpose or mission differs for each person, but identifying work one truly loves, that uses one's talents in ways that have significance, requires one's best self in that work. For many internal consultants, work has significance when the results are that employees learn, leaders inspire, and organizations become effective.

Ability and Competence

The success of the internal consultant according to the discipline of personal mastery is more than competence, although it is grounded in competence and skills. Several consultants interviewed for this book cite the importance of competence in gaining respect, although they quickly add that respect and credibility are also based in the quality of the relationship with the client. One consultant phrased it as "doing honorable work that is organic to the organization and makes sense to the managers." A former internal consultant with the life insurance industry talked about getting access to senior management by working hard and ensuring that his technical competence was good and above average.

Credentials Are Important

Internal Journal

For internal consultants, credentials are important. They need to know the theory and know why they are doing what they are doing. Consultants can come in with a bag of tricks. But managers are pretty smart, and a bag of tricks bottoms out quickly. If you have basic theories of groups, organization, and so forth, you are in a better position to genuinely help the client system.

June E. Delano, director, executive and management education, Eastman Kodak Company

Just to get through the door, internal consultants must possess expertise in a specific discipline, knowledge of theories of change, hard business skills, and good interpersonal skills. This book is directed toward consultants with expertise in such disciplines as OD, HPI, and HRD. Because these are change disciplines, the internal consultant must also be well versed in the theory behind and knowledge about individual and organizational change. Prior chapters emphasized the importance of business knowledge—the "hard" skills necessary to understand what drives the strategic and financial results of the business. Credentials and competence in these areas build internal consultants' confidence and trust in their abilities to perform and achieve results. Finally, interpersonal competencies help the internal consultant build client relationships and develop the trust and confidence needed for clients to make commitments, take risks, and initiate change. The pace of change today requires internal consultants to maintain their competence and knowledge base by constantly learning and improving their craft. Internal consultants should periodically take stock of their abilities, practices, skill development, and knowledge to maintain effectiveness. Appendix 1 is an inventory for performing such an evaluation.

Continuous Learning

Internal Journal

We have to be continuously learning. We need to spend a percentage of our time upgrading our own skills and ourselves. Things are changing so fast that we can fall into old habits of using what worked in the past and failing to keep pace with new developments. We must have a high commitment to go to professional conferences, seminars, personal-development workshops to stay abreast of what is happening in our field. It is so important to take the time to learn!

**Bob Farnquist, Bob Farnquist Consulting Group,
former internal consultant with Santa Clara County**

Continuous Self-Development

Confidence and the ability to address organizational challenges and difficult clients come from the internal consultant's lifelong process of conscious self-development. Self-knowledge comes from exploring one's self through the perspective and assumptions of a variety of frameworks. Although true believers argue the virtues of specific frameworks, all of them provide benefits in terms of insight and self-knowledge. The Myers-Briggs Type Inventory and other assessment tools provide feedback on the consultants' style of leadership, communication, and approach to conflict. Participating in a 360-degree feedback process, which includes clients, peers, external colleagues, superiors, and subordinates, will ensure genuine feedback. One internal consultant admonishes, "Don't fall into the 'cobbler's shoes' syndrome."

Internal Consultants Need to Know Themselves

Internal Journal

Internal consultants need to know themselves, where they are willing to negotiate, and where they are unwilling to negotiate. When you first start out in consulting, you are going to be pushed. Knowing your boundaries is very important . . . I have a very strong value-based orientation, and I let people know when they overstep the boundaries or if they are not aligned. For example, when a manager in another organization for which I had worked asked me to do a 360-degree assessment, I discovered he had already made up his mind to fire the person and just wanted to use the assessment data to support his position. I said no. There is no room for negotiation with me on that issue.

Bob Browning, director, Global Career Planning and Development, Colgate-Palmolive Company

Another avenue for self-development is using a therapist, coach, or group-support session to explore the relationship of current challenges to significant life experiences. The internal consultant should explore some tough questions:

- What are the issues that hinder me, trip me up at unexpected times, or undermine my effectiveness?
- Is it collusion or cowardice when I say that the client is not ready to hear it yet?
- If I confront the client will I lose the client relationship or am I just avoiding conflict?
- Why am I in such a hurry to please and get approval?
- Is my assessment of the client system on target, or am I unwilling to take a risk?

Know Your Shortcomings

Internal Journal

Knowing your shortcomings and potential conflicts is critical. I have to be real clear about my priorities and what value I bring as an internal. I used to think I could take the job and shove it. Now I wonder if I am as clear as I should be. Have I changed because of machismo or defense mechanisms? Or is it about fear or my identity being tied up in this job?

Michael Horne, director, organization development, Marriott International

Recognize the Shadow

The lifelong learning process for the internal consultant also means continuing to seek understanding of the shadow side of the self—that part of ourselves that we have not yet examined. Because it is in the shadows and hidden, it holds a great deal of power. Acknowledging these hidden parts of the self helps to minimize their influence and not let them hinder you in a tough client situation. It is recognizing and exploring the signals of tension and anxiety, such as leaping to answers, practicing one-upmanship, tightly controlling emotions, or eagerly, but insincerely, agreeing with the client.

Clean Up Your Own Issues

Internal Journal

As an external consultant, you can get by with charisma and some tools. If you are not clean with your own issues, they probably won't haunt you. As an internal consultant, if you are not clean with yourself and how you use yourself, you will get a reputation, and you will stumble over your own issues . . . Attention to your own use of self and how you deploy yourself is critical. We can get lazy and forget how important this is. For example, if we can't manage our own anger about downsizing, it plays out with our clients.

**June E. Delano, director, executive and management education,
Eastman Kodak Company**

One internal consultant discovered that she had projected her feelings about her father onto the senior-level management of her company. Such "little-girl" deference diminished her power and limited her value as a consultant. She was able to identify this issue, work through it, and reduce its influence on her senior-client relationships. Another consultant found that he had problems with clients in authority, which he traced to a very authoritative grandfather. He was able to remind himself that the individual in front of him was his client, not his grandfather, and so avoided being reduced to childhood terror when the client got angry.

Clients pick up on the consultant's shadows, which can contaminate and erode the quality of the relationship. The consultant is no longer comfortable and confident and can quickly lose the relationship he or she worked hard to build. Practicing the discipline of personal mastery means confronting internal shadows, searching out old ghosts, and embarking on a personal quest to move toward the internal consultant's best self. Ashmore, a former internal consultant and spiritual coach, has developed a process by which internal consultants can safely acknowledge and tame their shadows. The method—a series of exercises, really—is included in appendix 2.

Beliefs

Much of human behavior is habitual. Habits engender ease and efficiency, thereby enabling us to move quickly through our morning routines or drive familiar routes without much thought. Habits are based on belief; for example, beliefs about health or cleanliness support the habits of our morning routines. Other beliefs influence how we respond to the behavior of others or how we go about our work.

Those beliefs can result in habits that undermine or diminish our power. One internal consultant interviewed for this book shared the beliefs behind her need for extensive details about a situation before she would answer a question. This tendency drove her boss crazy and although she had tried various alternatives, she had been unable to change her behavior. Then she discovered that a belief she held, rooted in childhood experience, lay behind this irritating habit. She held the belief that she always had to have the "correct" answer, and without all the detailed information she might be wrong. Another believed that if he offered his opinion or ideas, he would be humiliated or laughed at so he had become a great listener but seldom offered any of his own perspectives. Uncovering such personal belief systems leads to greater freedom in choosing more constructive behaviors. Changing beliefs can lead to deep individual change.

Principles and Values

The power and influence that internal consultants wield in their organizations demand ethical constraints and a set of values to guide the consultant's behavior. Credibility and competence in building relationships, handling resistance, coaching clients on sensitive issues, and providing personal feedback require a clear set of professional values to tether and guide the internal consultant's consulting practice (DeVogel et al. 1995a,b).

During the interviews for this book, many consultants referred to their own values and the values of their practices. Most frequently, they emphasized a respect for the trust placed in them by the client and treating the client's information as strictly confidential.

Client Confidentiality

Internal Journal

I was asked by one HR manager for one of the business units if I would tell him what issues I was working on with a particular coaching client. He wanted to discuss the individual's issues with other HR people to define how he should intervene with this person and his organization. I refused to tell him, because I believed that all the client's data should be held in strict confidence. He lectured me saying, "You are an employee of this organization, a member of HR, and we are a team. You need to support this team." I told him if it came to breaking confidentiality, I would leave the organization first. He then began to back off.

**Monica McGrath, Resources for Leadership,
former internal consultant**

The issue of confidentiality is constantly tested for internal consultants. Immediate bosses, HR managers, and senior executives often request that the consultant share information. Several consultants recounting such experiences emphasized their belief that information is inviolate even at the risk of losing a job. Practicing this value is based on more than principle. It is also very practical; violating it compromises the consultant's credibility and reputation with clients. One consultant recounted the loss of credibility by colleagues who did not keep this trust.

Being open, truthful, and authentic also reflects important values, which guide consultants' interactions with clients. Without behavior that consistently matches these values, it is almost impossible for the internal consultant to build trusting relationships, serve as stewards for the organization, or partner for critical changes. Making a commitment to the client's success requires an ability to move beyond the needs of one's own ego and desires and the demands of those in authority to rise to the higher level of values and ideals required by internal consulting.

Knowing Professional Values

Internal
Journal
I have always associated and felt more affinity with my profession than with the organization. As an internal consultant you need firm grounding in your professional perspective. When I was new in one organization, a client wanted me to have a prearranged solution before I did the needs analysis. I was very distressed. I got strength to confront the situation by consulting an outside colleague and mentor. I highly recommend finding external resources to help you sort out your position or to reinforce your own values when there is conflict with your client or the organization.

**Nedra Weinstein, Catalyst Consulting Team,
former internal consultant with communications industry**

If a consultant's personal values do not align with the company values, then, as one consultant put it, "Don't go there." To be congruent as a consultant, it is important to work in an organization with corporate values that the internal can support. However, another consultant advised, "Remember we are here to help the business, we are not on a religious quest." If the values of the organization change as a result of a merger or a change in leadership, and there is a mismatch, then it is time to move on.

Corporate Versus Personal Values

There is the issue of corporate values versus personal values which at times are in conflict. If your personal values are harmony, balance, and stability and corporate values involve change, then get with it or get out. Find a company that reflects your personal values so that you can be a happy person . . . Your values have to agree with the corporate values or you will not be successful or personally happy.

**Kevin B. Wheeler, Global Learning Resources,
former internal consultant with Charles Schwab Corporation**

Energetic Integrity

Human beings, like everything else in the universe, are composed of energy. Energy provides the vitality, vigor, and the will and the capacity to motivate and move toward a vision and goals. Positive energy can transform. It can

Being Grounded and Centered

Internal Journal

Working as an internal requires a consultant to be very centered and self-confident. If you are not grounded, then you won't add enough value to be worth being on the payroll. Lots of people are deferential to authority. Not many people are provocative and effective in their interaction with senior management nor are they able to provide a perspective that wouldn't be there otherwise. Many internal consultants don't have that grounding. They end up being a pair of hands and doing trivial work in the larger scheme. When internal consultants are well grounded and know who they are, they can be a really valued voice at the center of power.

**June E. Delano, director, executive and management education,
Eastman Kodak Company**

bring light when others are anxious or demoralized. Internal consultants can bring the possibilities of hopefulness, choice, empowerment, and opportunity. Allowing the shadow side to dominate saps energy from others and projects negative emotions on the clients.

Keep Your Cool

Internal Journal

As an internal consultant you are on all the time. You may be walking in the hallway and see someone who wants to talk to you. Or someone may walk into your office to complain about a manager or something that you feel similarly about. Although you might like to agree with them and blast that person or policy, it is necessary to stay centered, balanced, and objective. Otherwise you run the risk of loosing your integrity and power as a consultant.

**Nedra Weinstein, Catalyst Consulting Team,
former internal consultant with communications industry**

In many organizations, internal consultants live in tumultuous environments buffeted by the swift waves of change. Internal consultants move from one intervention to the next with little or no time for recharging; they often handle multiple projects and may have limited choice or control over their work. Maintaining personal balance, energy, and focus amidst the fast-paced business realities of changing strategies, new leadership, cost cutting, and process-improvement initiatives is a constant challenge that can be overwhelming.

To continue to bring the hopeful possibilities, internal consultants must stay in touch with their own physical and emotional energy to be grounded and centered. Appendix 3 describes a grounding-and-centering technique to give one access to natural balance, intuition, intellect, and the heart. It enables internal consultants to be more aware and available for their clients and to practice with emotional and energetic integrity.

Minding Personal Boundaries

As a native it is imperative to mind your boundaries. It is always a dilemma to keep your objectivity and your personal boundaries in check when you are internal. I don't take work home on the weekends. I try not to work more than 45 hours per week to keep a sense of myself and not overwork like the managers I am trying to help.

Molly Smith-Olsson, team leader, organization effectiveness, Blue Shield of California

An internal consultant who is grounded and centered can avoid taking on the negative emotions, anxieties, and fears of his or her clients. It also means being present and open for clients, with empathy, warmth, and caring but not taking on their issues personally. Using the grounding and centering technique also minimizes the risks of storing up the minor irritations and annoyances or the toxic, angry frustrations from others in the organization.

In addition to staying grounded and centered, other practices are also important to ensure that internal consultants maintain vitality and full energy. Many internal consultants talk about the importance of balance, pacing, and keeping boundaries between work life and personal life. The holistic care of mind, body, and spirit is essential to handle the speed of change, the demands of clients, and the challenges to consulting success. Mitani d'Antien, a spiritual teacher and coach, lists seven fundamental areas of self-care to help stay healthy, productive, and energetic:

- *Nutrition:* Proper nutrition varies for each individual. For some a vegetarian diet works because they carefully balance their protein intake. For others, animal protein is important to maintain good health. Some must avoid dairy and wheat products because of dietary allergies. Eating the proper diet and ensuring good nutrition is important for good health and energy.

- *Water:* Drink at least eight glasses every day. Just as car batteries used to need water, our own internal batteries need to be flushed and recharged with water. The physical body can become stiff and arthritic if it is not kept hydrated.

- *Exercise:* The evidence is overwhelming in support of 30–60 minutes of exercise daily to prevent serious illness and promote good health. A half-hour walk is a wonderful way to relax and release stress and tension.

- *Rest and solitude:* Everyone needs time to recharge internal batteries. Consultants give a lot of themselves. Taking time alone to reflect, meditate, close the eyes, or take a catnap is a good way to rebuild internal resources.

- *Breathing:* Taking deep breaths brings fresh oxygen to the whole cellular structure of the body. Breathe in new life through laughter, a walk in nature, or a deep, grounding breath. A deep, long exhalation also releases tension and tight muscles.

- *Fun:* Fun and laughter bring health and healing. Work can become too serious with daily confrontations with organizational and personal challenges. Friends and fun relationships bring joy and deep nurturing to our lives and our hearts. With a heart full of love and joy, we can give to our clients with warmth and caring.

- *Meaningful work:* It is important to ask regularly, "Is my work meaningful?" and "Am I striving toward my goals with my work?" Our lives and our work suffer when work no longer has meaning. If the answer to these questions is no, it is time to review alternatives and perhaps make a change.

How Am I Managing Myself?

Internal Journal

I am in it for the long haul. I need to pace myself. My mantra is that this company is just another important drop in the ocean of life. It is not the end of the world but part of the world. When I feel pressured and stressed, I stop, breathe, smile, let go, and then continue with my work. Since I use myself as a tool, I continue to ask how well am I managing myself? Can I bring myself to the table and be effective? It is a way of both giving and receiving, of nourishing and giving nourishment. I tried to keep pace with the crazy hours of the executives. Then I had to say no. I now live a sane and healthy balanced life with quiet time every morning, exercise, and good food. I don't schedule back-to-back meetings. I need breathing space. I often say no. Sometimes I say yes knowing that the next two or three weeks will be very busy. It is like training for a race knowing that it will take extra effort, but then there will be time to recover. I let clients know that they are not the only ones, although when I am with a client I am there 100 percent.

Michael Lindfield, senior OD consultant, Boeing Company

Summing Up and Looking Ahead

To serve as stewards and be authentic partners with their clients, internal consultants must know themselves through a lifelong pursuit of self-knowledge. This requires the discipline of personal mastery to focus not only on building competence, exploring the inner self, searching for integrity with emotional and physical energy, but also continuously learning through work. Internal consultants can meet the challenges they face and find reward and accomplishment in their work by staying grounded and centered, and consciously in touch with their intuition, intellect, and emotions. If internal consultants practice personal mastery to be fully themselves, they will bring their best selves to their work.

The final section of this book provides a step-by-step guide to the consulting process with checklists, resources, and suggestions to help internal consultants be most effective in serving their clients and their organizations.

References

Bergman, L. (1996, Spring). "An Interview with Dick Beckhard." *Vision/Action*, 4.

Block, P. (1993). *Stewardship: Choosing Service Over Self-Interest.* San Francisco: Berrett-Koehler Publishers.

DeVogel, S., R. Sullivan, G.N. McLean, and W.J. Rothwell. (1995a). "Ethics in OD." In *Practicing Organization Development: A Guide for Consultants,* W.J. Rothwell, R. Sullivan, & G.N. McLean, editors. San Diego: Pfeiffer & Co.

DeVogel, S., R. Sullivan, G.N. McLean, and W.J. Rothwell. (1995b). "Ethics Statements for OD." In *Practicing Organization Development: A Guide for Consultants,* W.J. Rothwell, R. Sullivan, & G.N. McLean, editors. San Diego: Pfeiffer & Co.

Palmer, P. (1994). "Leading from Within: Out of the Shadow, Into the Light." In *Spirit at Work,* J.A. Conger, editor. San Francisco: Jossey-Bass.

Senge, P.M. (1990). *The Fifth Discipline: The Art & Practice of the Learning Organization.* New York: Doubleday.

Wheatley, M.J., and M. Kellner-Rogers. (1996). *A Simpler Way.* San Francisco: Berrett-Koehler Publishers.

The Consulting Process: A Step-by-Step Guide for Internal Consultants

Chapter 8

The Process of Consulting

Many well-known writers, among them Peter Block (1981) and Geoff Bellman (1992), have described a consulting process with linear steps (table 8-1). However, real life seldom follows such a rational, tidy process. The process for internal consultants is often messy and organic. Some phases of the consulting process must be repeated several times, and others are skipped, only to be taken up again later in the cycle. The nonlinear nature of consulting is represented in figure 8-1.

The Consulting Process is Not Linear

Internal
Journal

The consulting process is not linear for internal or external consultants. We had a corporate university, which was an ideal forum for internal consulting. We had a group of people with a broad variety of skills and expertise who could cover all of the HRD areas. We assigned one person to a business group to "hang out" and have discussions. They spent time with the business partner, listened, made suggestions, and were available. This resulted in an informal contracting process. A client might say, "Our production is down, can you give me some help?" Then we could go in directly and do the intervention. We had a formal process, as well. We usually did the diagnosis quickly. We didn't do a formal diagnosis except with an organizational survey, because we had the informal knowledge of what was going on.

**Kevin B. Wheeler, Global Learning Resources,
former internal consultant
with Charles Schwab Corporation**

Table 8-1. Consulting model comparisons.

Consulting Model	Murray Hiebert	Peter Block	Geoff Bellman	Charles Margerison
Consulting Activity	Defining the business need	Entry and contracting	Entry	Contact
	—	—	—	Preparation
	Clarifying expectations and reaching agreement	—	Contract	Contracting
	—	—	—	Contract negotiation
	Gathering information	Data collection and diagnosis	Data collection	Data collection
	—	—	Analysis	Analysis diagnosis
	Recommending options	Feedback and decision to act	Feedback	Data feedback
	—	—	—	Data discussion
	—	—	Alternatives	—
	—	—	Decision	Decision
	—	Implementation	Action	Implementation
	Taking stock or closing	Extension, recycle, or termination	Evaluation	Review
	—	—	Exit	—

Reprinted, by permission from Murray Hiebert & Colleagues, Inc., from Hiebert, M. (1999). *Powerful Professionals: Getting Your Expertise Used Inside Your Organization.* E. Hiebert, editor. Calgary, Canada: Recursion Press.

Eight Phases of the Consulting Process

The eight phases of the consulting process and the goals sought by the consultant in each phase are listed below. Each phase is discussed, beginning in chapter 9 with the contact phase.

- *Contact:* Seek an understanding of the client's organization or business need; lay the foundation of the consultant-client relationship.
- *Agreement:* Confirm the agreement on consultant and client roles, expectations, and the actions each will take. Define the need to be addressed and the goal or outcome to be achieved.
- *Information and assessment:* Gather information about the issue, the business, performance, and the organization. Assess or analyze the data and information collected. Gain an independent view and interpretation of the issues.
- *Feedback:* Provide the client with the information or data; seek acceptance or "ownership" of the data. Offer a consultant's analysis or interpretation.
- *Alignment:* Seek alignment with the client on the desired outcomes or future state and the approach or intervention to be used to achieve it.
- *Change targets and transition strategies:* Clarify which components of the system need to be changed, and identify necessary support and resources. Develop a transition strategy to navigate from the current state to the desired future.
- *Implementation:* Complete the intervention by providing guidance, coaching, facilitation, and leadership to implement the planned change.
- *Evaluation and learning:* Evaluate the success of the project with the client system by supporting the client's reflection and identification of learned skills, knowledge, and self awareness. Explore enhanced knowledge, skills, and self-awareness.

These phases often overlap and are not completed in neat, orderly fashion. The purpose of this section is to discuss in an orderly, linear manner all eight phases, which are integral to any internal consulting project. Keep in mind, however, that the natural tendency is for projects or interventions not to proceed in such a straightforward way. As was diagramed in figure 8-1, a project may require revisiting an earlier phase. Sometimes an initiative or an intervention is prematurely terminated because of leadership changes, demands of customers, changes in the competition, or because the sponsor of the project loses interest and turns to more pressing issues.

Despite the challenges of shifting ground and the need to cycle back to earlier phases, a consultant's commitment to achieve the goals of each phase must remain steadfast. Experienced consultants confess that less successful project results can usually be traced to moving too quickly or overlooking a step in the process.

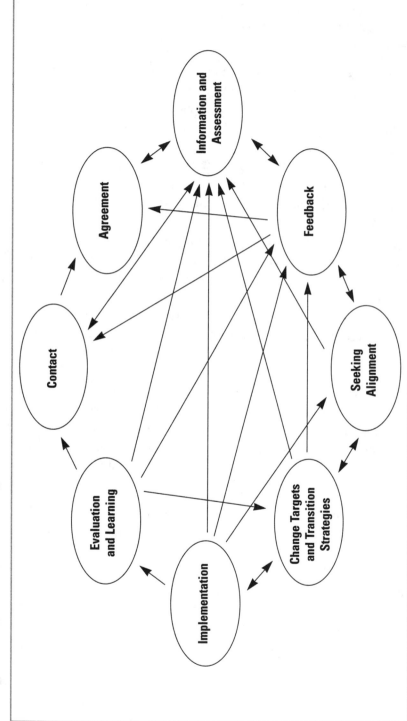

Figure 8-1. The process of consulting.

Summing Up and Looking Ahead

Here we introduced the eight phases of consulting that comprise every consulting project, although it is likely that the process will not proceed in linear fashion. The following chapters in this section will explore each of the phases with detailed suggestions, examples, and tips to achieve success with references to how the phases often overlap.

References

Bellman, G.M. (1992). *Getting Things Done when You Are Not in Charge* (Fireside edition). New York: Simon & Schuster.

Block, P. (1981). *Flawless Consulting: A Guide to Getting Your Expertise Used.* San Diego: Pfeiffer & Co.

Chapter 9

Phase One: Contact— Defining the Need and Building the Relationship

Internal consultants already have intimate knowledge of the organization, know what many of the issues are, and have already established relationships. As Lacey (1995) suggested, internal consultants have an understanding of the root cause of the "presenting problem," because they not only know the people, processes, and operations but are also aware of "sacred cows, waiting guns, sources of power" and are comfortable with the "company anachronisms and jargon." External consultants must spend time learning about the organization and exploring the presenting problem to determine if the project is appropriate. External consulting models often characterize this first phase of the consulting process by using the term *entry*.

Knowing the Problem

Internal Journal

When you develop a close relationship and understand the company, you can go to a senior client with a suggestion or to propose addressing an issue. I went to my boss (the president) and said that as a team we have had the same year's experience several times over. We were not capturing and using the knowledge we'd gained from our past experience in the budgeting and planning process. He proposed using the case study method because he was familiar with it. I collected cases from the top 15 managers who each wrote up two cases with successful outcomes and two cases with unsuccessful outcomes. In a follow-up meeting, we discussed these case studies in small groups. We looked for patterns and proposed an approach to address the problems with a checklist to follow in the future to ensure success. This turned out to be a powerful way to work with any client—raising an issue that needed to be addressed and using an approach familiar to the client to design the solution.

Gerald R. Pieters, EverChange Institute, former internal consultant with Signetics Corporation (now Philips Semiconductor)

Contact

The term *contact* captures the beginning phase of internal consultants' work more accurately. The contact may begin with a brief conversation in the hall with a client known only by reputation, it may be a point or observation raised with a senior executive with whom there is an already established client relationship, or it may be a follow-up to a successful team-development session. In reality, the intervention begins with this first client contact. For internal consultants, it is seldom entry into the organization except when the internal is first hired in the position.

Whether it is the first contact with the client or a scheduled meeting to follow up a serendipitous or spontaneous encounter with the client in the hallway, here are some helpful tips:

- Prepare for the meeting.
- Use open-ended questions.
- Confront your own fears and issues before the meeting.
- Model or practice the behaviors you desire from the client.
- Use language and dress that are similar to the style of the client group.
- Take a flexible approach and use a style that works with the client.
- Clarify any confusion of communication or expectations as it occurs.
- Hold difficult meetings at peak performance times.
- Use strong interpersonal skills.
- Adjust to changes in expectations or plans and be comfortable with ambiguity.
- Take notes on both the content and the process.

Remember that the first meeting is an exploration for both you and your client to determine whether to move forward. Although the client may know the consultant by reputation, the first contact officially launches the consulting relationship. At the first meeting the consultant has the most leverage to establish the parameters for the work and the best opportunity to build a strong foundation for the client-consultant relationship. Because future success is influenced so heavily by this first meeting, it pays to take time to prepare (figure 9-1). Seek information through resources or colleagues to gain information about the client's business and organizational unit.

Keys to Success at the Contact Phase

Several factors are critical for successful completion of the contact phase for internal consultants. They are

- setting the stage at hiring
- building the relationship with the client
- seeking clarity and support from multiple clients

Figure 9-1. Preparing for the first client meeting.

Do you understand or know your client's

- business?
- organizational-unit function or purpose?
- level of decision-making authority?

What might you expect or surmise about your client's

- expectations and experience in working with consultants?
- personal style?
- fears and concerns?

In your understanding, is the need or request

- clear and focused?
- common across the organization?
- related to an initiative that is underway?
- something you have the time and the knowledge base to address?
- better met by someone else?
- tied to business outcomes?
- a potential way to address a vexing problem?

Are you clear about

- your consulting charter and the parameters of your work?
- your personal goals?
- your consulting style and approach?
- the boundaries of your competence and knowledge base?
- other resources available to address the need?
- your response to resistance?
- your needs and expectations?

- determining client readiness
- identifying the business or organization need
- approaching this phase with a spirit of inquiry.

SETTING THE STAGE AT HIRING

Establishing agreements when internal consultants are first hired sets the stage for success. This stage will not only define the expertise they bring to the organization but will provide the basis for promoting consulting services to potential clients. This initial effort begins to establish the internal's reputation. With each successful consulting project, the good word spreads and the internal consultant's reputation builds.

Sometimes in the hiring process the candidate may ask questions that the hiring manager has never considered, or perhaps the manager does not understand why they are important. It helps if the candidate is matter-of-fact in tone and is prepared to explain why these points are important. This may take time. In cases like this, the hiring phase helps educate the client about the role of an internal consultant.

The following steps will help internal consultants develop their charter in a new organization:

- clarify the match between organization needs and the expertise the consultant brings
- determine title, grade level, and reporting relationship
- seek to report to a high-level, credible manager
- agree on the level of potential clients and how to get access to them
- establish parameters about confidentiality, autonomy, and workload
- establish the consultant's authority to refuse unreasonable or inappropriate requests
- agree on the introductory "story"
- contract with the immediate boss and the highest-level manager who will be a client.

Negotiating at Hiring

Early in my hiring interviews I got a sense of what they wanted and needed, and how much commitment and resources they were willing to put into it. Once I was satisfied with their commitment, resources, and the identified need, I came back with a 10-year plan. It included staffing, budget, outline of structural changes to support the effort, regular meetings with the general manager, the development of a council or a guiding coalition, and a plan for management development and training, as well as cultural interventions. I did that because if they couldn't buy into a 10-year plan, then I couldn't take the job. It helped me make a career decision, and it helped the top manager make a decision about his commitment. We negotiated aspects of the plan until we were both satisfied that we could live with it.

Internal Journal

**Jim Harley, director, organization development,
Westinghouse Electric Company**

RELATIONSHIP BUILDING

The goal of relationship building in this phase is to develop rapport and trust with the client. Trust is critical, because it allows clients to confide in the consultant without fear of reprisal or loss of reputation. Clients need to be able to share their fears and hidden agendas without judgment and raise issues of conflict without feeling embarrassed. The consultant, in turn, must be able to confront the client about such difficult issues as lack of leadership or support that may undermine the project or the client.

The Power of Relationships

I got to design a worldwide managers meeting where we were thinking strategically in a global way. The relationships made it possible. The chief operating officer was my client. He empowered the design team. Having a really good relationship was the key to the success of the design. He was available, I could confront him, and it was easy to modify the contract.

Betsy Merck, former internal consultant with the fashion and manufacturing industry

Clients may have suspicions, fears, or concerns that they find difficult to express. They may become so enmeshed in the issue that they lose perspective. Some clients worry that working with a consultant will affect their reputation and that others will assume that they are incompetent. If the consultant is from corporate headquarters, field managers may limit the information they provide about their business issues because they fear it will get back to upper management. Awareness of potential client fears will help the internal consultant address and perhaps allay them. Success ultimately depends on the internal consultant's ability to overcome clients' fears, help them feel safe, and support them as they face the risks of initiating change.

Fears and concerns may plague the client and seriously impact the interaction in the contact phase. Assure the client that many concerns, including the following, are commonplace:

- Others will see me as incompetent or unsuccessful.
- Negative information will get back to headquarters, the boss, or others who pass judgment.
- The consultant is not competent to handle this problem.
- I must be incompetent if I cannot handle this without a consultant.
- It will take too much time, money, or attention.
- I should be able to solve this myself.
- The consultant does not understand my business or the situation.
- I won't be able to control it.
- The potential for failure is too great.
- I will look stupid if it does not work.
- It might make things worse.

- I don't understand it.
- If it doesn't work, I will lose too much.
- I don't understand what a consultant does anyway.

Even with an established client relationship, it is important to take time to ensure that trust and rapport are present. Meetings during the contact phase may take place in person or over the phone and may occur over a couple of minutes, a few days, a few weeks, or even a few months. There may be sensitive issues to raise or feedback to deliver at this time that will increase the client's self-awareness or improve his or her effectiveness in leading change. The consultant and client should be of one mind when it comes to handling sensitive communication. Review mutual understandings and raise feedback and leadership issues.

The Advantages of Client Trust

Internal Journal *This was a huge culture change project. The organization had no prior performance accountability and we were introducing 360-degree feedback. This was a huge step. The sponsor's credibility was on the line. No one really wanted performance accountability. Her trust in me allowed her to listen and make adjustments that made the project more successful. I did a pilot project and discovered the leaders were not as skilled in change management as I expected. For example, one of them said, "I feel like I've been sent out on a horse and it has been shot out from under me." They were concerned about success. They knew that poorly done feedback makes both parties feel worse. I created a skill development piece for the change process called, "Chief as Change Leader." It meant a longer timeline for the whole project. I was able to add this extra time because of the trust I had developed with the client. I was able to calibrate what was needed because I knew the culture.*

Emily C. Jarosz, Emily and Associates, former internal consultant with health-care industry

CLARITY AND SUPPORT FROM MULTIPLE CLIENTS

Serious consequences ensue when an internal consultant does not get the support, authority, or leadership to ensure a successful project involving two levels of clients. Project requests from senior executives can generate suspicion and potential distrust with secondary clients. It is critical to explore the issues of potential resistance, lack of support, or distrust early in the consulting process. To help address these issues,

- Discuss the issue with the primary client to develop an agreement about which information will be reported back, critical support and leadership functions, and methods for resolving differences.

- Acknowledge to the secondary clients that initially they may be uncomfortable expressing disagreement, disapproval, or sharing personal concerns or confidential information.
- Work together to begin to establish trust.
- Offer secondary clients information about the agreements with the primary client concerning what will and will not be shared.
- Seek an agreement with primary and secondary clients that the secondary client will not serve as a buffer and limit the consultant's access to the primary client.
- Ask secondary clients about issues or problems they have with the intervention, project, or activity.
- Raise potential concerns and propose alternatives to address them, and ask the secondary clients about their perspectives.
- Bring the primary client together with secondary clients at the next level and facilitate a dialogue to address the issues.
- Bring the second-level managers together without the primary client to air their reservations, and allow members of the group to exert leadership and influence the others in positive support of the project.
- Give the primary client feedback from the secondary clients. Obviously this requires an agreement with primary and secondary clients specifying the information to be shared.

Lack of Sponsorship

Internal
Journal

I had marching orders from my boss, although the real sponsor was his boss. His sponsorship was nominal because he didn't understand what was required. It took two years of my life because it was very labor intensive. We revamped our training programs based on managerial competencies, but it was never really implemented. We didn't have the support base or the authority to make things happen. I lost my own commitment and ultimately left. It was a huge project, expensive, and involved promises to employees that we didn't live up to.

**Chrissa B. Merron, senior consultant, Concentrics,
former internal consultant with financial industry**

CLIENT READINESS

It is imperative to determine the extent to which the client is ready, willing, and able to carry out changes. Many projects stall or fail because the change required becomes too threatening. Change is high risk. Clients need not only the consultant's personal commitment and support, but they must also believe that although the change may be a stretch, it is an acceptable risk.

Proving Myself to the Client

Internal Journal

I had a new client who did not want me in front of his management team until I had proved myself to him. He needed to trust that where I would go with the group would match where he wanted to go. He also wanted to be sure that I was competent. He wanted intellectual rigor. I needed to earn my stripes by planning and facilitating meetings for him.

Scott Burton, internal consultant with consumer products industry

Without a prior relationship with the client, these fears and concerns may necessitate an agreement about a few, first steps. Taking a few preliminary steps increases the comfort and the trust level of the client. Propose spending time in the business, on the shop floor, in the warehouse, riding the delivery trucks, or calling on customers. This serves two purposes: the consultant learns more about the business, and the client may be more willing to trust the consultant. Schaffer's (1997) advice is also useful when a client is reluctant to move forward: encourage the client to divide a large project into subprojects with incremental steps. This not only enables the client to see short-term successes, thereby boosting the client's confidence and motivation, but it also makes the change process more manageable and less risky.

Another question regarding client readiness revolves around the client's capacity to give attention to the proposed initiative. Managers today have enormous demands on their time and attention. If clients have so much on their plate that little time can be devoted to the change effort, they may expect the internal consultant to lead it or to solve the problems they face. One senior-level client was initially so overwhelmed after his promotion by the serious problems he faced that he wanted the consultant to "just handle" several of the organization's issues. He did not understand the importance and value of his leadership in making the needed changes.

Fallout from a Lack of Readiness

Internal Journal

It is critical to establish boundaries regarding what I am going to do and not do—the scope. The company had undergone mass reengineering of a 200-plus HR function from transactional to a shared-services concept. They flipped the switch in June, and I arrived in November. It had not gone well, and they wanted me to help by running the change management portion. They were operating as if change management was something different than the business initiative. I laid out an integrated approach. I also said that the vice presidents had to be part of the solution. In fact, we got ownership from the line HR and from the execu-

tives. I had to prod and pull because executive visibility had not been present before.

Laura J. Christenson, director, global organization effectiveness for a pharmaceutical/health-care company

Test the client's readiness by clarifying the consulting role and what is needed from the client in terms of availability and commitment to lead the project and staff resources to support the project. It may be helpful to divide the project in bite-sized pieces, suggest a postponement, or even ratchet up the client's awareness of the issues to promote readiness. Although many of these concerns may not be fully answered until later, it is wise to begin exploration early. The checklist in figure 9-2 can be used to assess the client and the client system's readiness to embark on a change effort. Remember that clients are not always aware of their own mixed emotions regarding a change initiative, so some concerns may not show up until a later phase in the consulting process.

BUSINESS OR ORGANIZATIONAL NEED

In addition to building a relationship with the client, the ultimate success of this phase depends on the initial definition of the business or organizational need behind the client's request. In this first phase, the consultant is seeking the client's perspective of the need and why it is a problem. In addition, the internal consultant must learn the answers to several questions, among them: What is the effect on the business, customers, or performance results? How is it affecting the employees, the ability of the team and organization to function effectively?

Internal consultants often already have an informed perspective on these issues, and if they have been in the organization for a while, the client expects them to be well versed. In fact, the client may come to a knowledgeable consultant because the consultant has a reputation of being informed and helpful. Despite the urge to agree to the request, it is worth asking a few questions to ensure a clear understanding of the client's perspective on the issue.

To jump-start a client meeting, Henry Leget, senior HR/OD consultant with PCS Health Systems, asks open-ended questions that can help the internal consultant understand the specific request and the client's perspective:

- How can I help you?
- What is happening now?
- What are the issues?
- How do your managers and employees view the issue(s)?
- What is your vision?
- What are your roadblocks?
- What do you see as possible solutions?
- What has been tried?
- Where do you want to go from here?

Figure 9-2. A readiness checklist.

Drivers and Motivation

- What are the drivers for this project? Are there business or organizational drivers to make this change?
- What is the client's motivation for this project? Does the client have positive energy and enthusiasm, or is the client's energy for the intervention flat, resistant, or negative?
- Is senior management pushing this intervention? If so, who?
- What does the client believe are the reasons?
- What are the potential outcomes anticipated by the client?
- Who is supportive, antagonistic, or apathetic toward the change?
- To what extent does this project support the business strategy or business goals that are deemed important?
- How did this need arise? How long has the client been aware of it? Have there been efforts to address it? What has worked or not worked?
- Who suggested using consulting assistance to address it?
- Are there other issues?

Environment for Change

- Where is the pressure for change in the client system?
- How much change has the organization experienced recently? What has been the impact?
- Will the organization's culture support the kinds of changes required by this project?
- Is there an openness to new ideas and learning in the culture of the organization?
- Are there other issues?

Client-Consultant Relationship

- Have you established a partnership relationship with the client? Have you established credibility with the client? Do you have the client's trust?
- Have you worked with this client before? Has the client worked with other internal or external consultants?
- What is the client's perspective on these experiences? What have you learned from those experiences that you can draw on for this project?
- Do you and your client have a common understanding, use the same language, and share expectations for the results of this intervention?
- Are there other issues?

Client's Understanding and Skill in Managing Change

- What is the client's change leadership capacity? Do recent experiences inform you about the client's ability to implement the changes that will be required?
- Has the client demonstrated interest and ability to learn new ideas, knowledge, and skills, and how to use them advantageously?
- What is the client's experience with or knowledge about the specific issues that will be the focus of this intervention?
- Is the client open to feedback about his or her leadership and communication on the project? Is there a willingness to engage in self-reflection and learning?
- Are there other issues?

Figure 9-2. A readiness checklist (continued).

Commitment, Resources, and Attention

- What is the client's view of the energy, commitment, support, and attention that the project will require?
- Where does this issue rank on the client's priority list of issues demanding time and attention? Is it a top-priority issue or something that seems far down the list?
- At what level of involvement or responsibility is the client willing to participate? Is the client willing to do his or her part?
- Has commitment or participation been secured from members of the client system? Senior management? Other functional areas?
- Is it clear what the budget will be? Does the client's view of appropriate costs match yours?
- Is the client willing to commit administrative or other support resources to the project?
- Are there any other issues?

Client Understanding of the Intervention or Project

- Has the client identified outcomes or goals for this intervention? How will the client measure success?
- Does the client have a vision of the desired future for the organization?
- Does the client understand the potential impact of the intervention on the organization and the business?
- How does this intervention relate to other, ongoing change projects in the organization?
- What is to be the specific output or result of the project?
- Are there other issues?

Scope and Timeline

- What is the client's view of the scope of the project? Does the client want or understand the value of breaking it into small pieces?
- Does the client understand other systems and processes that will need to be changed to support this project?
- How soon does the client want concrete results?
- Are the timeframes expected by the client realistic?
- Are there other issues?

Asking Questions

I interview the client to understand the scope of the request. I ask questions: How will the organization benefit? What are the barriers? What will it look like? How does the staff feel? How will they be involved?

Mila N. Baker, system director, learning and organization development, Baptist/St. Vincent's Health System

By getting the client's perspective on the issue, the internal consultant is doing a preliminary assessment to determine if there is a match with the consultant's approach and expertise and what Henning (1997) calls relevance and fit. Internal consultants often believe that they have to accept all requests. However, it may better serve the client to say no if the consultant is overloaded or there is not a fit between the need and the consultant's expertise. A mismatch provides an opportunity to help the client find alternative external or internal resources. The client ultimately will appreciate the internal consultant's candor about declining an assignment or being willing to help the client find other resources.

Avoiding the Trap of Just Saying Yes

Many of our clients tend to call after the fact and ask, "We have this mess, can you come and help us clean it up?" rather than calling us further upstream. A typical request might be phrased, "We are up against a deadline, this product must be delivered" or "We are stuck, can you help us?" Until recently the requests were to help facilitate meetings. The trap is to say, "Yes, I will be your facilitator." Instead, we need to say that facilitation may be one possible intervention and explore the need.

Michael Lindfield, senior OD consultant, Boeing Company

Nevertheless, the consultant may not be able to assess the match between consultant expertise and the client need during the contact phase. An "independent view" is needed, according to Henning (1997). Then the discussion focuses on what is needed—observations, interviews, or surveys—to obtain this independent view. This is the information and assessment phase that gives the consultant not only an independent view of the situation but also the data to plan the change intervention. An advance discussion of the information and assessment phase during the contact phase helps educate the client and expand his or her understanding of what will be required for the project.

Educating the Client

Consulting is an educational process with the client. Consulting means educating clients about the consulting process, the ways we will work together, their needs, and about how I can be helpful. It is also figuring out ways that they can learn. Another part of it is educating them on follow-through and keeping commitments and goals. My consulting style is very practical. I don't go off on theoretical or conceptual views. I try to bring the intervention to a practical solution.

Jan M. Schmuckler, Consultation, former internal consultant with high-technology industry

SPIRIT OF INQUIRY

The contact phase is an opportunity for the internal consultant to approach the client with a spirit of inquiry and openness to learning about the client, the organization, and the current situation that precipitated the request. Consider asking about the client's beliefs and prior experience with change initiatives in addition to questions about present issues. Leading the client through questions about hoped-for outcomes and views of the ideal situation stimulates the creative tension between the current situation and the desired future. This tension offers an approach that will engage positive energy and build the motivation needed to address unpleasant issues and move toward the ideal or create the desired future.

The Foundation is Laid

The foundation of successful internal consulting is laid in this phase. The keys to success just outlined contribute to the strength of that foundation. Each internal consultant's situation is unique, and each client request is unique. Figure 9-3 offers a set of potential questions from which internal consultants can pick and choose to develop their own set to fit their unique practices.

Benefits of Completing this Phase

This phase is the best forum for establishing project parameters and ensuring that the consultant's expertise matches the client's needs. Many consultants later lament those times they did not carefully complete this phase when problems emerge that were traceable to the very beginning of the project. The consultant-client relationship and the scope of the project will influence the length of time needed for this phase. When internal consultants have an already-established relationship and know the business, it is especially tempting to rush ahead and get started. Yet, there are many advantages to taking the time to complete this phase:

- building rapport, trust, and the interpersonal basis for the relationship with the client
- increasing knowledge of the current business and organizational context
- determining the client's willingness and availability to participate actively in the project
- exploring the client's readiness for change
- gauging the fit between the consultant's approach to the change process with the client's beliefs about change
- establishing the positive-change process and building the energy needed to inspire and motivate the client and the client system to make the changes needed
- flagging any differences or difficulties that may undermine the project so that they can be addressed

Figure 9-3. Potential questions for client contact meeting.

Change

- What are your personal beliefs and experience with change?
- What benefits and difficulties have you experienced in implementing other change efforts?
- What did you learn from a recent effort similar to the one we are discussing?
- What motivates you to make changes in behavior, the organization, or business processes?

Business/Organization

- What is the background that led to your decision to call me?
- What have you done or tried so far?
- What business issues are you currently facing? What is the background?
- What employee/organization/performance issues are you currently addressing? What is the background?
- How is this issue affecting the business, customers, or employee results?
- How is it affecting the employees and the ability of the team or the organization to function effectively?
- What has been successful in the past?
- What is working now?
- If these issues were resolved what would the business/organization/performance look like?
- What may impede or get in the way of accomplishing the desired outcomes?
- What will support or help achieve the desired outcomes?
- What opportunities are opening up for your business or organization?
- How would your ideal organization function?
- How do you see the organization three to five years from now?
- What are your ideal performance outcomes/results?
- Who else needs to be involved in this project?
- May I talk to your boss/employees/colleagues to get a broader perspective?
- Whose commitment do we need for this project? How will we secure that?
- Are there parts of the project we can break into smaller pieces?
- I would like to spend time on the shop floor/riding with the sales team/listening in on customer service calls/ or ——— to learn more about your business. Can you set that up for me?
- What administrative or other needed support is available?

Client

- What is driving or motivating your interest in this effort?
- What interests you in doing X?
- What else is taking your time right now?
- How much time and attention are you willing to devote to this initiative?
- What role are you willing to play?
- What are your personal goals for the future?
- Have you had prior experience with a similar change effort before?
- What benefits and difficulties did you experience?
- What did you learn?

Figure 9-3. Potential questions for client contact meeting (continued).

> **Relationship**
> - How do you see us working together?
> - How will we resolve differences or conflicts?
> - How will we communicate? How often?
> - How will decisions be made?
> - How will we manage changes from outside the project?
> - How will we handle changes needed within the project?
> - What ground rules or agreements will guide our work together?
> - How and when would you like to hear feedback about your support and leadership of the project?
> - How often do you want progress reports?

- determining the preliminary parameters of the project and agree to revisit them after data is collected
- addressing assumptions and expectations about both the consultant's and the client's roles
- constructing a foundation for shared partnership and responsibility for the project's success.

Summing Up and Looking Ahead

This contact phase focuses on preparing a solid foundation for a strong client-consultant partnership. Matching the consultant's expertise to the client's need and readiness is critical. If there is not a match, the internal consultant may conclude this phase with an agreement not to meet the client's request but to find other resources. This is the beginning phase of building an open, trusting relationship. By approaching the client with a spirit of inquiry and clarity about the relationship, the consultant seeks to lay a solid foundation. This foundation is seldom poured in one meeting. It may take several meetings, and the consultant may serve as facilitator or meeting planner or take other short-term steps, which are preliminary to launching the project. Gradually the foundation of consultant credibility and client trust is built. This foundation enables the internal consultant to partner with the client to address a significant intervention or confront a sensitive leadership issue. The next chapter will discuss the agreements with the client, which flow from the discussion in this phase.

References

Henning, J.P. (1997). *The Future of Staff Groups*. San Francisco: Berrett-Koehler Publishers.

Lacey, M.Y. (1995). "Internal Consulting: Perspectives on the Process of Planned Change." *Journal of Organizational Change Management, 8*(3), 77.

Schaffer, R.H. (1997). *High Impact Consulting: How Clients and Consultants Can Leverage Rapid Results into Long-Term Gains*. San Francisco: Jossey-Bass.

Chapter 10

Phase Two: Finalize Agreement

In many ways this is the conclusion of the contact phase. It memorializes the understanding between the client and the internal consultant. A common consulting term used for this phase for external consults is contracting. For internal consultants and their clients the term *contract* may imply a legal agreement or too much formality, even though this is a social and not a legal contract. Nevertheless, because *contract* is a term frequently used by many consultants, both terms, *contract* and *agreement*, will be used in this book. The agreement confirms the match between the needs of the client and the consultant's approach and expertise, establishes the parameters of the project, and clarifies the expectations of both the client and the consultant.

A Contracting Struggle

I was brought in to help a client who headed a major unit pull together an organization, which consisted of four or five units each with different functions, products, and ethos, to create one department. I did interviews, we conducted training, and held off-site retreats. She was very pleased but I didn't see it as successful, because she was not willing to see her role in any dysfunctional behavior. I also did not believe that the group could really be pulled into one unit, because they were so disparate in function and goals. Nevertheless, she wanted to bring them together. She was not willing to hear the feedback about her behavior, and I was incapable of shaping it in a way she could hear it. We had really struggled in the contracting phase to be clear about what was to happen and about giving feedback. My level of satisfaction was light-years behind hers. She was thrilled.

Jim McKnight, OD consultant, California Federal Bank

Internal Journal

Do Not Gloss Over the Agreement

Because the agreement is the culmination of the contact phase, it is tempting to gloss over finalizing the agreement. This is especially true when consultant and client know each other and have worked together before. Nevertheless, many internal consultants who were interviewed for this book cautioned against this oversight. Each project brings different issues, roles, and expectations. Even with a contract or agreement, the client may be unwilling to address the issues that arise during the project. In addition, with the fast pace of today's business environment, there are likely to be new stakeholders, changing business demands, or a restructured organization. Experienced consultants advocate taking the time to review the client's perspective and expectations, confirm the client and consultant roles, and verify the actions that each will take to support the project.

Let's Talk About Our Expectations

The up-front agreement is probably the most important—and the most neglected—step for internal consultants. For external consultants, the agreement is part of entry and part of their planned strategy. Because internal consultants are part of the organization, it is hard to sit down and negotiate agreements. I don't use the word agreement or contract. I would rather say, "Let's talk about our expectations, what we are going to do, and how we will approach it." Jargon turns people off, and the terms are too formal. The process is the most important part. I believe you also need to review the agreements frequently—not just at the beginning of the project . . .

Jim Harley, director, organization development, Westinghouse Electric Company

Clarify Administrative Support

Internal consultants become involved in issues that are seldom experienced by the external consultant. Because they live in the organization as an employee, clients may expect them to drive the project, provide the leadership, or do the administrative work. Internal consultants need to ask themselves if they are willing to let the client off-load these responsibilities and what support the client should provide. One consultant emphasized the importance of seeking an agreement to use the time and expertise of the client's administrative assistant. Developing a strong relationship with the assistant will yield immeasurable benefits in accessing senior-level clients, obtaining approvals, and arranging schedules. In addition, such support supplements the internal consultant's own administrative support in sending out announcements and communicating with the client system. Even if leadership or administrative responsibilities are not part of the agreement, the internal consultant may end up being the organizational *nudge,* who reminds people of meetings, time-lines and goals, and just "keeps the trail warm," as one internal consultant put it.

Pressure to Change the Agreement

Internal Journal

It is easier for external consultants to maintain boundaries and agreements. For internal consultants, no matter how clear we are in contracting, the agreements end up sliding and getting mushy. The high-level executives to whom internal consultants report change their minds and agreements get broken. Internal consultants can challenge only so much without backing down because of the executives' positional power. For example, I had an agreement with a team of executives on a design for an intervention that was geared to communicate a "trust" message to middle managers. The executives got anxious, believing it was too great a risk, and wanted to change the design. I pointed out why it wouldn't work. I pushed hard without success. I felt I had to back down when I got nowhere. We ended up doing it their way, and it blew up. Later one of them had the decency to say "You were right." I had to back down because I couldn't jeopardize my position and my relationships.

Emily C. Jarosz, Emily and Associates, former internal consultant with health-care industry

Sticking to the Agreement

As the vignette related by Emily Jarosz suggests, another issue is pressure from superiors to change an agreement. Keeping agreements builds credibility, promotes open communication, and builds trust. Keeping agreements also means taking risks sometimes. For the consultant that may be communicating bad news, and, for the client, that may mean going forward with an intervention.

The parties should make only agreements that they intend to keep and avoid making or accepting unclear or open-ended agreements. Give early notice if an agreement must be broken or changed, and clean up any broken agreements promptly (Atlanta Consulting Group, unpublished material from workshop). There is no guarantee that senior-level managers will not demand changes in the agreement, but there are steps to take to minimize that possibility, including the following:

- Make clear agreements between primary clients or sponsors at the senior or executive level and the secondary clients who are more closely involved in the project.
- Ensure that all stakeholders are kept informed and involved in key decisions.
- During early consulting phases, discuss with all the appropriate clients how to use your consulting expertise. Resist pressure to take a different approach to avoid being accountable for less-than-successful results.
- Take time to address concerns and resistance.

- Involve HR and other critical functional units in the contracting process.
- Review the importance of keeping agreements as a consultant and ask clients if they are willing to follow the same practice.

I am a Consultant, Not a Subordinate

Internal Journal

I had a senior vice president as a client who was three levels up in my reporting structure. I said, "I need an agreement with you. When I am with you I want you to see me wearing a hat like an external consultant so I can give you honest feedback that someone in your reporting structure would find hard to do." He agreed. It was useful and served well in that assignment. It was the first time I decided to ask because I had a good relationship with him. Now I do that in every situation.

Michael Lindfield, senior OD consultant, Boeing Company

Agrèements Regarding Feedback

Another important area of agreement with your client is how bad news or critical feedback will be delivered and received. Delivering bad news or critical feedback can place internal consultants in a vulnerable position where clients can retaliate or shut them out if executives do not like what they hear. A candid discussion can be painful, but frankness can reduce the risk later. Explore the client's openness to tough messages and issues of confidentiality, power, control, personal style, and authenticity. Will differences of opinion be governed by power and authority or by mutual respect and competence? Having the discussion and including it in the agreements psychologically prepare your client for hearing bad news and sensitive feedback. This way, the internal consultant receives permission to address the tough subjects that the client may not hear from others.

Can We Talk?

Internal Journal

I say to my clients that to do my best work for them, I need to be able to tell it like it is and give my honest opinions, my perspective, and my recommendations. If you don't want to hear the truth, then I am not the right person to do the work. I did that when I was hired, and I do that with individual clients. I have to be able to tell clients the good with the bad and work with them to remove the inhibitors. I have gained credibility. People know I am honest and will tell them the truth.

Laura J. Christenson, director, global organization effectiveness for a pharmaceutical/health-care company

Clarification of Expectations

Whether the project is with a new or long-term client, clarifying expectations about the work and the internal consultant's role before the agreement is finalized will enhance the project's success. The client and the consultant must be clear about what they expect from each other. Some items that should be considered by the parties and included in any agreement—verbal or written—are the

- model to be used and approach to change
- other assumptions that underlie consultant's work
- role(s) of consultant and how much emphasis to place on process versus expertise
- role of the client
- handling of information and data
- boundaries of confidentiality
- scope and parameters of this project
- responsibilities of the consultant
- responsibilities of the client
- clarification of how consultant's expertise is to be used
- nature of consultant's relationship with the client
- agreement on delivering sensitive feedback and bad news
- deliverables and timetable
- resources and support needed from the client
- access and availability of the client
- measures of success for evaluation.

The Agreement—Verbal or Written?

With assumptions and expectations clarified, it is appropriate to finalize the agreement. The level of detail in the agreement depends on both the business and the relationship issues involved in the project. It may also depend on the clarity of the defining issue and what additional information is needed. During many projects, clarifying expectations, reaching agreements, and gathering information is cyclical. In this ongoing process the consultant gains a different, independent view of the issues through data collection, or as the project unfolds the client makes additional requests. Then, it is necessary to cycle back to the agreement phase.

For example, a new senior manager might ask the internal consultant to collect information from the members of his or her department about their development concerns and performance goals and to make recommendations about next steps. Clarification of agreements can be as simple as saying, "So, I am going to contact each of the members of your department, solicit information on performance and development, prepare a summary and recommendations, and meet with you in three weeks." Then, clarify what is expected from the client: "And you are going to let them all know to expect a call from me and to set aside time to meet with me." Experienced consultants strongly suggest that every client telephone call or meeting end with a statement of mutual expectation and confirmation of agreements. This effort alone can save days of misdirected work not to mention the frustration that is bound to occur when unwanted work is done.

For projects of a few hours to a few days, a verbal agreement is often sufficient. However, some consultants and some clients prefer putting the agreements even for shorter projects in writing. If you are unsure in the beginning of a client relationship, send a confirmatory memorandum by email. Most clients will be grateful to receive a clear, brief note outlining expectations. Appendix 4 provides a sample memorandum that would memorialize an agreement for a short-term project.

A verbal agreement may also be all that is needed if the consultant is only going to take one or two steps before meeting again with the client to define and confirm a longer or more detailed project. For a new client or one who needs to see agreements in writing, it is useful to confirm the agreements for the next steps in a memo. Appendix 4 includes a sample agreement memorandum for a long-term or detailed project.

What Goes in the Agreement?

Emily Jarosz, a former internal consultant, offers a useful checklist (figure 10-1) for items that should be included in the agreement memorandum. Some items, labeled "always include," are critical items for all projects. Others are suggested "as needed" by the client, the stage, or the character of the project. Some items are more likely included after the information and data collection phase with alignment and agreement to move forward to implement an intervention.

A Formal Written Agreement

For longer projects of a several days to weeks, months, or even years a more structured agreement with a description of the presenting issues and potential opportunities to be addressed, a list of the key activities, timeframes, and the expected measurable results is useful. A statement regarding the consultant's role and agreements about the partnership with the client and the approach to the work can be included. In some organizations a one-page memorandum is more customary; in others a longer more detailed document is appropriate. A sample of a longer contract or agreement is included in appendix 5. The contract for a leadership and team development project, provided by former internal Marilyn Blair, is similar to a contract that might be used by an external consultant. However, some organizations prefer to take this more formal approach with internal consultants, as well.

Figure 10-1. Project contract items.

Background and Scope

Include as needed:
- [ ] need for the project/intervention
- [ ] brief definition of the project
- [ ] organizational background.

Desired Outcomes

Always include:
- [ ] goals and tangible outcomes of the project.

Process and Timeline

Always include:
- [ ] project steps
- [ ] target dates.

Logistics

Always include:
- [ ] roles (who will make room reservations, serve as contact person, and so forth)
- [ ] location
- [ ] time
- [ ] refreshments
- [ ] materials.

Resources

Always include:
- [ ] clerical support
- [ ] resources that the client is dedicating to the project or intervention (salary, hours of participants, and so forth).

Communication

Include as needed:
- [ ] preferred communication method
- [ ] method for communicating with those affected by, but not directly involved in, the project or intervention.

Next Steps

Include as needed:
- [ ] contingency plans
- [ ] actions needed before project begins.

Confidentiality

Always include:
- [ ] confidentiality level of data collected
- [ ] confidentiality level of results
- [ ] any confidentiality issues associated with union regulations (if necessary).

Barriers

Include as needed:
- [ ] any barriers to success as discussed with the client.

Support

Always include:
- [ ] one-up contracting and support expected from client's boss
- [ ] consultant's time commitment
- [ ] other necessary support mechanisms.

Follow-up

Include as needed:
- [ ] actions that consultant or client will complete to achieve the desired outcomes of the project or intervention.

Emily C. Jarosz, Emily and Associates
Former internal consultant with health-care industry

Summing Up and Looking Ahead

The product of the agreement phase is a confirmed agreement between the consultant and the client. This agreement may be verbal or written. It may only specify the next steps of data and information collection, or it may detail the phases of a long, complex project. The clearer the consultant and the client are about their expectations, the greater the chance for success of the intervention. The agreements should include clarity about outcomes, the process, and next steps to be taken by consultant and client, timelines, and the support and resources needed. With this clear agreement, the internal consultant is ready for the next phase—information and assessment.

Chapter 11

Phase Three: Information and Assessment

This is the phase of data collection and analysis. The purpose is to collect and evaluate information on the strengths and weaknesses of the client system, identify problem areas, and analyze the root causes. The internal consultant may conduct structured or informal interviews, observe cultural norms, employee interaction or performance levels, distribute questionnaires, mail out customer surveys, or review operating statistics and company documents. Input may come from the front line, supervisors, managers, customers, senior executives, or customers, as appropriate. Conducting formal or informal benchmarking with data from internal or external locations may also be helpful. Here we will explore in more depth the tools of interviews and employee surveys. They can be supplemented by observation, operating data, and company documents.

After the information or data is collected, the consultant must analyze or assess it to draw conclusions and make recommendations. In most internal projects, the conclusion of this phase will take the internal to the feedback phase, but sometimes the consultant may need to return to the agreement phase to renegotiate with the client. The collection of data or gathering of information enables the consultant to gain an independent view of the organization, learn more about the business and the current challenges, and generate data to mobilize the positive energy in the organization. It is also an opportunity to get members of the client system involved, and ensure that their perspective is represented, and give the client another perspective of the problem.

The Importance of Data Collection

Internal consultants differ in regard to how much they emphasize the information and analysis phase. One senior, experienced consultant, June Delano, said that she is very committed to extensive interviewing of everyone involved, summarizing the data, and using it as a diagnostic tool to determine an appropriate intervention. Another experienced senior consultant, Kevin Wheeler, stated, "It was very hard to really listen to the need, ask questions, and do a good diagnosis. Internal consultants shouldn't have to ask many questions. They need to know what is going on and be very connected to the real issues."

Traditional consulting practices have emphasized the importance of collecting information, analyzing or "diagnosing" based on that data, and arriving at the correct interpretation before presenting recommendations to the client. The consulting process is not a series of discrete steps. As the internal consultant gains knowledge, awareness, and data about the client system, a continuous process of analyzing and assessing evolves. This process in turn revises the earlier interpretation and hypothesis about the issues in the client system. This process is comparable to the Gestalt approach to organizational assessment described by Nevis (1987). He illustrated the Gestalt approach as using both "active, directed awareness," which includes interviews and surveys, and "open, undirected awareness," which includes observation and sensing of activities, emotion, and interactions in the client system.

The observation and sensing data that the internal consultant possesses from living within the client organization always supplement structured information and data. Therefore, it is easy to slip into not collecting structured data before conducting an intervention in a known client organization. Internal consultants, however, are cautioned to remember that long-term work with a client or living in the client organization can lead to absorbing and accepting the perspectives of the clients and colleagues and losing the consultant's objective posture. A structured data-collection process supports the internal consultant's efforts to maintain a more neutral view.

Limitations and Suggestions

Each internal consultant brings his or her own lens that focuses on certain facets of the information. To limit either the collection of data or the analysis to those components that draw the internal consultant's attention is limiting for clients and the consultant. The result is potentially championing the wrong strategy or tackling the wrong issues. Block (1993) suggests that gathering information from the client organization is, in some ways, analogous to an onion with many layers. The outside layer is the organizational or business issue the client is experiencing. The second layer contains the perceptions of how others are contributing to the issue. The third layer is the individual's contribution to the issue. Other alternatives to avoid this consultant bias are to review the following topic list or to use an organizational model to ensure data is collected from all the relevant areas.

The extent of the need for data and information depends on the consulting engagement, the organizational environment, and the consultant. Collecting and analyzing data may help clients understand the problem better when they see the issues documented and interpreted during a feedback presentation. On the other hand, the environment may be changing so fast that clients cannot wait for a complete information and assessment phase. What is most important to remember is that having an independent view is vital whether that view comes from in-depth knowledge of the organization through experience and tenure or the collection of data and information.

Doing "On-Your-Feet" Consulting

Internal Journal

I began with a basic assessment—interviewing team members for 45–60 minutes, reporting back themes, and making recommendations to both the client and the entire group. As time went on, I shortened this process not only because I knew more, but because of the rapidity of change and some of the things I was taught were obsolete. I was doing more "on-your-feet" consulting than using a planned process.

**Jan M. Schmuckler, Consultation,
former internal consultant with high-technology industry**

Methods of Gathering Information

Internal consultants use several methods of gathering information, which are described here.

INTERVIEWS

Interviews can be structured or unstructured. Structured interviews consist of a fixed number of prepared questions asked in order with established response choices. This option addresses a set number of issues and provides easier comparison across respondents. Unstructured interviews consist of open-ended questions. The interviewer then formulates additional questions based on the response. This approach allows the interviewer to follow-up and probe unanticipated areas. Most internal consultants use a blend of these two approaches. A structured set of questions might begin the interview with later modifications based on the responses. In other cases, the interviewer uses an established set of open-ended questions to ensure coverage of the areas of concern but allows follow-up in each area.

QUESTIONNAIRES

A wide variety of questionnaires can include structured or open-ended questions. Questionnaires can be short and informal to collect data for a team building. Figure 11-1 provides an example from former internal consultant Perviz Randeria.

Questionnaires can also be longer and structured for use as an employee survey. Standardized questionnaires with existing databases are used as feedback

Figure 11-1. Example questionnaire.

Pre-work and preparation for the first October meeting:

- Read the attached articles and handouts.
- Complete the following questionnaire and bring your responses on a flipchart and notepaper for the whole-group meeting in October. Send a legibly written or word-processed copy of the questionnaire to John Doe by September 24th.

Questionnaire

1. My key objectives as division manager are:
2. My strengths and abilities as a manager are:
3. Areas for improvement and change for me are:
4. My expectations of HR are:
5. My expectations of my peers in this group are:
6. My definition of accountability is:
7. Key obstacles or impediments to my effectiveness are:
8. Areas where I can contribute or be a resource to others are:

Perviz Randeria, organization and management development consultant
Former internal consultant with city government

instruments; examples include 360-degree feedback instruments for development and organization-wide employee surveys. Online questionnaires are easy for participants to complete, and it is a simple task to tabulate the results.

OBSERVATION

Useful observational data is collected as the internal consultant works in the organization. For specific interventions, recording the observations of targeted behaviors on a structured observation sheet with space for notes for each category helps to focus the observations. Specific observation data for some interventions, such as a team meeting, employee performance, or a senior executive's leadership style, may be the best and easiest method, because it offers the advantage of giving immediate reinforcement or making suggestions for improvement. Observation does have its drawbacks, however. The bias of the consultant is hard to control, the mere presence of the observer changes behavior, or a single observer may miss some actions and behavior.

REVIEW OF DOCUMENTS

To learn about a new client system, it is often helpful to review existing data and information about the organization. These documents include performance and financial reports, notes from essential meetings, annual and long-term planning documents, and other data on HR, customers, or operations. Document review, as a preliminary data-collection step, is a way to get a quick overview and gather potential quantitative data for measurement and evaluation. In this discussion of methods of data and information collection, we will provide detailed instructions for using interviews and employee surveys as data-collection tools.

Using the Interview

PREPARATION

Internal consultants frequently collect information and data about their client systems by conducting interviews with their clients, the employees, managers, and other critical stakeholders. It is very important to establish ground rules with the client and the participants about how the data will be used, for example:

- Will it be shared in the team or client system?
- Will it be kept within the team boundaries?
- Will anyone's statements be identifiable?

Making and keeping these agreements about the ground rules will help build trust among the participants to candidly share their perspectives and concerns.

Conducting effective interviews requires skill and preparation. The interviewee can significantly affect the process. This requires that the consultant be skilled in managing the process. The interview and the questions constitute an intervention in themselves and do affect the client system. For this reason, it is wise to plan carefully the approach and the questions so that the internal consultant can effectively manage the interview process and the ripple effect throughout the client system. The issues presented by the client, the organizational culture, and the internal consultant's style all influence how the interview is conducted and the focus of the questions. Several topics must be considered when preparing interview questions, among them,

- position, role, job responsibilities (current and past if relevant)
- tenure with the organization
- perspective on the history and culture of the organization
- feelings about company, department, and job
- prior successes of the organization, role, and contribution
- view on what is going well in the organization
- understanding of the vision, desired goals, or outcomes of the organization
- understanding of the business, industry, competition
- potential opportunities
- understanding of metrics and financial picture of the business
- relationship with boss, subordinates, and peers
- relationship with other key departments

- barriers or impediments to achieving vision, desired goals, or outcomes
- barriers or impediments affecting business results, customers, or employees
- efforts to address barriers, successes, and failures
- experience and learning from other change efforts, benefits, difficulties
- changes respondent is motivated to make
- projects, initiatives, or other activities taking time and attention
- view of the ideal organization
- view of the organization three to five years in the future.

ADVICE FOR CONDUCTING THE INTERVIEW

Carrying out effective interviews not only requires preparation, but also demands alertness. Jones and Bearley (1995) called the method "slippery" because of the ease with which people being interviewed can influence the process while it is occurring. The interviewer is signaling a willingness to listen and the exchange can be "sidetracked" easily as the respondents are tempted to gripe about the boss or the organization. Some interviewees may ask their own questions. Because peers often discuss interviews, people may come with prepared answers or messages they want to convey. Finally, the interviewer's own biases and judgments can seriously sway the data.

Figure 11-2 demonstrates some advice from Jones and Bearley, who are masters at the interviewing process.

ASKING QUESTIONS

The types of questions consultants use in the interview can expand or broaden their role, communicate their own biases, establish their neutral position, and build a relationship with the respondents. Questions can be content-focused, close-ended, or open-ended questions. Content questions usually pursue an explanation and use words, such as *what, where, when, how much.* They can be very useful follow-up questions but may serve as leading questions if they are used to open a topic, as in "When did you start having conflict with Sam?" Such a leading question biases the answer and communicates the interviewer's biases, judgments, or conclusions. Close-ended questions usually elicit a limited response—yes or no. Using close-ended questions can be very helpful to confirm details and obtain direct and specific answers. Nevertheless, it is seldom helpful to rely on them extensively because they yield very little information and the client may feel interrogated.

Open-ended questions have the potential to provide the most informative responses. These are broad questions that allow respondents to tell their story, explain their perspective, and express their feelings. By inviting the respondent to be forthcoming, the consultant is more likely to gain insight and information that might not be available through other means. Many consultants do not even begin with a question; they say, "Tell me about your experience with . . . " or "I'd like to hear your perspective on . . . " As the respondent tells the story, the consultant has

Figure 11-2. *Do*s and *don't*s for conducting an effective interview.

*DO*s

- Do keep to now. Ask about the person's observations, opinions, attitudes and feelings "right here, right now."
- Do ask what and how questions. These open up the interviewee. Follow up on the interviewees' responses. Asking, "What is it about...?" is an excellent way to get more precise and detailed information rather than opinions or vague descriptions. Another good approach is, "Tell me more."
- Do accept what the person says. The interviewer is only interested in the reality that this person is experiencing. All employees have a right to see things the way they do, and they have a right to feel the way they do.
- Do move from general to specific. It is important, however, not to develop an atmosphere of interrogation in the process of honing in on what the person is saying.
- Do make verbatim notes. Experiment with abbreviations and other shorthand methods, and go over the notes with the person when the questions are completed. Sometimes people want to change what they said.
- Do develop the relationship. It is important to prepare the person to cooperate with the intervention by explaining what the interviewer's role is and to reinforce that person's participation in the activity.
- Do control the conversation. Empathy is almost narcotic, since it is so rare in day-to-day interactions among people at work. Consequently, when interviewees are listened to completely and accurately, they often open up to say many things that may be out of the scope of the interview. The interviewer has a job to do here, and it requires that he or she retain control of the flow of the interchange.
- Do keep the task clear. The task is to gather information that you need for the intervention.
- Do check understanding frequently. We believe that it is vital to stop from time to time during sensing interviews to paraphrase what the person is saying and reflect that person's feelings. The interviewer needs to be ready to be "wrong" about what is fed back to the interviewee. Sometimes people who are being asked questions deny their responses.
- Do probe both the positive and the negative. It is important to ask people about the good news about working the organization, as well as about their negative perceptions.
- Do coach for participation. End each interview by suggesting how the person can contribute to organizational improvement in their later participation in the intervention.

continued on page 136

the opportunity to explore and probe for specific information and details. Although they tend to be more time consuming, open-ended questions or "tell-me" statements also help the consultant build rapport and a relationship that will be advantageous later in the project. Here are some reminders about asking questions:

- Questions communicate information about the consultant and solicit information from the respondent.
- A strategy is useful when selecting questions to communicate the desired message, elicit the desired information, and establish rapport and relationship.

Figure 11-2. *Do*s and *don't*s for conducting an effective interview (continued).

DON'Ts

- Don't gather a lot of history. What is needed is the present state of the organization as experienced by the interviewee.
- Don't ask *yes–no* or *why* questions. The *yes–no* questions close down the interviewee; they are restricting rather than enabling of response. *Why* questions simply elicit people's theories and that is not the purpose of the interview.
- Don't judge what you hear. This is a challenge, of course, but it is important that the interviewee feel accepted.
- Don't jump topics randomly. Show order in the sequence of questions; point out the model if necessary.
- Don't edit what is said. Take whatever people say as data, and record it all. It is frustrating to be interviewed when the interviewer is taking notes selectively.
- Don't carry tales or be impersonal. Don't say, "So-and-so (or everyone) said such-and-such." This can destroy a sense of confidentiality and safety. On the other hand, people need to be related to in human terms, not as simple numbers of "subjects." Show friendliness and interest in what they say.
- Don't permit the other person to ramble. Keep to the tasks of the interview. Practice saying such things as, "Thanks for sharing that with me. Let's move on to another topic."
- Don't make assumptions. This is impossible, of course; it may be better to notice when the interviewer is making assumptions and test them with the interviewee.
- Don't ask for problem diagnoses. This a sore temptation and should be avoided. Anyone who has studied problem solving recognizes the tendency to "jump to conclusions" or to talk about what should be done before there is a common acceptance and understanding of the problem.
- Don't let the person surprise you later. Explore how the person perceives the proposed intervention. If it is negative, suggest ways in which the person might cooperate for his or her benefit, as well as that of the organization.

Reprinted, by permission, from Jones, J.E., and W.L. Bearley, *Surveying Employees: A Practical Guidebook* (Amherst, MA: HRD Press, 1995).

- Open-ended questions expand the scope and communicate interest in the big picture.
- Close-ended questions narrow the problem and communicate interest in the details.
- Content questions are useful as follow-up questions.

GROUP INTERVIEWS

The group interview is an option that allows the consultant to collect much information in a short amount of time, to gain a perspective of the client system quickly, and to test the commonality of perceptions within the organization. Group interviews build relationships and involve members of the client system that the consultant may not be able to reach through individual interviews. However, there are some disadvantages. In groups, employees do not contribute equally, and the consultant may not get accurate data because some people are hesitant to participate. In addition, the process needs to be well facilitated and focused on the subject. It is easy for employees to want to solve the problem instead of discuss the real source of the issue.

In convening group interviews, it is useful to identify someone from the client system or from HR to assist the consultant in identifying participants and arranging for the meeting. Choose participants who will help meet the objectives for collecting information. If involving more than one level in the group, do not include a boss with employees and do not include more than two levels in the group. Options include

- a cross-section to get a sampling of perspectives at a particular level
- representatives from two levels in the organization
- everyone in a unit to observe the group dynamics
- a random sample to get as much data as quickly as possible from a large population
- selected individuals who will speak up and express opinions readily.

Send out a clear purpose and agenda for the meeting in advance. In addition to a facilitator, a recorder can capture all the comments for members of the group to review and correct if a comment is inaccurate. At the meeting, be sure to explain the roles of the facilitator and the recorder. Reviewing the purpose at the beginning and several times during the meeting will help stay on track.

A critical issue in group interviews revolves around confidentiality. Although the consultant assures participants of confidentiality, members of the group may fear other members' judgment or that they will carry tales after the meeting. If the issues are too sensitive, it is wise to collect information in more private settings. However, developing ground rules about confidentiality will help reassure some participants. The following are additional suggestions for ground rules to review with the participants to help the group interview go smoothly:

- Speak for yourself; make *I* statements.
- Build on the comments of others.
- Be specific instead of general.
- Give examples of what you are saying.
- Keep what is said here confidential.
- Listen actively to everyone.
- Do not gripe. Describe the issues.

Using Employee Surveys

The employee survey is a tool that enables the consultant to collect data from a large population and partner with the executive team to take action to move the organization to a higher or more effective level of performance. The major objectives of employee surveys identified by employee survey experts Jones and Bearley (1995) are:

- identifying situations that need attention
- uncovering latent conflict
- measuring the effects of changes
- providing bottom-up feedback to managers
- improving management-employee communication
- pushing down problem solving.

Conducting employee surveys is more than just taking the pulse of the organization, identifying weak supervisors, or isolating problem areas. The process of implementing the employee survey is just as important as the outcome. This approach is a powerful intervention in the organization and, to be successful, the primary clients must be prepared to feed the data back to the employees and to act on the "problem" areas. The internal consultant's role is critical in helping senior management make the commitment to involvement, share the data, and solve problems. Involving managers and employees in the process improves the receptivity to receive the data and develops ownership of identified problems.

Because employee-survey technology is widely available, it is important to capitalize on what others have learned as effective implementation strategies. Jones and Bearley offer some principles to guide the internal consultant and client managers as they determine whether and how to use this intervention (figure 11-3). Many of these principles apply to later phases in the consulting process. It is important that both client group and consultant discuss openly how to use this intervention from the beginning steps through the entire process before collecting the data.

These principles are intended to be discussed by senior managers in strategizing the overall activity. The accountability and reward systems of most organizations do not directly support the survey-feedback process, and it is important that top leadership think openly about how to use this technology well. Rewarding managers and groups who cooperate with the intervention and use it well and holding people accountable for helping the organization look at itself candidly and improve its functioning are two powerful ways of making sure that survey-feedback efforts deliver what they promise (Jones & Bearley 1995).

Once the consultant has collected the data, the next demanding step is to analyze, assess, or interpret the data. In the feedback phase, clients need to explore and seek their own interpretation of the data to develop "ownership" of it. However, they will want to know the consultant's interpretation. A frequently asked question is, "What does this mean?" The consultant needs to be prepared with an answer.

Traditional models of consulting often refer to the term *diagnosis,* which assumes a model of illness rather than wellness. Many projects are not based on a

Figure 11-3. Guiding principles for employee surveys.

- Plan to include as many people as possible, and make sure that everyone gets the results. Since commitment to making action plans effective is a direct function of feeling influential in effecting the plans, it is imperative to involve everyone who could possibly help in the specification of what needs to be done.
- Involve representatives of several levels in planning and carrying out the intervention under the direction of top management. Make sure that all "constituencies" of the organization are listened to in the planning of the intervention. This may involve communicating with union leaders.
- Feed back the overall results of the survey to everyone. Let all personnel know the summary statistics of the survey, preferably with commentary by the chief executive.
- Work with senior leaders to communicate their action plans to everyone. Facilitate the feedback session with the top-level group, and encourage them to "go public" with what they decide.
- Make sure that the feedback and action planning are conducted in a timely manner. Make the interval between administering the questionnaire and feeding back the results as short as possible.
- Consider using task forces or employee-involvement groups to work on organization-wide situations that need attention. Use the intervention to extend the participatory management strategy throughout the organization.
- Carefully evaluate the intervention through follow-up study. Interview individuals and groups, do a small-scale survey of managers, and review action plans of work groups.
- Hold individual managers accountable for holding survey-feedback meetings with their subordinates. Encourage the senior executive to indicate his or her expectation that everyone will cooperate fully and completely with the activity.
- Publicize action plans and implementation outcomes that are generated by work groups at all levels. Gather nonconfidential reports and working documents from teams, and communicate them to everyone.
- Provide consultative assistance to individual managers and their work groups to use the survey results effectively. This is done by using "outside" consultants, internal HRD personnel, and specially trained managers to act as process consultants in the survey-feedback meetings.
- Do not raise expectations unduly by including items on organizational "givens." Focus only on what seems to be correlated with organizational goals and is open to improvement.
- Reward people who use the intervention to make lasting organizational improvements. Work with top managers to devise ways of providing special recognition to individual managers and teams who make significant contributions to organizational excellence as a result of the intervention.

Reprinted, by permission, from Jones, J.E., and W.L. Bearley, *Surveying Employees: A Practical Guidebook* (Amherst, MA: HRD Press, 1995).

disease or problem condition but are focused on prevention, improvement, development, or learning. The analysis and assessment phase applies whatever the condition of the client system. Once the data is tabulated, the consultant looks for themes, patterns, and connections. Using a model or framework is very helpful with the interpretation and analysis.

Models or Frameworks

There are many available. Weisbord's (1978) six-box model is an old standby. It includes purposes, structure, rewards, relationships, leadership, and helpful mechanisms. More recently published models include Henning's (1997) discovery model. It examines the social contract, management practices, and organization architecture that influences the distribution of organizational power—business literacy, accountability, choice, competencies, and access to resources. He recommends looking for opportunities to build organizational capacity by expanding these components of organizational power.

The appreciative inquiry model (Hammond 1996) explores past successes and achievements. This model offers opportunities to present the positive qualities valued by employees, why they are proud, what they appreciate. The data in this model allows the consultant to offer a "provocative proposition" about what the system can create or achieve by building on this positive and appreciative energy.

Bolman and Deal's (1997) four-frame model is another useful framework to consider. It has the following components:

- structure, which includes considering roles and functions; work processes; how individuals and teams are integrated vertically and horizontally; and how authority, rules, and policies are used
- human resource, which examines the fit between the organization and the people, whether people's human needs are being met, if they have the needed competencies to meet the organization's needs, and whether they know what is expected of them
- political, which explores the issues and impact of power, influence, dominance, control, and decision making
- symbolic includes the values, norms, stories, jokes, rituals, and ceremonies that give meaning to the activities and events of the organization.

An Interrelated Suite of Solutions

Internal Journal

The organization came knocking on the door with a particular problem. We were engaged to help understand the cause of the problem. We conducted employee meetings, and the richness of the issue was far greater than originally thought. We went back to the management team and laid out the complex picture. We laid out multiple problems and causes with proposed solutions. We had a highly interrelated suite of solutions actually, not just one solution. One solution would have little or no effect. We needed to address all the problems simultaneously. The measure of success was the organization's results in getting new products to market.

**Jim Fuller, Redwood Mountain Consulting,
former internal consultant with technology industry**

SYSTEMS VIEW

Regardless of which tools are used to collect information and data about the client organization, taking a systems view is imperative. A systems view of the presenting issue recognizes the interrelationships of the parts and the importance of their interaction to create the whole. This view is sometimes difficult for internal consultants and their clients, because they live in the system and it is hard to stand outside to see the whole. Figure 11-4 introduces some questions to help the client and internal consultant maintain a systems perspective.

The ability to stand at the edge, to see the patterns, connections, and underlying structures that create the dynamics of a situations is one of the most significant contributions a consultant can make. However, it is not only difficult to be a member of the system and to be marginal as discussed in chapter 1, it is also a challenge because of the Newtonian tradition in education and training. Both consultant and client are trained to dissect and analyze the parts based on the assumption that if they understand the individual parts they will master the whole. Simply focusing on events that the client presents as a series of parts limits the possibilities to a reactive stance. Look for patterns of behavior and the underlying structures that generate those patterns.

Figure 11-4. Systems questions.

- Are department and unit strategies linked to the organization-wide strategy?
- Who are the department's internal and external customers?
- What are the department's products and services?
- What are customers' requirements for those products and services?
- Is performance measured on the basis of how well those products and services meet customers' requirements?
- Who are the department's internal and external suppliers?
- Are clear goals established for the products and services provided by suppliers?
- Is there documentation of the department's role in the cross-functional processes?
- Is the department measured according to the degree to which it contributes to cross-functional processes?
- Is the "upstream" performance of the processes that flow through department measured?
- Are there tracking and feedback systems that effectively and efficiently gather performance information and provide it to the people who need it?
- Does the client have the skills to troubleshoot (remove the root causes of) performance gaps in the system?
- Does the client spend a large percentage of time working to improve the interfaces between the department and other functions and among the subunits within the department?
- Do employees work in an environment where their job design, goals, feedback, rewards, resources, and training enable them to make their maximum contributions to process efficiency and effectiveness?

Perviz Randeria, organization and management development consultant
Former internal consultant with city government

The new, science approach teaches that organizations are fluid, interdependent, and in constant change. To harness the positive energy in the system, the consultant must recognize the organization as a living system. The value the internal consultant adds is to make visible the connections and interrelationship beneath the surface of a series of events. Only by discovering the structural underpinnings for behavioral patterns can we truly implement successful organizational or performance change.

Engaging the Whole System

Internal Journal

I worked with a director and her team engaging the whole system in their own process of sharing information about jobs, customers, services, and what kind of feedback they were getting. The goal was to be more integrated and not duplicate work or services. We got into all the changes the department was facing, understanding the different disciplines from a merger, who does what, why, and how it fits into the department. It was a success because I had the trust and involvement of the department director, and we worked diagonally across the organization, did just-in-time training, and problem solving. I also knew the other parts of the organization and what other changes were going on. I was able to keep a larger, systems focus.

Perviz Randeria, organization and management development consultant, former internal consultant with city government

Beliefs About Change

The internal consultant's beliefs about change will also affect how he or she approaches this phase. The traditional problem-solving diagnostic model of asking "What is wrong?" or "What problems are you having?" will expose the negative underside of the system and potentially amplify the problem. On the other hand, approaching this phase in the spirit of inquiry raises the tension between the desired future and the dissatisfaction with the present, which can motivate change. Remember that by observing and asking questions, the consultant influences the system. This is a sensitive balance. The value of a consultant is to bring a perspective, a view that the client lacks. Therefore, identifying and diagnosing the barriers and roadblocks that impede the achievement of desired goals, outcomes, and visions is necessary. Yet, focusing too heavily on what is wrong can result in a loss of motivation, create resistance, and demoralize the members of the system. Change strategies will be explored further in the next chapter.

The Hornet's Nest

Internal Journal

We were reorganizing and merging departments. Some were more prepared than others, but I made the mistake of dealing with them in the same way. In one area, I underestimated the animosity and the conflict, which turned out to be monumental forces. I had had no prior affiliation with them. Each group distrusted the other, and one group didn't trust me. When I tried to listen to both sides, one side thought I had joined sides with the other. It was very political. I had walked into a hornet's nest. I had underestimated the power of the situation and not learned about it before I tried to work on the merger. It is so important to know what you are dealing with before you try to change something. I would work with them individually if I were to do it over again.

**Mila N. Baker, system director, learning and
organization development, Baptist/St. Vincent's Health System**

Summing Up and Looking Ahead

Collecting information or data about the organization gives the consultant an independent view and helps the long-term internal consultant keep a more neutral perspective of the client system. This process is essential to successful consulting. It also provides additional benefits, such as offering the client an alternative view, and begins to prepare the client system for the intervention. Interviews, questionnaires, observation, and document reviews all yield valuable information. This chapter specifically explored using interviews and employee surveys. Regardless of the tool used to collect the data, a framework or model to analyze and interpret the findings brings value to what is otherwise just a collection of information. Using a model in conjunction with taking a systems view of the organization will help the internal consultant find the patterns in the structural underpinnings that influence outcomes or behavior to be changed. In the next chapter, we review the critical process of feeding back the information to the client and provide a step-by-step process for the feedback meeting.

References

Block, P. (1993). *Stewardship: Choosing Service Over Self-Interest.* San Francisco: Berrett-Koehler Publishers.

Bolman, L.G., and T.E. Deal. (1997). *Reframing Organizations.* San Francisco: Jossey-Bass.

Hammond, S.A. (1996). *The Thin Book of Appreciative Inquiry.* Plano, TX: Kodiak Consulting.

Henning, J.P. (1997). *The Future of Staff Groups.* San Francisco: Berrett-Koehler Publishers.

Jones, J.E., and W.L. Bearley. (1995). *Surveying Employees: A Practical Guidebook.* Amherst, MA: HRD Press.

Nevis, E.C. (1987). *Organizational Consulting.* New York: Gardner Press.

Weisbord, M.R. (1978). *Organization Diagnosis.* Reading, MA: Addison-Wesley.

Chapter 12

Phase Four: Feedback

The results of the information gathering and assessment phase are shared with the client in this phase. The consultant has assessed the information and formed an independent view about the business processes, the organizational culture, how departments interact, the strengths and hopes of the people, the opportunities for increasing the capacity of the organization, the employee competencies, or the team performance. Other questions the consultant must answer based on the data are

- Is there a match or fit between the consultant's knowledge base and the needs and opportunities in the client system?
- Is there a match between the organizational culture and the approach the consultant brings?
- What alternatives can the consultant offer to the client as next steps?

Presenting the findings from the information gathering and assessment phase is a critical step not only in the relationship between consultant and client but also in determining the client's willingness to move forward with the project. Many internal consultants lose clients and the opportunity to complete important projects because this phase does not go well. However, carefully planned and delivered feedback will continue to build a valued consultant-client relationship.

A Missed Opportunity

Internal Journal

To create content for a leadership development initiative, I conducted a conversation assessment with an external consultant. We got groups of people together, used questionnaires with quantitative analysis, and small-group interaction that was recorded. We were looking for principles of leadership that were most important and how they were defined. The principle of external focus was not valued throughout the organization.

No one talked about it or referred to it. They were not paying attention to customers or meeting customer needs. I took the results to the CEO who totally disagreed, saying that customer orientation was not a leadership issue, it was a business issue. I was very frustrated. My boss chickened out and the whole leadership program fell apart.

Internal consultant with high-technology Internet company

In preparation for the feedback meeting, remember that clients want to know what to do. That does not require brilliant, strategic recommendations. Clients need a clear picture of the situation, as if looking at the picture on the jigsaw-puzzle box to help put all the pieces together. They also need time to digest, absorb, and accept the data. A clear presentation of the data using an interpretative framework or model with time to discuss and reflect will help the client see that picture and understand how all the pieces fit together.

Successful Feedback Process Leads to Positive Outcomes

Internal Journal

I worked with a department of ambulatory surgery at an academic health center. It was fraught with conflict among the professional, clerical, and surgical staff. There were high turnover, high stress, and flaring tempers. I did a needs assessment and gave them the feedback engaging them in the development of their own solution. The intervention lasted over a number of months. The outcomes were: reduced turnover, people feeling positive about being at work, more efficient patient flow, and greater collaboration between the administrator and managing physician. Giving them the feedback and getting them to buy into their own solution was the ingredient for success. The managing physician was a hard sell and a real challenge. I insisted he be a part of the solution and attend the meetings and participate in all the activities. If he couldn't make the meetings we would reschedule. His isolation had been part of the problem. I also coached him in working with his administrative manager. That enabled him to see that he could work on his issues with her, as well as the other issues. It was also important to get the clerical buy-in. By working issues in a public forum and letting them see they had some capacity to improve their working environment, they were empowered. We created ground rules that were implemented with a trial period. They originally didn't believe anything would change or that anyone would listen to them. They felt powerless.

Chrissa B. Merron, senior consultant, Concentrics, former internal consultant with financial industry

Presenting a clear picture requires the consultant to spend time working with the data, massaging it, finding the key messages, and condensing it to a form that the client system can absorb and handle. Consultants may be tempted to provide the data almost "raw," including all phrases or sentences captured from the interviews. This catch-all approach yields too much data, and the clients will be overwhelmed. It is better to sort through the data to

- identify repetitive themes that are critical to the client's objectives and desired outcomes
- report areas the client has some control to influence or change
- choose issues that have energy in the organization
- explore the layers of the problem: how it presented itself, perceptions of how others contributed to it, and the client's own contribution to it.

Feedback Themes—An Example from an Internal Consultant's Experience

The following excerpted paragraphs exemplify how themes can be developed during the feedback phase. They can serve as a model for other internal consultants. In this case, we saw several patterns, which were holding the organization back from a path of healthy and prosperous growth. These were blaming and judging, pairing, and a culture of security. In these paragraphs, we addressed blaming and judging.

It is always easy to focus on others as the cause or reason for that which one does not like; after all, that's the American way! While it helps one to be innocent of existing problems and supports wiping one's hands of responsibility, we see it as a path to nowhere.

In the popular and powerful book, The Wisdom of Teams *(Katzenback & Smith 1993), the single, most astounding piece of information reported is that high-performing teams have one potent characteristic that is lacking in teams that are successful but not high performing. That characteristic is this: Every member of the team is as dedicated to the success of his or her teammates as to the success of themselves.*

We believe this means that there is no blaming and judging. Rather, each member of the team becomes fully self-responsible for his or her behaviors and equally responsible to team members. Thus, if one part of the organization is not doing well, everyone on the team takes responsibility for that condition and works with teammates to correct the situation. Similarly, one member's success is viewed and publicized as a team's successful endeavor.

The wisdom of this belief is that it saves face and time! The time it takes for an individual to recover from failing is primarily dependent upon two factors: (1) actively seeking support from one's family, friends, and col-

leagues; and (2) being able to begin anew (resiliency). Over the course of time, each one of us will have our time of being less than perfect and of creating some kind of organizational or business mess. To know that our teammates will support us because they are committed to our success is a powerful factor.

The matter of trust is an important consideration. No one can or will trust others if those others are continually blaming and judging. Most of us are smart and savvy enough to know that if a person blames and judges others, she or he will blame and judge us when the opportunity presents itself. Trust levels within a team are high when each member can count on peers and colleagues to be supportive even when failures occur. While trust is a complex consideration, it is a necessary characteristic of teams that are successful.

**Marilyn E. Blair, TeamWork,
former internal consultant with 3Com Corporation**

Author's Approach

When I approach a stack of notes from client interviews, I read through them a couple of times. Then I set them aside and begin a list of key repetitive themes, review them against the points listed above, and then check back over the notes to see if I have missed anything. The next step is to select words or phrases in the language of the interviewees to expand or explain each theme. If I am using a particular model, such as Weisbord's (1978) six-box model or Bolman and Deal's (1997) four-frame model, I place the themes in the appropriate box, frame, or category. The final step is to formulate recommendations.

Preparing for Survey Feedback

When the feedback data comes from an employee survey, much of the same advice applies. The workgroup manager or supervisor may request to look at all the basic statistical data, but if that is extensive, it pays to also provide a summary of the key points from the survey: the highest response items, the lowest response items, averages of related items grouped together, and so forth. Such a summary will help a busy manager gain a clearer picture of the organization and understand where to focus improvement efforts.

Sensitive Information

Prepare carefully for feedback of sensitive information, such as data that is new or contradicts the client's perspective, that is critical of the clients, or that they may not support. The internal consultant is more vulnerable than the external consultant to the accusations of incompetence, insubordination, or retaliation if the client is not prepared to hear negative or unwanted information. Even though the clients may have agreed that they want feedback, that is not always the case. Here is some advice to consider:

- Prepare with the needs of the client in mind. Use the knowledge of the client gained from the contact and agreement phases. Review the agreements about bad news and critical feedback. Does that discussion and subsequent experience with the client give you any clues about the best way to present the data?
- Do not blame senior management or others. They may be your clients in the future and word can travel. In addition, blaming others undermines your credibility with current clients who will wonder what the consultant will say about them to other departments. Help the client accept the reality of the situation and focus on what is within the client's control.
- Think about possible client objections and resistance to the data. Identify opportunities to bring them to the surface and discuss them.
- Avoid projecting feelings and issues on the client. The internal consultant might be upset at hearing that subordinates think the boss is meddling and controlling, but the client may be upset and deserves to hear the feedback. Clients are often relieved to find the situation is not as serious as they expected. In addition, a client cannot act to change behavior without information that it causes a problem.
- Be willing to confront the tough issues. Clients may be avoiding dealing with poor performance or a peer relationship. If the data confirms that the issue is having a serious impact, do not minimize it because of a suspicion that the client does not want to address it. Raise the issue and help the client face it and find a way to deal with it.
- Acknowledge and confirm the positive data in the feedback. It provides a firm foundation and reassurance to take the risks to change.
- Remember the data could be wrong or the interpretation could be off-base. Be sure to invite the clients to provide their interpretation first.

Framing the Data

This is an opportunity to influence how the issue is framed by organization members. A frame is the boundary around the presenting "problem" or issue. Reframing implies viewing the situation with a different frame, from a different perspective, shifting beliefs in such a way that the situation looks different, much as picture can look very different with different framing around it. This process is based on the assumption that the way that the data is framed and interpreted influences how members in the client system receive the information and affects the level of their motivation to tackle serious issues.

This framing can be done within the theoretical model chosen for the analysis or assessment. The model might be considered the mat used to display the picture of the organization within the perspective of the frame.

Clients Unwilling to Accept Feedback

Internal Journal

We were brought in where management perceived there was a clear issue—a lack of documentation that kept the organization from using a piece of new software. What we discovered was that it wasn't the documentation at all. People didn't want the software because it turned them into mindless button-pushing zombies. Given this perspective, they didn't want the problem to be fixed but wanted management to continue believing in the documentation problem. It became clear to us that the department members could dream up more problems to be fixed than we could possibly solve. We went back to management to say this will not be successful. They said to make it successful. We explained the issues, but they would not accept them. We ultimately wished them luck and disengaged.

**Jim Fuller, Redwood Mountain Consulting,
former internal consultant with technology industry**

Presenting the information or the assessment from a critical frame by identifying all the problems and issues that are wrong with the organization is usually ineffective, just as a poor choice of frame detracts from a painting. A frame of criticism tends not only to create resistance and a lack of willingness to admit the problems and individual contribution to them, but may also limit possibilities. It tends to generate more negativity and shoot down a fragile future dream. It can become a negative vortex, drawing others into the swirl of counterattacks, complaints, and resistance, as well.

Reframe the presentation of data and interpretation to include the strengths and successes upon which the system can build and highlight opportunities for improved capacity, higher performance, achievement of goals, and other positive outcomes. When the clients can begin to envision these positive outcomes, they have more energy and motivation to work hard and take unpleasant but necessary steps to reach the desired results. They can begin to see their own and others strengths and contributions that will make success possible. By sharing information about what is working well, the internal consultant is also reassuring the client that the positive future can be leveraged from the familiar present. In the journey to the unknown future, clients will have more confidence if they know they can carry forward some of their familiar past. In addition, reframing can also give team members an empowering sense of control, creating positive movement that becomes reinforcing and infectious and inviting others to get on board.

Working with Resistance

Resistance is a normal and natural response to change or feeling a lack of control. Despite all the planning and the efforts of reframing and presenting the strengths and successes of the system, the internal consultant must be prepared to address resistance from members of the client system. Some of the strongest resistance from clients will surface during feedback meetings. If it is not addressed, it can undermine or sabotage a change project.

Resistance has many faces (chapter 5). When it is expressed directly through open opposition or disagreement, it is easily recognizable. When it is subtle, covert, and camouflaged fear or discomfort, often even unconscious to the resister, it may be harder to recognize and address.

Expressions of resistance are messages to the internal consultant that something important is happening with the clients. The most important response to resistance is to listen actively and to encourage more expression. Here are some tips to effectively handle resistance:

- Do not take it personally.
- Respond without arguing in a clear, even tone.
- Try rational responses first.
- If the resistance continues, state observations or feelings without blame and then be quiet. (This is particularly useful for resisters who are postponing activities or canceling meetings.)
- Do not back down from the touchy issues in the feedback.
- Continue active listening.
- When the expression has "slowed down," review the vision, goals, objectives, and agreements.
- Continue listening.
- Cycle back and repeat some of the above suggestions.
- Ask for continued or demonstrated support.

Remember, resistance is not to be overcome, it must be understood and expressed. Although consultants are prepared for resistance, it is important to remember that some resisters are really "persisters," who have a different perspective and a valid reason to resist the anticipated changes. It is important to listen carefully and to consider concerns and reasons seriously as the project moves forward.

Personal Feedback

A client relationship based on trust provides an opportunity to give the client feedback on personal style or behaviors that are self-defeating or potentially undermine the success of the project. During the courtesy feedback meeting with the client manager before organizational data is presented to the group members, there is an opportunity to provide personal feedback. Below are tips for giving useful personal feedback:

- *Timing:* Feedback is most useful when your client has the time to listen and to give full attention. Use recent events and examples of behavior. If examples are too distant, the client will not remember or find them useful.
- *Agreement:* It is helpful to review agreements about giving feedback; remind the client about the agreement regarding discussion of difficult issues.
- *Descriptive:* Use an objective description of behaviors that can be changed. Avoid judgmental or critical statements. A general evaluative statement, such as "You are dictatorial," is not helpful and will probably create resistance.
- *Examples:* Include examples of specific actions, words, or statements if possible without violating the confidentiality of the source. Draw upon personal observations.
- *Balance:* Include both positive and negative feedback.
- *Impact:* Help the client understand the result or affect of the behavior, words, and statements. Understanding the negative impact helps to motivate changing the behavior.
- *Support:* Solicit reaction and allow the client to express his or her own frustration or disappointment. Provide support and listen with empathy.
- *Learning:* Ask the client what he or she learned and what could be done differently next time. You may need to provide coaching and suggestions.

Making a Difference in People's Lives

Internal Journal

I feel that I have done good work when I can look a client in the face and tell him the truth. The most valuable process we are able to accomplish is to hold up mirrors and tell a story. I worked with a CEO whose company had hit the wall. His shadow side was coming out, and he was lashing out at his own executive team in very harsh ways. He was very close to losing members of his team at a very critical point. He knew something was wrong. He wanted to just build the team. I convinced him that it was important to get some data first.

I did the interviews, and the data was very negative. People were ready to leave. People had no hope. They believed he would not change, and they had given up on him. I gave him the data privately and worked him through it. I got him ready to hear the same data in front of his team. He gave his own heartfelt response. He said, "I need your help." It turned everyone to putty. This was the first day of a three-day retreat. One of the members of the team, who had been acquired from another company, was very quiet, and the others had not known how to read him. Because the CEO was so open, this very quiet person opened up, and everyone saw what a leader he was. Three or four years later he became CEO of the company. If I had not given the feedback and the CEO had not been so open, people would have left. If this person had not responded so openly, he would not have become CEO. We can make huge differences in people's lives!

Eddie Reynolds, consultant, executive and organization development, former internal consultant with high-technology industry

Feedback on the client's personal style or behaviors that negatively affect the organization is the hardest data to report. Nevertheless, it may be the most helpful information your client receives. Provide it in a straightforward but supportive way.

The Steps of the Feedback Meeting

The first feedback meeting is a courtesy feedback meeting with the manager or executive of the client system. In this meeting the internal consultant is not only presenting the feedback and the assessment, but also preparing the client to partner in the presentation of the data to the client's organization members. Thus, it is important to allow the client to express feelings of disappointment, fear, anger, and frustration, and to work through any resistance. As a result, the process may require more than one meeting. Appendix 6 consists of a step-by-step process to use for the courtesy feedback meeting and the feedback meeting with the organization's members. The appendix includes a clever metaphorical approach to presenting the consultant's observations.

The following are some ground rules for feedback meetings:

- Everyone participates.
- Listen without interrupting others.
- Express disagreements with others without criticizing.
- Accept others' views and attitudes as true for them.
- Keep to timelines.

Survey Feedback Steps

There are many approaches to organization survey feedback. Experienced consultants and employee survey experts believe that the data belongs to those who provided it and that it is important to feed it back to them and to use it to improve organization effectiveness. The feedback process to individual units or work groups can be time consuming and resource intensive.

Figure 12-1 depicts a survey feedback process that involved mid-level managers, who had been trained as facilitators, working as partners with workgroup

Figure 12-1. Survey feedback flowchart.

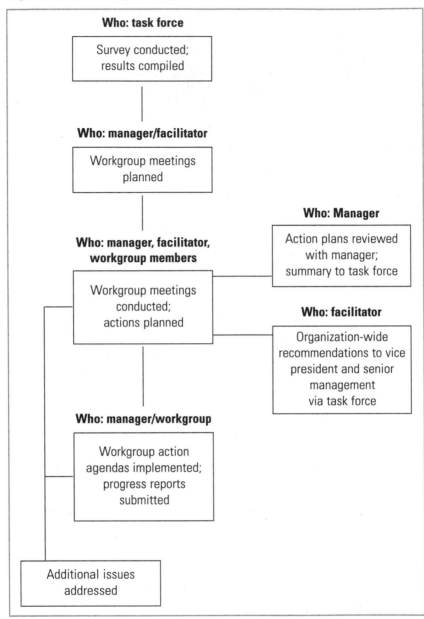

managers for the feedback process. In this feedback scenario, the main elements of the workgroup manager's role were to

- use consistent decision-making method
- present data overview
- respect expectations of participants
- not be defensive

- define expectations of facilitator
- set overall purpose of the meeting and the agenda.

The key elements of the consultant/facilitator's role were to

- maintain neutrality
- keep the group focused on the task
- protect group members
- make sure everyone had a chance to participate
- give process suggestions
- make a contract with group members and the manager regarding the consultant's role
- create a record of the discussion by writing down key words of the participants.

The group members were to

- participate in the meeting
- listen to and solicit other's contributions
- have a win-win attitude.

The responsibilities of mid-level managers, who had been trained as facilitators, were to

- plan for meeting with workgroup managers
- meet with workgroup manager
- facilitate the workgroup feedback meeting
- conduct the workgroup-action-planning meeting
- perform follow-up activities as needed.

The facilitators schedule meeting(s) with the workgroup manager. They opted to hold an initial meeting for 15–20 minutes to introduce and review data. Then the facilitators could let the manager study before meeting again to plan feedback session. To prepare for this meeting, the facilitators reviewed the data and prepared a draft agenda for the first workgroup meeting. They developed a plan on how to review the data and copied survey results and other relevant material.

The meeting with the workgroup manager was designed to build rapport, check for understanding on each section of the survey, and clarify the purpose of the survey-feedback intervention. The goals for the meeting were to

- understand the survey results
- plan the subsequent feedback meeting to deliver results of the survey to the workgroup
- clarify the purpose of the feedback meeting (understand statistical results, identify opportunities, plan action steps for problem solving)

- review critical guidelines about data confidentiality and remind manager not to ask direct-reporting staff to share their data
- clarify feedback process and answer pertinent questions
- orient manager to data format and work systematically through the data
- design the workgroup feedback meeting
- help manager focus on listening and being open to input.

The feedback session itself would probably require about two hours. The facilitators confirmed the number of employees who were in the workgroup at that time, as well as the date, time, and location (workgroup manager's responsibility) of the session. The agenda provided to the facilitators for the feedback meeting appears in figure 12-2.

Figure 12-2. Proposed agenda for survey-feedback meeting.

Agenda

Purpose:	To understand the survey results and to begin taking action on improving our work together
Today's outcome:	Understand the survey results compiled by company, organizational unit, and workgroup. Identify problems and issues based on the survey and our discussion. Prioritize issues to be ready to initiate action plans.

Time	Activity
15 min	Welcome to first feedback meeting Review purpose and outcomes listed above Explain agenda Define roles of manager, facilitator, workgroup members Discuss and get agreement on ground rules
30 min 15 min	Review of data: explanation, questions and answers What does this mean to us? Members individually read and make notes on good news and opportunities
10 min	Break
60 min	Record good-news items on flipchart Record opportunities on flipchart
30 min	Acknowledge good news Rank opportunities by priority
15 min	Group agrees on final list Classify high-priority items by workgroup, organizational unit, or company
5 min	Note how organizational and company issues will be addressed Review agenda and set time for next meeting

The action planning and implementation process included several steps, such as

- studying the results and alternatives suggested by employees
- involving employees in determining what actions to take and preparing an action plan
- reviewing the survey summary results, the top three to five issues, and the action plan with the next level manager
- implementing the action plan
- providing follow-up reports to the manager and the survey taskforce on action plan progress.

The agenda for the action-planning meeting appears in figure 12-3.

Summing Up and Looking Ahead

Feeding back the findings generated by the information and assessment phase is an intervention in itself that can have a major impact on the system. The internal consultant has already "disturbed the system" by his or her presence in asking questions, distributing surveys, and collecting information. Conscientiously preparing for the feedback meeting by selecting key themes, using a theoretical model to help

Figure 12-3. Proposed agenda for action-planning meeting.

Agenda	
Purpose:	To begin problem-solving issues and agree on actions to improve our work together and prepare plans for implementing agreed actions
Time	**Activity**
10 min	Review first meeting quickly Review ground rules Review purpose

60 min	Use problem-solving process on top workgroup issues:
	    Define the problem
	    Define the objective
	    Determine criteria
	    Generate alternatives
	    Evaluate alternatives
	    Choose the best solution

60 min	Prepare action plans
30 min	Review and identify company and organizational unit issues
15 min	Determine next steps Set up follow-up meeting.

interpret the data, and framing it with the opportunities, successes, and strengths of the client organization are essential for success in this phase.

If the information is particularly sensitive, approach the meeting with an awareness of the client's needs and potential resistance. Internal consultants must not project their own feelings on the client or waver about presenting the tough issues. Such careful preparation contributes to productive feedback meetings, builds the consultant-client relationship, and leads to successful project outcomes in the future.

The next phase, alignment, confirms that the consultant and client are aligned and in agreement on the next steps of the process and the desired outcomes. Alignment leads directly into the planning process, choosing change targets and developing transition strategies.

References

Bolman, L.G., and T.E. Deal. (1997). *Reframing Organizations.* San Francisco: Jossey-Bass.

Katenzenback, J.R., and D.K. Smith. (1993). *The Wisdom of Teams.* Boston: Harvard Business School Press.

Weisbord, M.R. (1978). *Organization Diagnosis.* Reading, MA: Addison-Wesley.

Chapter 13

Phases Five and Six: Alignment and Change Targets and Transition Strategies

After presenting the findings and discussing the observations and recommendations, the internal consultant often needs to cycle back to the original agreement phase to revise or extend the agreement to the next steps. With agreement to move to the next steps, discussion then may focus on educating the client on the change process and the alternatives the consultant is recommending. The client's willingness to move forward, to take risks, and to invest his or her personal reputation and performance is influenced strongly by the strength of the partnership relationship built by the consultant. The client's sense of confidence and competence to handle the risks and challenges of change contribute to that commitment.

Phase Five: Alignment for Next Steps

In this phase the consultant and client agree on the alternatives they will use to address the organizational issues, seek alignment regarding the goals and outcomes they will strive for together, and determine the measures of success to be applied in evaluation. The internal consultant may propose generating a vision of the desired outcomes or performance results. Alternatively, the consultant may create a "provocative proposition" as propounded in the appreciative-inquiry approach, which describes and captures the energy of the organization and offers an exciting possibility for members to create. Examples of this approach (Hammond 1996) include organizational creeds, such as, "Our customers have a pleasant experience when they talk to us" or "The information we need to answer their questions is available to us at the touch of a finger." It is also important to continue to reinforce the client's personal learning and increasing self-knowledge and to emphasize the value of processes or structures to build organizational learning.

Often the original contract is with a primary client; before finalizing plans and agendas, it is helpful to clarify expectations and needs with the secondary clients. Other areas of alignment are provided in appendix 7, which consists of a useful checklist to ensure that all the important areas for this project or intervention are covered.

This Was a Contracting Issue

I was working with a group, which had been underperforming for many years. The project was pushed by a high-level staff person who did not have strong credibility with them. They were going along from a compliance stance and because they were in a lot of pain. It turned out they wanted more structure and more facilitation in the approach I used. It was too personal for them. This was a contracting issue.

Scott Burton, internal consultant with consumer products industry

In this alignment phase, the internal consultant becomes a co-navigator with the client, because the client's visions for the organization become the consultant's, too. This helps the client create and use symbols that capture attention, communicate and frame the vision, and provide energy and motivation for change. The process of alignment is not a single, isolated event. It is often a continuous process as internal consultants repeatedly check back with the clients. It is complicated when multiple levels of clients are involved. Success requires vigilance and persistence to ensure that client alignment is maintained. Some of the areas listed in the checklist (appendix 7) will actually carry the consultant into the next phase—change targets and transition strategies.

Continuous Alignment with Multiple Clients

When I first came on board in a prior organization, it had spent $10 million on quality training, none of which stuck. It was the supervisors' "fault," so management wanted to put the supervisors through two more days of quality training, hoping that would solve it. As a new internal consultant without established credibility or currency, I knew I couldn't say no. I tried to position the initiative to gain support from the target audience. I went back and forth between the stakeholders, the senior leaders, and the supervisors to ensure support. I would say to the senior leaders, "Here's what I hear you saying . . . " or "Here's what the supervisors are saying." I recommended an action-learning approach, which was very nontraditional for this organization accustomed to two-day training programs.

Despite the negativity and resistance, in four months I had pushed these supervisors in directions they had never considered before. I was constantly visiting the supervisors and the senior leaders, explaining what was to be expected. I worked the boundaries and built relationships with the constituents to learn about their needs. Although the initiative had a terrible reputation at the kick-off, it was eventually very successful and won the chairman's best-practice award.

Bob Browning, director, Global Career Planning and Development, Colgate-Palmolive Company

Ending a Contract

Internal consultants often feel that they cannot say no or end a bad contract. The immediate boss, senior management, or an influential client may be applying pressure. Moreover, internal consultants may find at the alignment phase that alignment is not possible. As Weisbord (1997) put it, "Better a clean death than lingering agony." It is time to confront the client, test the level of commitment, and perhaps end the agreement if the following occur:

- The client continually forgets the agreements.
- Meetings, activities, and events are continually postponed.
- There is not a match in style, approach, or competencies with the client and the client's needs.
- The internal consultant is more committed or has a higher emotional stake in the outcomes than does the client.
- The client expects the internal consultant to perform tasks or assignments that are the client's responsibility as a manager or leader of a team or organizational unit.
- There is so much change and activity happening in the client system that no attention can be given to the project.
- The client system is functioning well and the consultant is no longer needed.

Sometimes the client system is not ready, and the consultant must raise questions or postpone the proposed intervention. Those actions may lead eventually to a more successful effort in the future, or they may end the project.

Is the Client System Ready?

I learned about client readiness. I had a proposal designed to meet client needs, which included roles, expectations, responsibility, decision making, and guiding principles. But there was no support for it. They weren't ready. Later, after an outside assessment when the people were in more pain, they were ready to move on it. It has been very successful. When I first made the proposal, the timing was off. Internal consultants need to pay attention and look for signs of when there is readiness to address specific issues.

Internal Journal

Molly Smith-Olsson, team leader, organization effectiveness, Blue Shield of California

Putting on the Brakes

Internal Journal

> *I had a philosophical difference regarding a pay-for-performance initiative. I didn't feel the organization was ready for it. I believed what was requested was not in the direction the organization needed to go. I voiced my concerns. Sometimes we are successful, and sometimes we are not successful in influencing decisions tied to the philosophical issues of our profession. I often handle this by asking clarifying questions, such as, "What are our goals here, truly?" I first ensure that my clients can see my support. Then I ask if we can find another way to reach the goal. If they believe that I'm not seeing their perspective clearly, I ask them to educate me or change my assumptions.*

Internal consultant with government agency

Phase Six: Change Targets and Transition Strategies

Change, as discussed in earlier chapters, is complex and chaotic. It can generate anxiety, fear, and a loss of control in executives and employees alike. Managing change and the transition from the current reality to the way they would like it is a challenging task for most executives and managers. They dislike uncertainty and want to take action by jumping right in to create the envisioned result. In fact, in organization or performance change efforts, the first action executives frequently want to take is to change the structure. Restructuring is often viewed as a solution to any number of performance issues and may look easy to accomplish. However, leaping into a new structure is only a temporary fix in many cases and also denies the systemic nature of organizations and performance. Bolman and Deal (1997) remind us that the structure is only one of the four frames to consider.

Avoid Command and Control

In addition, the practice of many executives and managers still is to announce changes and to expect those affected to accept such change and fall in line without question. The old patterns of "command and control" continue to be the leadership style of too many executives despite the evidence that it is seldom as effective as allowing employees to manage and organize themselves to produce results (Wheatley 1997). The internal consultant has an important role to play in educating managers regarding the value of self-management and self-organization not only for increasing productivity but also in managing the change process.

Go Slow to Go Fast

Convince the executive client to take time, that is, to go slow is to go fast in organizational change. Going slow means taking time to create a vision and goals for the desired outcome and enrolling members of the organization in the vision.

Developing this shared understanding of what is important, why the change is needed, and the common goals for which everyone should strive guides the energy and work of organization members toward creating that outcome. Communication, networks, teams, and other structures emerge to support the movement toward the future. To lead change in this way requires that leaders trust their employees' capacity to create and commit to the future of the enterprise. Leaders who take that risk are often surprised, pleasantly so, by the results.

New Ways to Look to the Future

We used communication centers where things were published and posted to describe changes taking place, what was in process, and what could be anticipated for the future. One team had full responsibility to collect and disseminate information using all kinds of media ranging from videos, to focus groups, and interviews.

Jim Harley, director, organization development, Westinghouse Electric Company

Chaos and Order

Educating employees about the messy, organic, complex nature of change builds the capacity to organize and manage their own work and move toward future goals. Michael Crnobrna, an internal consultant, uses a model of chaos and order to help employee teams understand the need for both. See the chart in figure 13-1, which portrays the classic hierarchy in either an organizational chart or in a defined process. These are defined and ordered relationships. The balls represent more chaotic relationships, which are complex and changing. The words *more orderly* and *more chaotic* are used because the orderly components can have a fair amount of chaos, and there is order to the chaos even though it is not initially visible.

The left side of the chart does not encourage innovation; the focus is on following a defined path. However, do not expect to complete a job quickly, efficiently, or consistently by using the right side. Chaos generates possibilities; structure will make it happen. Most government and corporate organizations try to manage by using the orderly, structured method. It is the Newtonian-machine model. But chaos may be more representative of today's turbulent environment. One side is no better than the other, both order and chaos are needed.

Change Leads to Personal Transition

Bridges (1991) introduced a model of transition that clarified the personal, internal psychological process individuals go through to adapt to change. The process begins with an "ending" in which a change occurs. The hurdle of transition is the "in-betweens," a period that seems unproductive, chaotic, out of control, and dis-

Figure 13-1. Model of chaos and order.

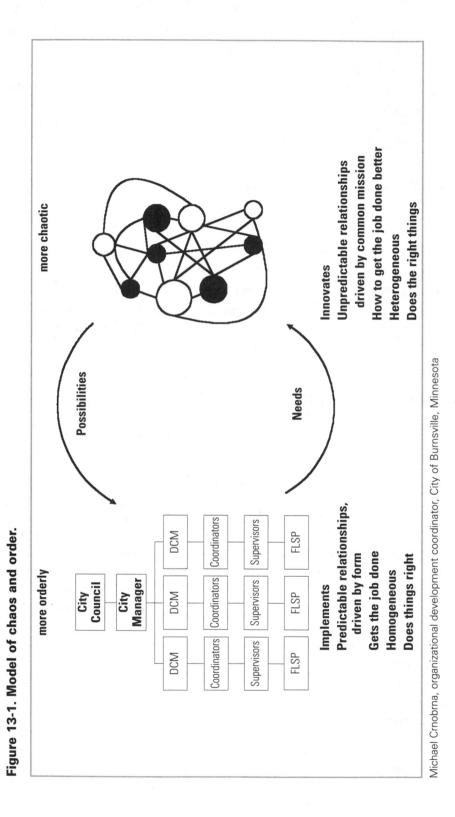

Michael Crnobrna, organizational development coordinator, City of Burnsville, Minnesota

connected from both the way things were and the desired future. Ultimately, people reach a sense of "new beginnings" with the energy and excitement of a fresh start, the challenge of opportunity, and organizational renewal.

Whether the consultant is introducing personal behavioral change, new skills through feedback, performance improvement, team building, coaching, or implementing systemwide change, it is helpful to consider suggestions to support and assist the internal personal transition process. Bridges recommended the following steps for "endings":

- Be clear about what is ending or what will be changed.
- Allow time to express feelings of loss or even grieving.
- Take the opportunity to honor the past and the achievements of the past.
- Offer emotional understanding and support.
- Communicate and share information repeatedly in many ways—group meetings, newsletters, memos, bulletin boards, one-on-one sessions, and training sessions.
- Honor the past; avoid making fun of or degrading the past.
- Identify what will replace that which has been "lost."

For the "in-betweens," Bridges suggested the following:

- Let people know that the feelings of confusion, chaos, and lack of control are normal.
- Create a dual system: Continue the old way while the new way is tested.
- Spend extra time with people to give support, reassurance, and encouragement.
- Use a transition team. (See appendix 8 for a sample charter.)
- Encourage and foster new ideas, innovations, and creativity.

And finally, for "new beginnings," Bridges offered these recommendations:

- Acknowledge mixed feelings of fear and excitement about the unknown.
- Recognize that individuals emotionally reach the new beginnings at different times.

The following actions will ease the transition process:

- Involve people in creating the vision, establishing goals, and developing action plans.
- Continue to communicate about the purpose of the change.
- Carefully plan actions to help move through the transition process.
- Score some quick wins to reassure the believers, convince the doubters, and confound the critics.
- Celebrate successes.

Change is a Learning Process

Change is a learning process; all learning is change. Supporting the organization change requires change in knowledge, skills, understanding, behavior, or attitudes. Provide training for new skills and behaviors that are required, accommodate processes that provide time for individual reflection and identification of personal learning, and set up structures to promote shared learning in teams, groups, and task forces. Remember that structures and processes for shared and continuous learning are imperative to cope with the pace of change in the 21st century.

Change Targets

The process of identifying change targets is informed by the data collected. The vision, purpose, or goal provides focus, energy, and motivation, fueled by the desire to achieve those ends, to do the work. Educating the client and the client organization about the systemic nature of successful change is important. Looking underneath problems or events to identify the patterns and structures that created them is crucial. Even if the consultant has covered it in earlier phases, it often needs to be reemphasized. Regardless of the specific target of the project, many components of the system must be addressed to ensure that a change is lasting. Some of those components are rewards, communication, selection and promotion, learning and development, and even structure. Kotter (1995) suggested that it is important in any change to focus on structure, skills, supervision, and systems to ensure that a change is lasting. Ulrich (1998) recommended the following six-part framework to help guide a companywide or organization-wide transformation process:

- *Shared mindset:* Do we have the right culture to reach its goals?
- *Competence:* Do we have the required knowledge, skills, and abilities?
- *Consequences:* Do we have the appropriate measures, rewards, and incentives?
- *Governance:* Do we have the right organizational structure, communication systems, and policies?
- *Capacity for change:* Do we have the ability to improve work processes, to change, and to learn?
- *Leadership:* Do we have the leadership to achieve our goals?

Transition Team

A useful vehicle to support the change process is a transition team whose charter might be

- to keep a pulse on the process of change in the organization, identify barriers, and recommend actions
- to develop the new models, structures, and processes for the organization
- to plan the transition process from the current state to the desired future state.

See appendix 8 for an example of a transition-team charter.

Planning and Managing the Project

In large projects, plans need to be developed to define the measurable goals, outline the strategic success factors, detail the steps for implementation, and outline how commitment will be obtained from key decision makers. See figure 13-2 for a project management guide and table 13-1, a project-tracking chart, which can help manage large, complex projects. Transition planning might also involve cre-

Figure 13-2. Project management guide.

Stage One: Initiating

Stress the development of a vision for the project and establish clear goals. Key individuals form the core project team. In this phase,
- determine what the project should accomplish
- define overall project goal
- set down general expectations of customers, management, and stakeholders
- outline the general scope of the project
- select initial team members.

Stage Two: Planning

Define the resources needed to complete the project, devise a schedule, and develop a budget. Identify objectives and describe means for achieving them. In this stage,
- refine project scope
- establish a balance among results, time, and resources
- list tasks and activities that will achieve the goals of the project
- sequence activities in the most efficient manner
- develop a schedule and budget; assign resources to activities
- get plan approved by stakeholders.

Stage Three: Executing

Coordinate and guide team members to get the work done according to the plan. Keep resources and people focused on priorities. In this stage,
- lead the team
- meet with team members

- communicate with stakeholders
- fight fires and resolve problems as they arise
- secure the resources to carry out the plan.

Stage Four: Controlling

Watch over the project: measure progress and correct deviations. Expect and respond to the unexpected and solve problems. In this stage,
- monitor deviations
- take corrective actions
- receive and evaluate project changes from stakeholders and team members
- adapt resource levels as necessary
- change (usually cutting) project scope
- return to planning stage to adjust goals and gain reapproval of stakeholders.

Stage Five: Closing

This is the time for celebration and reflection. Ensure effective closure and acceptance of the final product. In this stage,
- acknowledge achievement and results
- shut down and disband the team
- learn from the project experience
- review project process and outcomes with team members and stakeholders
- write a final report.

John D. Adams, manager, organization consulting, Blue Shield of California

Table 13-1. Example project-tracking chart.

Meeting Team: Meeting Date:

#	Task	Person responsible	Plan date	Actual date	Deliverable [what, to whom]	Customer/Comments
	Add a module on mental models to off-site agenda	Kate	[6/11] postpone		Mental models module developed to share with organization-change (OC) staff	OC/ Not done due to lack of time on agenda of 6/11. To be rescheduled at a later date, if still requested.
	Add time for discussion of budget to off-site agenda	Karen	[6/11] postpone		Time added to 6/12 agenda	OC/ Not done due to lack of time on agenda of 6/12.
	Develop individual goals, values, and behaviors for consultation and culture survey Bring to next off-site event	All	[6/12] postpone		Goals, values, and behaviors relating to consultation and culture survey brought to 6/12 meeting.	OC/ Done, but didn't review all at 6/12 meeting. Do we want to finish this activity?

Table 13-1. Example project-tracking chart (continued).

#	Task	Person responsible	Plan date	Actual date	Deliverable [what, to whom]	Customer/Comments
	Capture lessons learned, results, etc., on the culture survey as you come across them. Archive for later use in Denison's book.	All	Ongoing through '98		Documentation of culture change results, lessons learned, etc., archived for easy retrieval.	Daniel Denison
	Type up sheets for off-site	Jen	8/12	8/19	Give to Nancy electronically	Team/ Typed and distributed by Nancy
	Draft memo/proposal of structure/plan	Nancy	8/21		Draft circulated to team	OC
	Provide input on draft	All	8/24		Input provided to Nancy for incorporation into document. Document sent to Karen.	Karen

John D. Adams, manager, organization consulting, Blue Shield of California

ating new processes, writing job descriptions, and establishing performance expectations. The internal consultant must identify which cultural norms and patterns, decision-making processes, and political environments need to be changed. Transition planning may involve developing the ideal organizational design. This is a time of running interference with senior-level stakeholders, ensuring their commitment offline, and confirming that the resources are available. John Adams, an internal consultant, offers the following 12 "golden rules for project management success":

1. *Gain consensus:* Stakeholders and team members must agree to goals and expectations.
2. *Build an excellent team:* The team must get smart quickly and remain ambitious.
3. *Develop a comprehensive and viable plan:* Make sure changes get communicated to everyone.
4. *Make sure you have the resources:* Line up the personnel, capital, and equipment to do the job and renegotiate as needed.
5. *Have a realistic schedule:* The fastest way to lose credibility is to change the schedule without a good reason.
6. *Do not try to do more than is possible:* Scope is the depth and texture behind the goals.
7. *People count:* Projects are mostly about people.
8. *Establish and maintain formal support from managers and stakeholders:* Make the approval process a formal event.
9. *Be ready to change:* Be prepared to be surprised.
10. *Keep people informed:* Communicate, communicate, communicate!
11. *Try new things:* Think outside the box.
12. *Be the leader, as well as a manager:* Plan, track, control, guide, motivate, and support.

In most organizations, it is absolutely critical that top management be committed and understand the changes to be implemented. A project's success or failure hinges on that support. Three things are essential—communication, communication, and communication—to inform all those who will be affected by the change. To manage a large organizational change, the accountabilities of all levels of the organization and key functions or departments must be clear. See table 13-2 for a sample outline of project accountabilities and deliverables.

Small Projects

On the other hand, if the project is a small one, this planning phase is primarily the responsibility of the consultant. With limited projects, such as a team-building event, a preliminary step to a larger intervention, or the delivery of an already designed training program, the consultant will move from the alignment phase to

Table 13-2. Example project-accountability chart.

Position/Function	Accountability
Executive Office	• Owner/sponsor of Project ABC • Owner/sponsor for vision, values, and culture for entire organization, including Project ABC • Monitor alignment across the organization • Ensure availability of necessary resources
Senior Executives	• Establish leadership behaviors and management practices to support companywide implementation of Project ABC • Approve and provide necessary resources • Establish targets, measures, and plans in support of Project ABC • Ensure companywide integration of Project ABC outputs • Ensure successful business operation during Project ABC
Project ABC Program Office	• Owner of Project ABC master plan • Establish key success factors and decision processes for Project ABC • Manage Project ABC budget • Build appropriate structure and ensure integration across the project
Process Team Leads	• Coordination with program office, content stewards, senior executives, and all process teams • Owner of process team plans, structures, and budget • Manage process team operations in executing plan • Communicate findings regularly to all stakeholders
Process Teams	• Develop and execute process team plans • Ensure regular coordination and communications among all subteams • Meet all deadlines with high-quality, consumer-focused deliverables
Content Stewards	• Coordinate between senior executives and process teams • Provide content ideas and tangible support to process teams • Ensure that consumer point of view is maintained in all process team activities • Communicate progress regularly to rest of company
Managers	• Serve as primary communications link between Project ABC and company management; provide regular information, and solicit and pass on ideas • Ensure effective operations of ongoing organization • Work with relevant Project ABC process teams to implement their outputs

continued on page 172

Table 13-2. Example project-accountability chart (continued).

Position/Function	Accountability
Employees	• Meet all ongoing business deliverables • Assist in implementation of Project ABC outputs • Provide regular feedback and ideas to Project ABC
Organization Effectiveness	• Develop and implement change management plan for overall Project ABC • Work actively with each process and team to support effective delivery of their plans • Ensure active regular coordination of all Project ABC activities
Organization Consulting	• Deliver organizational consulting and training to the ongoing ABC organization • Identify integration needs at interface of company and Project ABC • Develop and deliver services to ensure smooth integration of Project ABC output

John D. Adams, manager, organization consulting, Blue Shield of California

the implementation phase. However, preparing the organization may require more than the consultant initially believes. Organizational resistance can be covert and unexpressed until the implementation begins. At that time, it can seriously undermine the intervention and challenge both the client and the internal consultant.

It Was Blatant, Overt Resistance

My client was the new corporate vice president of marketing. I had worked with him in his prior position as a general manager. He had an organization of folks who saw themselves as the real marketing experts and had been with the company since the early days. They were an elitist group, hierarchical, and had been running the second level of the organization for a long time. The vice president did a lot of preparatory work for the intervention. He talked everything over with his four directors. When we began the meeting with the full department, these four directors let the vice president and me have it. They were very critical of us. It was blatant, overt resistance expressed in front of 50 people. The vice president fell apart, because his success was bound up in this position. I did not prepare the client sufficiently for this resistance. I should have cascaded the process before bringing the whole group together. I should have worked individually with each director in the organization. I should have recognized that there is history in some groups that requires doing a lot of work before you can address the issues in the whole group.

Marilyn E. Blair, TeamWork,
former internal consultant with 3Com Corporation

Summing Up and Looking Ahead

In seeking alignment, the internal consultant continues to build the client relationship and reach agreements on their work together. Ensuring alignment avoids failed projects and destroyed relationships later. The phase of change targets and transition strategies is both an educational and a planning phase. The internal consultant's role as an educator is greatest in helping traditionally trained command-and-control managers learn more about the organic and systemic nature of change.

The seemingly chaotic complexity encompasses self-organizing order. The internal consultant can help the manager who understands and trusts employees to manage and organize themselves to manage change. As a planner, the internal consultant must use a systems framework to plan the change targets for large organizational change projects and pay attention to the personal transition needs of both clients and employees. Once the planning of change targets and transition strategies is completed, the consultant moves to phase seven, implementation, which is discussed in the next chapter.

References

Bridges, W. (1991). *Managing Transitions: Making the Most of Change.* Reading, MA: Perseus Books.

Bolman, L.G., and T.E. Deal. (1997). *Reframing Organizations.* San Francisco: Jossey-Bass.

Hammond, S.A. (1996). *The Thin Book of Appreciative Inquiry.* Plano, TX: Kodiak Consulting.

Kotter, J. (1995). *The New Rules.* New York: Free Press.

Weisbord, M. (1997). "The Organization Development Contract." In *Organization Development Classics,* D.F. van Eynde, J.C. Hoy, & D.C. van Eynde, editors. San Francisco: Jossey-Bass. Originally published in *OD Practitioner,* 5(2), (1973).

Wheatley, M. (1997, Summer). "Goodbye, Command and Control." *Leader to Leader,* 21–28.

Ulrich, D. (1998). *Delivering Results.* Boston: Harvard Business School Press.

Chapter 14

Phase Seven: Implementation

Implementation is the exciting action phase in which the consultant and client take the steps to create the outcomes they envisioned. Remember that the intervention began with the contact phase of the consulting process. All the earlier phases laid the foundation for the success of implementation. Because the consulting process is not a stepwise process that follows a straight line, for some interventions, such as team development or coaching, the feedback and alignment phases may be included in the implementation phase.

In very large projects, the early phases take many months of high energy and creativity. The actual implementation of organizational processes, a new structure, or the action plans recommended from the employee survey feedback may seem like a letdown compared to the earlier phases. Implementation snags and unanticipated problems are frustrating. The creative glow and excitement may dissipate as design or transition teams pass their responsibilities to others for implementation, and the members move on to other projects and tasks. One internal consultant in an international manufacturing company recounted how the steps and responsibilities of implementation were not well defined. As a result, the efforts of many months of the design team fizzled and their recommendations spun away from them.

Success Requirements

From the perspective of the internal consultant, the success of this phase calls for coaching, communication, influence, project management, team leadership, troubleshooting, and feedback. From the client's perspective, successful implementation requires patience, leadership, communication, constant reinforcement, troubleshooting, development of new skills, influence, promoting and recognizing others, and changing personal behavior. The outcomes and results will not happen as quickly as the client wants. For the consultant and client partners, implementation requires steady focus on desired goals and outcomes, frequent communication, rewards for small wins, connection of actions to the vision and purpose, necessary adjustments, and realistic confrontation of challenges without minimizing them.

It Was a Great Success!

Internal Journal

The head of operations was a "fix-it guy." We were in a meeting going over some survey results, identifying items on which to work. We identified one problem. I wrote up the proposal describing the issue, providing cost data, looking at the time it took to solve problems, and proposing customer service training. I had four basic premises: reach for the best, do a big kick-off celebration, take a novel approach, and make an impact. I built support with the regional vice presidents by doing a session with them. We did executive overviews and asked, "How are you going to reinforce this and what measures will you use to track results?" It was a great success.

Linda Schomaker, director, corporate human resources, PG&E Corporation

In some cases, during the initial client contact, the intervention is determined and the phases of the consulting process all lead to implementation of that intervention. In other cases, selecting the intervention and choosing activities may occur gradually at certain points in the process as information and data are collected and analyzed, the clients wrestle with the feedback, and the planning and identification of change targets and transition strategies begin. This chapter will highlight the types of interventions most commonly used by internal consultants and draw on examples from their theory and practice.

Types of Interventions

There are several ways to categorize types of interventions: by the target of the intervention, the type or the focus of the issues, or a combination of the two. Here we will categorize commonly used internal interventions by the major target of the learning or change. The target can focus on improving the effectiveness of individuals, dyads, teams and small groups, or whole organizations or systems. Improving the performance and effectiveness of individuals, teams, and groups throughout the organization will also improve the effectiveness of the organization as a whole. See table 14-1 for examples of interventions typically used for each of these entities.

Individual Focus

Not all the consulting interventions under the umbrella of individual focus occur with just one individual; they may happen in a group setting, such as training

Table 14-1. Interventions by target focus.

Individual focus	Dyads, teams, and small group focus	Organization or system focus

Coaching
Education and training
Management/HRD
Life and career planning
	Team development
	Leadership development
	Learning
	Small-group work:
	  Training in decision making, problem solving, goal setting, action planning
	  Workgroup learning
	  Employee-involvement teams
	  Third-party facilitation
	  Conflict resolution
	  Intergroup relationships
	  Responsibility charting
	  Role negotiation
		Process improvement or redesign
		Performance improvement/HPT
		Organization restructuring
		Survey feedback
		Vision, strategy, and culture alignment
		Large-group intervention

workshops. The discussion here emphasizes interventions that focus on improving the effectiveness of individuals whether delivered in one-on-one or group settings.

COACHING

Coaching is a powerful teaching and learning process to enhance learning and effectiveness and effect personal change. Internal consultants serve as coaches for their clients throughout the phases of the consulting process. Coaching frequently is an integral part of the process of planning and implementing other interventions, such as team development, survey feedback, organization and process redesign, strategic leadership, and large-group-development activities. Most often, the agreement to provide coaching to a client occurs in the alignment phase. Alternatively, an internal consultant may conduct an initial intervention to build credibility with the client and then serve as a coach over a period of time when no other interventions are in process.

Executive coaching for senior managers is no longer used just for derailing managers. It is common for internal consultants to provide personal feedback to any of their clients for long-term development or guidance in managing change. In a coaching role, the internal consultant becomes a confidential advisor and an objective sounding board to senior executives who often wrestle with the implications of tough business decisions, need new insights on more effective management of interpersonal relationships, or need advice on leading a strategic initiative.

The internal consultant must be able to operate from the executive's point of view, understand strategy, handle the confrontation and power testing, and respect the conventions of the executive suite.

Successful coaching at any level also draws on strong communication skills—especially listening—and uses a facilitative questioning style. Using coaching with a client can

- help develop insights and self-understanding
- help client recognize the need to improve management and leadership skills
- provide understanding of the change process
- expand change readiness
- build client strengths
- help prepare mentally and emotionally for a tough meeting with employees or senior executives
- help prepare and rehearse for a confrontation with an employee
- develop and provide reinforcement for using new skills
- encourage continuous learning
- guide change leadership
- support risk taking
- help process strong emotions.

EDUCATION AND TRAINING

Education and training activities are designed to improve the knowledge, skills, and abilities of individual performers in the organization. The individual worker might use a computer-based learning program, attend an in-house workshop, or pursue an academic program on a college campus. Examples of content are technical skills required for task performance, academic knowledge for a degree program, or interpersonal awareness and leadership competence for supervisors and managers. The decision to participate in education or training activities often lies with the learner and his or her manager; but if groups of organization members receive the same training and it is reinforced by other management processes, it can be effective as an organization-change intervention. Increasing competence in leadership, teamwork, decision making, problem solving, or goal setting supports wider effort to raise the effectiveness of supervisors, managers, professionals, team members, or others. Training activities are often used as part of culture change in an organization realignment effort. Although effective as a part of a larger intervention, the primary target of training and education is the individual competence of the participants.

MANAGEMENT/HRD

These activities target individual performers and managers to prepare them for greater responsibility, to update or keep their skills current, or to increase productivity and effectiveness. Activities include development planning, coaching, training workshops, self-study, attendance at university development programs, mentoring, on-the-job learning assignments, and even team projects. Strategic management/HRD is linked to the business, strengthens the company leadership, and increases the productivity and effectiveness of employees if a system is established that

- builds competence to meet competitive business needs
- is required for those who are newly promoted
- develops common skill sets and approaches to business and management issues
- establishes consistency in language, style, and culture
- is an integral part of other HR management systems, such as succession planning, selection, and performance management
- holds managers responsible for the development of their subordinates
- is supported visibly as a high priority by senior managers who provide needed resources, participate as mentors and coaches, lead training or learning activities, and take advantage of development opportunities themselves.

Figure 14-1 provides an example of a strategic HRD process developed by experienced former internal consultant Kevin Wheeler.

LIFE AND CAREER PLANNING

The traditional covenant between employer and employee for lifetime employment no longer exists (Waterman, Waterman, & Collard 1994). The rapid pace of change with outsourcing, work elimination, business-process-improvement initiatives, and restructuring has engulfed our largest companies. Business has moved from an industrial economy to a knowledge economy with the customer-service revolution. Knowledge is expanding through technology, powerful information systems, and virtual teams communicating via email and the Internet. In the knowledge economy, a lifetime career is unrealistic.

Rather than employment, the focus is now on employability either inside or outside the company. This focus emphasizes a "self-reliant" workforce (Waterman, Waterman, & Collard 1994) in which employees take advantage of opportunities offered by their employers to build valuable skills, enhance their employability, and prepare for the rapidly shifting future. In exchange, companies gain increased productivity, a pool of developing talent within their own ranks, and some degree of commitment while the employee works there.

To build reliance into a company workforce requires a system or a structure with information about trends; changing needs; business developments; tools and vehicles for employees to assess their skills, interests, values, and temperaments; and training, education, and learning opportunities. Many progressive companies are providing internal career centers or supporting external centers that have resources and counselors to support their employees in managing their own careers and becoming self-reliant.

Figure 14-1. Human resources development process.

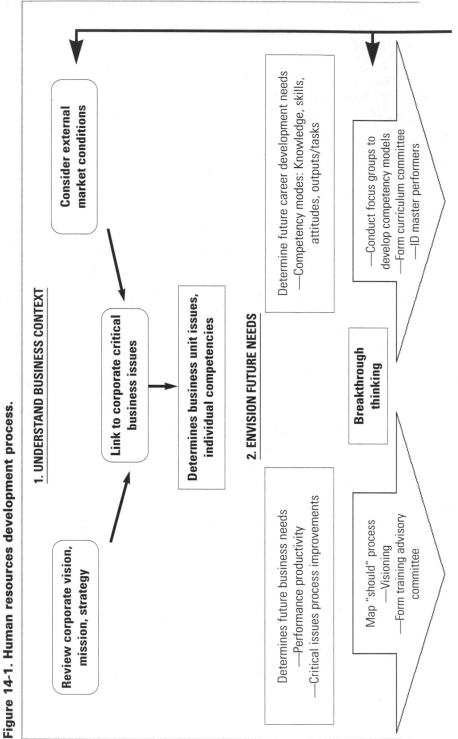

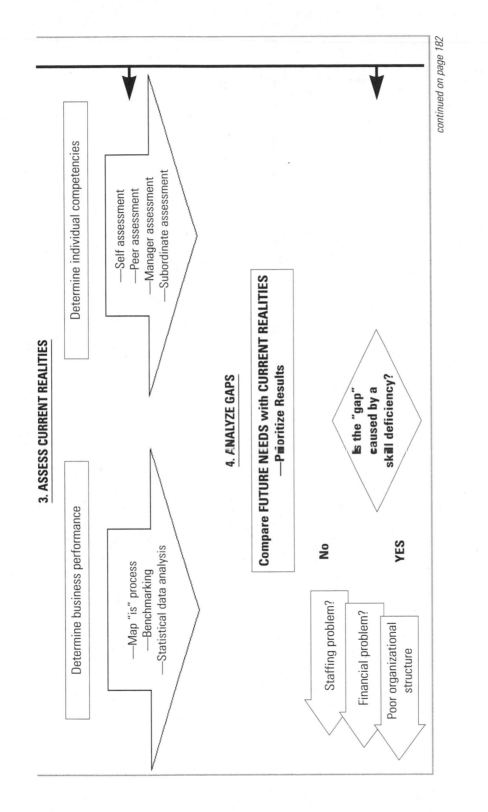

3. ASSESS CURRENT REALITIES

Determine individual competencies

—Self assessment
—Peer assessment
—Manager assessment
—Subordinate assessment

Determine business performance

—Map "is" process
—Benchmarking
—Statistical data analysis

4. ANALYZE GAPS

Compare FUTURE NEEDS with CURRENT REALITIES
—Prioritize Results

Is the "gap" caused by a skill deficiency?

No

YES

Staffing problem?

Financial problem?

Poor organizational structure

continued on page 182

Figure 14-1. Human resources development process (continued).

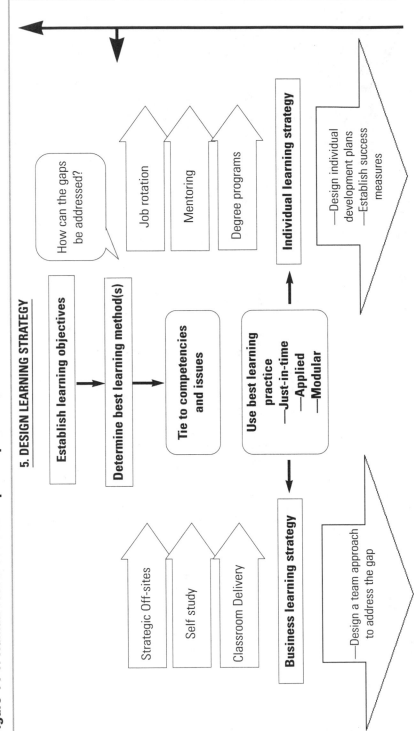

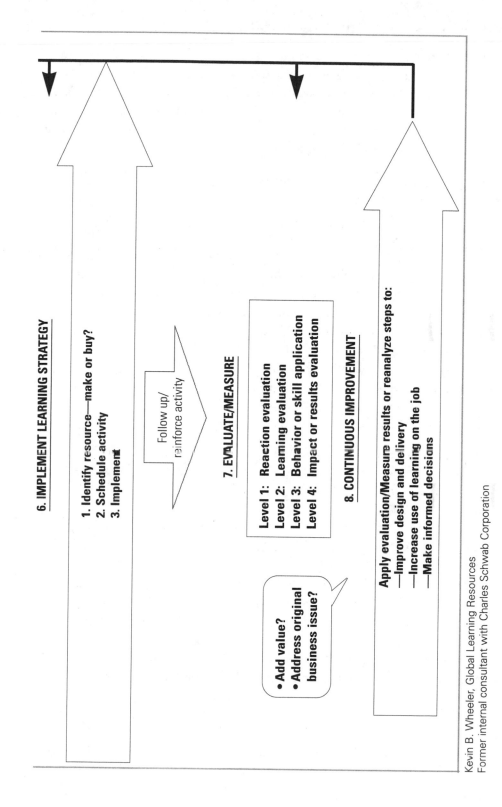

6. IMPLEMENT LEARNING STRATEGY

1. Identify resource—make or buy?
2. Schedule activity
3. Implement

Follow up/
reinforce activity

7. EVALUATE/MEASURE

Level 1: Reaction evaluation
Level 2: Learning evaluation
Level 3: Behavior or skill application
Level 4: Impact or results evaluation

• Add value?
• Address original
  business issue?

8. CONTINUOUS IMPROVEMENT

Apply evaluation/Measure results or reanalyze steps to:
—Improve design and delivery
—Increase use of learning on the job
—Make informed decisions

Kevin B. Wheeler, Global Learning Resources
Former internal consultant with Charles Schwab Corporation

Dyads, Teams, and Small-Group Focus

The work of internal consultants in small groups, teams, and dyads requires strong facilitation skills and grounding in group process and group dynamics. Group process includes facilitating a group's ability to accomplish tasks of problem solving and decision making while paying attention to group maintenance issues through communication, membership, norms, and leadership. Sue Blouch, an internal consultant, offers that the proficient facilitator

- designs the process to achieve objectives
- ferrets out and clarifies issues
- demonstrates flexibility by adapting to needs of the group on the spot
- keeps the group focused on the outcomes or task
- creates an open, positive, and participatory-learning environment
- asks questions that lead to reflection and insight
- helps the group own and take responsibility for outcomes
- builds rapport and relationship among the group members
- demonstrates self-awareness and self-expression
- behaves honestly and enthusiastically
- manages conflict and negative emotions constructively
- encourages and supports multiple perspectives
- pushes back without creating antagonism
- summarizes and integrates essential points from the discussion.

Internal consultant Elizabeth Schiff and her colleague Judith Sweet offer some of the tools a facilitator can use to work successfully in small groups in figure 14-2.

TEAM DEVELOPMENT

Team-development activities enhance the effectiveness of a group of people who work together so they can learn how to accomplish their individual goals and simultaneously accomplish the goals of the team. The goal is to create a work team that functions organically rather than mechanistically according to a series of rules, job descriptions, and a hierarchy of authority (Varney 1977). Team building, as it is also called, is a common intervention at all levels in the organization with payoffs in flexibility, creativity, productivity, leadership, and decision making. An ideal team is characterized by mutual trust, support, frequent communication, clear objectives, a process for conflict resolution, an environment that respects and uses individual differences, and members who take shared responsibility for task accomplishment.

Team development helps build a cross-functional team that must work together on a time-limited project, a new start-up team, or ongoing employee workgroups that must improve performance. The activities may focus on task issues, such as

Figure 14-2. Facilitator's tool kit.

1. **Establish ground rules, for example:**
   - Keep an open mind.
   - One person speaks at a time.
   - Share the air (give others a chance to share their ideas).
   - Stay focused on our agenda and objectives.
   If a problem occurs, refer back to ground rules

2. **Discuss consequences of breaking ground rules:**
   - What happens if someone breaks a ground rule?
   - How can we hold each other accountable?

3. **Discuss commitment to group/process/goals:**
   - What were the group's original commitments?
   - How did the members agree to proceed?
   - What is the group's common goals(s)?

4. **Validate group members' contributions:**
   - Accept or legitimize the member's contributions.
   - Deal with them now or defer, as appropriate.

5. **Focus and refocus:**
   - Ask questions or use a flipchart.
   - Create a "bin box" if needed (a place to keep track of important yet not immediately pertinent ideas).

6. **Give feedback/mirror:**
   - Say what is going on.
   - Describe how it is affecting the group.

7. **Ask the group:**
   - Use boomerang questions.
   - Take the group's "temperature."

8. **Brainstorm:**
   - Consider the presenting problems.
   - Discuss options.
   - Expand the discussion to related issues or other topics.

9. **Ask for specifics, for example:**
   - How does issue relate to the topic?
   - What effect does this information have?

10. **Use body language for maximum effectiveness:**
    - Sit, stand, or walk to change gears.
    - Use gestures and body language for emphasis.

Elizabeth Schiff, organizational development specialist, Administrative Office of the Courts, and Judith Sweet, Judith Sweet and Associates

the way things are done or the skills required to accomplish tasks, or they may focus on the nature and quality of the relationships between team members and between members and the team leader. Figure 14-3 outlines the areas of team development, the questions raised by that focus, and the topics that can be addressed.

The emphasis of the team building depends on the client goals and the needs identified in the information and assessment phase. In appendix 9 are examples of two designs for team building for workgroups provided by Jim McKnight, an internal consultant. The one-day design emphasizes group relationships, better understanding of each other, issues of trust, commitment, communication, and feedback. The six-meeting design emphasizes both group relationships and group-operating processes, such as work practices and shared learning.

Figure 14-3. Model of team effectiveness.

Group goals and objectives:

What is the purpose of the team? What goals or objectives is the team trying to achieve?

This topic includes direction, commitment, mission, vision, values, strategies, priorities, goals, objectives, performance, and ownership.

Roles and responsibilities:

What are the individual roles and responsibilities in the achievement of the team goals? Is there conflict among the roles? Are responsibilities clear?

This topic includes role clarity, integration, structure, job design, responsibilities, specialization, appropriateness, resources, and incumbent traits.

Group operating processes:

What are the processes used to get work done? Are there agreed upon procedures? How are decisions made, problems solved, differences handled? Do the processes support both task and maintenance needs? How does the team continue learning?

This topic includes systems, problem solving, innovation, decision making, learning, communication, recognition, appreciation, meetings, planning, implementation, and evaluation.

Group relationships:

Are the interpersonal needs of the members being met? Are all members interacting with all other members? What is the level of trust?

This topic includes acceptance, support, involvement, participation, trust, cohesiveness, diversity, conflict, listening, and feedback.

Infrastructure supports:

What does leadership look like? Is the larger organization extending its support? What is the access to resources? How autonomous is the team?

This topic includes leadership, intergroup relations, resources, empowerment, coaching, modeling, management, monitoring, representation, rewards, flexibility, and autonomy.

Team development with executives or senior-level professionals is often less structured with fewer activities. One option is using a conceptual framework that becomes the foundation for further activities, dialogue, and application. Such an approach is introduced by former internal consultant, Marilyn Blair, and is outlined in the following sections. She draws from concepts developed by Argyris (1993).

A Conceptual Framework for Team Development

Chris Argyris has long subscribed to the psychological theory that all people get embarrassed and become threatened. He believes that this theory underlies most of the group dynamics within organizations. Argyris and his research team have been testing this theory throughout the world and, as a result of the data, he is now convinced that people everywhere experience embarrassment and become threatened. Furthermore, he posited that all people bypass and cover up their embarrassment and their threatened feelings. In addition, they bypass the bypasses and cover up the cover-ups. All of us collude in this behavior, because all of us are embarrassed often and threatened, and we do not know how to work with these feelings.

Most of us wonder if human behavior is not more complex than this. Moreover, as a theory of the important underlying dynamic in organization life, it is not bad. All of us have noted that in a group that things go on below the surface that are generally not addressed, but seem to emit odors and tastes that frequently touch us at primal levels. Sometimes we speak about these things as the "garbage" we bring with us, meaning all of our past experiences—pleasant and unpleasant! Sometimes we are unable to put words to our feelings—we just know that something is going on, but that something remains unnamed and affects the group.

Marilyn E. Blair, TeamWork,
former internal consultant with 3Com Corporation

Action and Learning. "Learning occurs when we detect and correct error. Error is any mismatch between what we intend an action to produce and what actually happens when we implement that action . . . Human beings are designing beings. They create, store, and retrieve designs, or *theories of action* that advise them how to act if they are to achieve their intentions and act consistently with their governing values" (Argyris 1993, 49–66).

The research of Argyris identified two types of theories of action:

- the theory that individuals espouse and that constitutes their beliefs, attitudes, and values
- the theory individuals actually use (theory-in-use), which is often a fundamental, systematic mismatch with the espoused theory.

Also, individuals develop designs (theories of action) to keep them unaware of the mismatch. They do this when the issues are embarrassing or threatening.

"While there is considerable variance in the behaviors of individuals, there is almost no variance in theories-in-use in North America, Europe, South America, Africa, and the Far East. The same is true whether individuals are young or old, poor or wealthy, well educated or uneducated, male or female, and of any skin color. For example, the behavior called "face saving" varies widely. But the proposition or the rule that is followed to save face remains the same: when encountering embarrassment or threat, bypass it and cover up the bypass" (Argyris 1993, 49–66).

Marilyn Blair points out that Argyris's fundamental question for organizations is: How do we cease using the defensive routines and the organizational norms that protect those routines? Argyris believes that if we can answer this, we may well have the solution to moving forward into the new paradigms. He concludes that: "Changing the human predisposition to produce organizational defensive routines and the organizational norms that protect those routines requires altering both individual master programs and organization's protective norms."

Practice Exercise

Internal
Journal

This exercise helps to transfer this theory into practice: Identify two or three of the "organizational defensive routines" you imagine are present in your workgroup. For example, you can count on some team members asserting that collective time needs to be spent doing the work, not talking about it.

**Marilyn E. Blair, TeamWork,
former internal consultant with 3Com Corporation**

LEADERSHIP DEVELOPMENT AND LEARNING

Internal consultants often consult to a leadership team in their organizations. Although the work may begin as a team building effort, frequently the consultant also includes leadership-development topics, such as the roles of effective leaders, issues of empowerment, organization change, effectiveness, and performance. The internal consultant or, more often, an external person who introduces cutting-edge theories and may be the author of a successful business book delivers these activities. Although the internal consultant may not deliver the content, the internal consultant often facilitates the discussion, learning, and application of new ideas.

Another approach is to introduce a process for collective learning, such as dialogue. Marilyn Blair contrasts dialogue with linear communication in table 14-2.

Table 14-2. Dialogue versus linear communication.

Linear communication	Dialogue
Goal oriented	Undirected
To tell	To inquire
Win-lose	Win-win
Individual thought	Collective thought
Solve problems	Get to the root/find solutions
Negotiation is the point	Negotiation is the beginning
Sharing of content of opinions	Sharing of mind
Decisions are made	Complex issues are explored
Actions are the focus	New actions emerge as a by-product
Emphasis on analysis	Emphasis on shared meaning
Playing a game against each other	Playing a game with each other
Defend opinions	Think together
Concern with truth and conflict	Concern with shared meaning
Diverging	Converging

Marilyn E. Blair, TeamWork
Former internal consultant with 3Com Corporation

Dialogue—A Creative Space for Understanding and Learning

Internal Journal

The spirit of dialogue is the ability to hold many points of view in suspension, while simultaneously holding a primary interest in the creation of meaning. In dialogue we don't emphasize the parts. We don't have a means to an end. It doesn't work by trying to manipulate another individual or a group to an end. Rather, we are participating, exploring, creating together, and whatever emerges is owned by all of us.

Power and dialogue are antithetical to, or substitutes for, each other. The more dialogical skill you have in an organization or society, the less the need for exercising power.

Dialogue is not discussion. Discussion shares its root meaning with "percussion" and "concussion," both of which involve breaking things up. Dialogue is not debate. Both of these forms contain an implicit tendency to point toward a goal, to hammer out an agreement, to try to solve a problem, or to have one's opinion prevail.

Dialogue is nonlinear. It cannot have a goal, such as persuasion or debate. Scientifically speaking, it needs to be both particle and wave simultaneously.

Marilyn E. Blair, TeamWork,
former internal consultant with 3Com Corporation

Marilyn Blair has drawn from the works of Boehm (1994, 1996) and Senge (1990) to develop the following ground rules for dialogue:

- *Suspend assumptions:* Participants can speak of their assumptions, recalling that they are assumptions. Do not take a position; taking a position assists others to take positions and polarizes the group.
- *See each other as colleagues:* Participants are colleagues in the mutual quest for deeper insight and clarity. In the dialogue, participants can experience their differences and in so doing become more open with one another. When participants view one another as colleagues and not in their roles, they learn more from their differences but they can also celebrate their similarities. There is no particular hierarchy in the dialogue except for the facilitator who keeps the group on track.
- *Maintain a spirit of inquiry:* Explore the thinking behind the views people hold and what evidence they have that leads them to those views. It is appropriate to ask, "What leads you to believe . . . ?" or "What is your evidence for believing . . . ?"
- *Observe the observer:* Take the opportunity to watch and listen to fellow "dialoguers." Each one is each other's teacher.

Why Dialogue?

Boehm (1994, 1996) saw thought "largely as a collective phenomenon." He went on to assert that since thought is to a large degree collective, it cannot just be improved individually. "As with electrons we must look on thought as a systemic phenomena arising from how we interact and discourse with one another." His distinction between thinking and thoughts is important to remember. Thinking is an active, ongoing process. Thoughts are the result of that process that we often hang onto as the gospel truth; these thoughts become our assumptions.

Internal Journal

In the West, we have dismantled community, and understanding and acceptance are no longer the cornerstones of our national alliance. In our rush to individualize, we have created separateness, isolation, and alienation. To reverse this trend, we must heal one another and ourselves before we can move forward in our collective development. Dialogue allows for free flow of meaning to pass through a group and sharing meaning, or common understanding can be a healing experience.

**Marilyn E. Blair, TeamWork,
former internal consultant with 3Com Corporation**

SMALL-GROUP WORK

Small groups are one of the most frequently used interventions. Working with a small group or team may be the primary intervention or it may be an integral part of an intervention for the organization or system. Depending on the function of the group, small groups can be called teams, workgroups, task forces, cross-functional teams, planning teams, quality circles, employee-involvement teams, self-managing teams, or project teams. The focus of the activities is also very diverse: workgroup learning, decision making, problem solving, goal setting, action planning, or employee involvement. In some cases, the role of the consultant is to facilitate and offer groups a process to see alternatives and possibilities.

They Moved to the Domain of Possibilities (Lindfield 1998)

Internal Journal

One example comes from my work with a team of aerospace engineers who were very clear about why it was not possible to solve a particular problem because company politics and bureaucracy stood in the way. This was my approach: I invited them to listen to President Kennedy's historic challenge—the "impossible dream" of putting a person on the moon by the end of the decade.

I then asked them to imagine their response as aerospace engineers and come up with all the reasons why this was the craziest request in the world and why it would never get off the ground. After five minutes of animated conversation, I requested that they switch and now respond to the President's challenge as if this were the most exciting thing that had ever happened to them. Finally, this was to be a project that would release their creative energy and spiritual juices.

After five more minutes of intense role playing, we debriefed and compared not only the differences in language between the two conversations, but also the emotions and body energetics. The differences were startling. With these distinctions understood, I then brought them back to their reality as aerospace engineers, inviting them to reenact the discussion that occurred when they were first faced with the task that was currently causing them so much heartache. I heard the voices of the doubter, the victim, and the cynic proclaim the myriad of reasons why this would never work. The energy in the room became low and oppressive.

The final part of this intervention was to invite the engineers to get in touch with their professional pride and passion and step up to the challenge of the real business task facing them. I encouraged them to generate possibilities for success and find excitement in the task. The atmosphere in the room shifted, and solutions became the order of the day. They had broken free, if only for that session, from the confines of the domain of historical self-talk, which only knows why things will not work. They had moved into the domain of possibilities: the place of potential and where one can access "what you don't know, you don't know." For a few hours, the shadow had dispersed to reveal a different kind of group working relationship. Their con-

cern was how to maintain this. My coaching to them was that they should continue to observe the language and self-talk in the group and whenever it began to sound like a limiting pattern speaking, they could make the shift by choosing to speak themselves differently.

Michael Lindfield, senior OD consultant, Boeing Company

A frequent problem is the expectation of a leader or manager of the group that members will come together and function effectively to accomplish their task. Unless they have had prior training, employees seldom have the skills to work productively in small-group settings. The role of the internal consultant is often to train and coach employees to work effectively in small group settings. The training develops interpersonal skills, increases group competence, and builds teamwork and collaboration.

The pace of change in the global, competitive marketplace in the 1990s may be the basis for the widely recognized quote offered at the beginning of the decade by Arie de Geus (Senge 1990), former head of planning for Royal Dutch/Shell: "The ability to learn faster than your competitors may be the only sustainable competitive advantage." As organizations strive to become learning organizations, one of the most common practices is to promote team learning in workgroups, cross-functional teams, and task groups. Team learning and dialogue have been encompassed within the five disciplines (Senge 1990; Senge et al. 1994). Team learning is similar to the process of individual learning except that the reflection process is public. Public reflection leads to shared meaning, which allows joint planning and coordination of actions for implementation.

Sue Blouch, an internal consultant, describes the IAG process—identify, analyze, and generalize—the three basic phases of the experiential learning cycle. It is the *intentional* use of a series of *specific* questions selected to help participants to internalize any kind of experience. A good learner naturally applies the basic IAG process: We have an experience (what?), we think about why it happened (so what?), and we make choices about what we will do in the future (now what?). Figure 14-4 offers a series of questions to pose during the team-reflection process.

THIRD-PARTY FACILITATION FOCUS

Varney (1977) describes the role of the internal consultant in third-party facilitation as a skilled and knowledgeable facilitator to help in the assessment, understanding, and resolution of difficult problems existing between key individuals or among units or work groups. Four useful interventions with a third-party facilitation focus are highlighted: intergroup activities, conflict utilization, responsibility charting, and role negotiation.

Figure 14-4. The IAG question cycle.

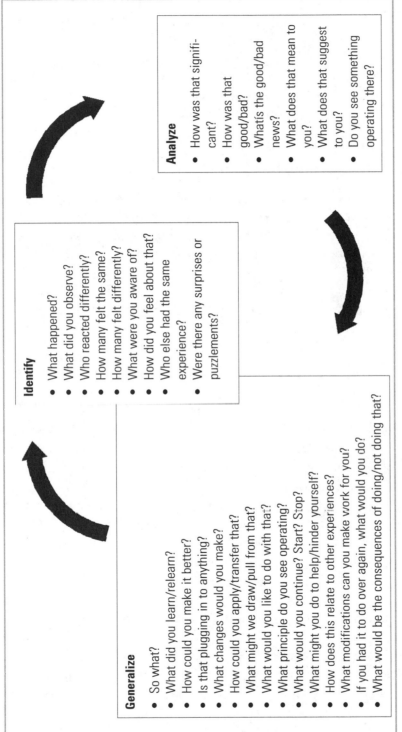

Analyze

- How was that significant?
- How was that good/bad?
- What is the good/bad news?
- What does that mean to you?
- What does that suggest to you?
- Do you see something operating there?

Identify

- What happened?
- What did you observe?
- Who reacted differently?
- How many felt the same?
- How many felt differently?
- What were you aware of?
- How did you feel about that?
- Who else had the same experience?
- Were there any surprises or puzzlements?

Generalize

- So what?
- What did you learn/relearn?
- How could you make it better?
- Is that plugging in to anything?
- What changes would you make?
- How could you apply/transfer that?
- What might we draw/pull from that?
- What would you like to do with that?
- What principle do you see operating?
- What would you continue? Start? Stop?
- What might you do to help/hinder yourself?
- How does this relate to other experiences?
- What modifications can you make work for you?
- If you had it to do over again, what would you do?
- What would be the consequences of doing/not doing that?

Sue Blouch, CSC
Former internal consultant with Taubman Company

Intergroup Activities. Intergroup activities focus on improving the effectiveness of interdependent work groups. The activities often involve understanding each other's work, integrating joint activities to produce common output, and improving interdependent work processes. Such activities might be part of the action planning results from an employee survey or part of a larger organizational process improvement or redesign effort. When conflict exists between work groups, the consultant may use third-party conflict resolution techniques. The model described in appendix 10 can be used for work between two individuals or between groups.

Process Consultant for Community Issues

I was seen as a content expert in performance management and in OD. I was also a process consultant helping define and work with process to get groups to think through issues together and to work with the community. They considered my skills in facilitating community meetings a valued expertise.

Internal Journal

Perviz Randeria, organization and management development consultant, former internal consultant with city government

Conflict Utilization. Conflict utilization is a process between two or more individuals or groups, which clears up a conflict and enables all parties to move ahead with little or no residue from the conflict. The activities are based on confrontation tactics, negotiation, and a search for common ground.

Because conflict tends to be scary for many people and is often hurtful and painful, it is frequently avoided and denied by members of workgroups and teams. Yet conflict or difference is unavoidable. Group members will differ about methods, objectives, values, or facts. They may have received different information, interpreted it differently, or have taken a different position based on their roles. If teams or workgroups can learn to use these differences to understand, learn, explore, and generate alternatives, conflict can become a source of energy and creativity.

Internal consultants not only help groups resolve conflicts, but also help groups develop the skills to utilize differences for creativity and problem solving. Appendix 10 provides a model to develop conflict-management capability in a team or workgroup drawn from Marilyn Blair's internal consulting practice.

Responsibility Charting. Responsibility charting is a process that documents decision-making roles for a group of individuals or across units, departments, or divisions. Using a skilled facilitator, the process provides a method to explore the conflicts, differences, gaps, and overlaps and to seek consensus about the roles that each person or unit plays in decisions (McCann & Gilmore 1983). This is a useful intervention at the senior or midlevel, with merged or acquired functional units, reorganized departments, or a newly formed team.

One way to define responsibilities is by applying the RACMI definitions:

- *R*—Recommend. Actor takes initiative for developing alternatives, assuring consultation, analyzing the situation, and making initial recommendations. This role ends upon approval of decision and assignment of responsibility.
- *A*—Approve. Actor signs off on or vetoes decision before it is implemented or chooses from among alternatives developed by *R* role and monitors results.
- *C*—Consult. Actor is consulted or asked for substantive input prior to sign-off but has no veto power.
- *M*—Implement. Actor is held accountable for implementation of decision once it is made, including notification of other relevant actors about decision.
- *I*—Inform. Actor is informed of decision but is not necessarily consulted before decision is approved.

Figure 14-5 outlines the RACMI process, and table 14-3 is a charted example.

Role Negotiation. With rapidly changing job assignments, new supervisors and team leaders, and merged functions, role confusion can arise easily. This intervention focuses either on the expectations between supervisor/manager and employee or among members of a team. The consultant serves as a facilitator to clarify expectations and build agreements for performance, interpersonal relationships, work processes, or frequency of communication.

Appendix 11 from Jim Harley, an internal consultant, consists of an outline for a role-clarification meeting. It outlines goals, pre-work, and a process for a role clarification or negotiation meeting among team or workgroup members. Appendix 12 offers a process used by Jan Schmuckler, a former internal consultant, to establish expectations and agreements between a new manager and a team of direct reports. This process speeds up the inevitable transition time, which allows for effective leadership.

Organization-wide or Systemwide Focus

Many of the interventions discussed so far can also be used as part of organization- or systemwide interventions. The focus of implementation of the intervention depends on the goals and the results the client desires. The purpose of large-system interventions is to make lasting change in the performance and culture of an organization, a business unit, or a large department. As clients and consultants alike acknowledge the systemic nature of organization change, interventions will focus on seeking alignment among the processes and systems of the whole organization to create high-performance work organizations.

Figure 14-5. Recommended process for discussion of RACMI decisions.

Explain process:

- Provide handout with RACMI definitions and discuss any questions about definitions
- Review steps (put on flipchart)
- Define and introduce decision
- Each person charts on chart at the table
- Report out and record on large chart for all to see
- Discussion
- Consensus

List benefits on flipchart:

- Gets the whole team involved
- Uncovers different expectations and perceptions
- Surfaces confusion about issues
- Provides opportunity to discuss and achieve clarity
- Connects strategy to implementation

Introduce decisions:

- Work with one at a time using copy of the chart as a handout for each decision
- Explain the decision and answer any questions
- Ask participants to record their suggestions for responsibility for the decision on their individual handout charts

Report out and post:

- Record individual responses on poster-size chart so all can see
- Note and discuss differences
- Seek consensus and finalize agreement
- Identify any action that needs to be taken regarding the decision and agreements reached

Repeat process for all decisions

Close:

- Summarize agreements and actions to be taken
- Identify what is left to do/next steps

A Whole-Systems Approach

Internal Journal

I had recently been hired into a newly created position. Up to that time the change processes in the company were driven by information services moving from the mainframe to a local-area network. Change was driven by the need for new systems. I asked the management team, "What is your vision or mission here?" They didn't have one and couldn't tell me what they were trying to accomplish. I suggested a socio-technical or what is now called a whole-systems approach. I told them that if you wanted to create satisfaction, just bringing in systems will mean a new system, but it will not create a new culture or a new ways of working. I helped them reframe their thinking to a more humanistic approach. We moved to a team-based organization, which gave employees variety, auton-

Table 14-3. Sample completed RACMI chart.

Decisions	President	Marketing	Management information systems	HR	Manufacturing	Finance	Operations
Actions							
1. List pricing	A	R	C	I	I	C	C/M
2. Acquisitions	A	C	C	C	C	C	C
3. Exempt salary administration	A	C	C	R/M	C	C	C
4. Develop and test-market ori-ented retention programs	I	R/A/M	I			I	CM

omy, and decision-making ability in their work. In six months, we were able to build a vision or purpose statement with the management team that was then shared with the rest of the division. Next, we divided into teams of 10 to react to the statement, reported out revisions or additions, and worked with cross-functional representatives from each team to pound out the final statement of purpose. Vision was one of four components we were addressing. The others were the culture they wanted to create, the image they wanted to project to vendors, the image they wanted to project to the organization as a whole, and the development of effective core processes. We realized three of the four components over time. The development of core processes is still a work in progress. But, people still remember what we did and think that was the best thing that happened throughout the change process.

Helm Lehmann, author, former OD manager, REI

PROCESS IMPROVEMENT OR REDESIGN

The last 10 years have seen a flurry of process improvement and redesign or reengineering efforts. The pressure for companies to reduce costs and to improve the bottom line has driven many executives to hire external consulting firms to reengineer and automate certain business processes in the hope there will be a long-term payoff. In some organizations, internal consultants are excluded from key roles in these projects. In others, the internal-consulting function partners with the external firm or has the lead role in process design projects (chapter 5).

Successful implementation of these projects relies heavily on

- participation of those affected by the redesign
- knowledge about the process and how it currently works or does not work
- innovative ideas about how to improve or change it drawn from the current players.

Clients who fear resistance among the current players often want to avoid such involvement. It is critical for the internal consultant to speak up about the importance of this involvement not only for the success of the project but also to reduce the dreaded resistance. Appendix 13 provides some excerpts from a two-year process improvement project led by internal consultant Helm Lehmann. The appendix includes an outline, description, roles, responsibilities, and outcomes for this large-scale intervention.

PERFORMANCE IMPROVEMENT

Performance improvement technology targets the gap between individual and group performance and business needs. The systemic and systematic approach to collecting information and analyzing the barriers that prevent people from achieving high performance often leads to a solution based in organizational processes. Human resource systems, such as rewards, incentives, recruitment and selection, or training, frequently must be changed. Organization values, management expectations, performance feedback, job design, and responsibilities are also potential performance improvement intervention targets. Other targets include work processes, environmental factors, information flow, tools, and technology. The focus is on the alignment of business requirements, organization processes, and the performer.

The key to a performance improvement intervention is to move from fixing individuals to changing the organization and system supports to achieve performance improvement.

ORGANIZATION RESTRUCTURING

This intervention is seldom successful in isolation. Nevertheless, restructuring is often an important part of process redesign or vision and strategy alignment. Organization restructuring can be as vast as reorganizing several large functions and the departments within them or limited to restructuring one function and its primary units. Traditionally, senior managers secretly have planned the restructuring and then publicly announced the results; they prepared to deal with the consequences of low morale, loss of productivity, and reduced employee commitment. Employee fears and reaction to restructuring are usually so intense, the wise internal consultant will counsel senior management to plan the intervention using change and transition strategies discussed in chapter 12. Involving employees who are affected by the restructuring or redesigning of jobs or the creation of the new processes and job responsibilities helps reduce the loss of employee commitment and productivity. Perviz Randeria, an experienced former internal consultant, provides an approach in a memorandum outlining a draft agenda and a plan for an ongoing restructuring and cross-functional teamwork consultation (appendix 14).

Shared Leadership and Ownership Were a Big Part

Internal Journal

We were moving from a matrix organization to product teams. It involved systematically eliminating 35 percent of the management jobs and creating new roles for those who remained as coaches, process leaders, and program directors. It involved creating more diversified teams so necessary resources were available and more disciplines were included on the teams. Shared leadership and ownership were a big part. Teams were able to select their process owner and team leader and establish policies and procedures. The organization became more efficient and effective as a result. Job satisfaction increased. Success was attributed to the process. I was the internal consultant; we used external consultants for specialized tasks. We brought in the first-line and employees early in the process. Every council and task force included a diagonal slice.

**Jim Harley, director, organization development,
Westinghouse Electric Company**

SURVEY FEEDBACK

We have discussed this intervention extensively in the information and analysis phase and the feedback phase. At the intervention phase in the consulting process, the activities involved in survey feedback included action planning at the work-group level, leadership development at management levels, and changes in organization-wide processes and vision, strategy, and cultural alignment.

VISION, STRATEGY, AND CULTURE ALIGNMENT

Activities with this focus usually begin at the top of the organization and may be precipitated by the arrival of a new leader or a new team. Changes in business conditions also frequently trigger a reexamination of the vision and strategy of the business. It is important to remember that vision and strategy are different. Vision is holistic, appeals to the heart and spirit, and draws people toward the end state. Strategy is linear, appeals to the rational mind, and pushes people toward the right direction with steps to get there. Organizations need both: the vision to attract employees to an exciting future and a strategy to provide a plan to get there. See appendix 15 for Marilyn Blair's suggested process to create a vision.

Research at the University of Michigan (Ulrich & Lake 1990; Ulrich 1997) confirmed that business performance is strongly influenced by a culture aligned with the business strategy. All too frequently executives change business strategies but do not invest in the important work of changing the organization culture to support that business strategy. Internal consultants have a pivotal role to play in educating senior executives here. The organization culture is developed and created through HR management systems and processes. Thus, executives must examine how people are managed, rewarded, trained, selected, promoted, and kept informed. Changing these processes and systems to align with the business strategy will change the culture and bring it into alignment. Chapter 13 included a six-part framework by Ulrich (1998) to guide systemwide change and transformation. Figure 14-6 demonstrates a model used by internal consultant Cecily Cocco for an intervention for one company.

What is Organizational Culture?

Culture is a by-product of a group working together over time. As people share a significant number of important experiences in the process of solving internal and external problems, those experiences lead them eventually to a common view of the world around them and their place in it. Culture operates much like a genetic code: a powerful yet invisible determinant of all that goes on in an organization. It is the internal "wiring," the system's core infrastructure. Because cultures exist to provide

Internal Journal

Figure 14-6. Transformational change model.

Guiding Principle: What people believe and how they think and feel has the utmost effect on everything they do.

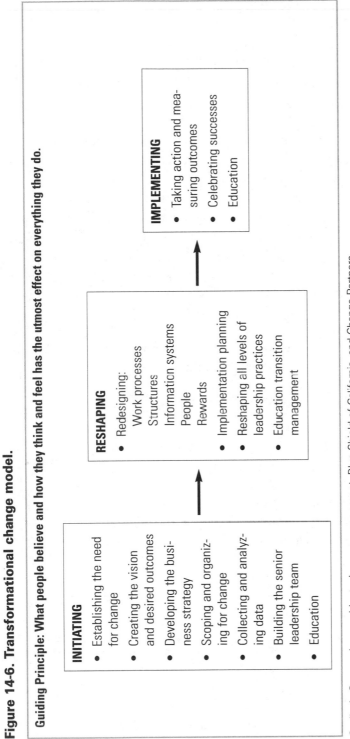

INITIATING

- Establishing the need for change
- Creating the vision and desired outcomes
- Developing the business strategy
- Scoping and organizing for change
- Collecting and analyzing data
- Building the senior leadership team
- Education

RESHAPING

- Redesigning:
  - Work processes
  - Structures
  - Information systems
  - People
  - Rewards
- Implementation planning
- Reshaping all levels of leadership practices
- Education transition management

IMPLEMENTING

- Taking action and measuring outcomes
- Celebrating successes
- Education

Cecily A. Cocco, vice president, change management, Blue Shield of California, and Change Partners

stability to social systems, it is inherently anxiety producing to give up the assumptions that stabilize our organizational world, even if other assumptions might be more functional.

Cecily A. Cocco, vice president, change management, Blue Shield of California, and Change Partners

LARGE-GROUP INTERVENTIONS

Earlier work with whole organizations used more of a "cascade" approach beginning with the top team and working through the whole organization (Bunker & Alban 1992) rather than "getting the whole system in the room" (Weisbord 1992). Groups larger than 25–30 were not seen as manageable. In recent years, however, using large-group techniques has succeeded with groups of 50–2,500. These technologies meet today's requirement for creating fundamental change quickly. These approaches include, among others, the Future Search Conference (Weisbord 1987), Open Space (Owen 1992) and Real Time Strategic Change (Dannemiller-Tyson Associates 1994; Jacobs 1994). Table 14-4 compares these three approaches. They are all highly energizing and move the change process for the whole systems very quickly by involving all levels and as many members and stakeholders of the organization as possible. Some managers, nervous and concerned about "things getting out of control" with such large groups, are unwilling to take the risk, but the increased potential for fast, fundamental change is worth the risk.

Using Open-Space Technology for Fast Change

Internal Journal

We needed to integrate a new area. The driver for it was the need to consolidate registration and patient-transportation functions of two hospitals. We needed to get an agreement very quickly—one that incorporated good practices from both groups. We needed to do this within 30 days. The impetus for change was there, and the vice president bought into it and was willing to take the risks because she trusted me. I thought using Open Space technology had the potential to get us there. I got the groups together who were in charge of the two areas. Their level of skill was high, and many people knew how the process could be done better. They bonded and it worked very well, almost seamlessly. I just had to monitor and check in to see how they were doing.

Mila N. Baker, system director, learning and organization development, Baptist/St. Vincent's Health System

Summing Up and Looking Ahead

The culmination of all the earlier phases of the internal-consulting process is the implementation of the intervention planned with the client and the client system. This chapter has described the types of interventions typically used by internal

Table 14-4. Examples of large-group interventions.

	Future Search Conference	Real Time Strategic Change	Open-Space Technology
Purpose	Create a future vision	• Systemwide change	• Discussion and exploration of ideas
Format	Past, present, future	• A basic model, adaptable to many issues	• Emergent design—least structured of large-group approaches
Characteristics	Minimizes differences Search for common ground	• Highly structured and organized • Intensively interactive • Uses "Arthritic Organizations"[1] and Beckhard's Change Models[2] —Common data and information base —Facilitated or self-managed small groups	• Large group creates agenda topics • Interest groups form around topics • Hold periodic town meetings for sharing information across interest groups
Resource needs	No experts No small groups Facilitators	• Outside experts as appropriate • Uses large- and small-group facilitators	• One facilitator who lays out format, ground rules, and "holds the space" —Requires an understanding of large group dynamics
Length	2.5 days minimum	2–3 days	Varies
Size	40–80 participants, sometimes larger	300–2,400 participants	Open

[1] Dannemiller-Tyson Associates (1994)
[2] Beckhard & Harris (1977)

consultants with several examples drawn from experienced internal consultants. Whether the intervention is focused on individual development, team effectiveness, or systemwide change, carefully built client relationships and successfully completing the earlier phases of the consulting process helps to ensure the success of this phase.

Once implementation is finished it is easy to move on to the next exciting project. Nevertheless, it is important to complete the final phase: evaluation and learning. The next chapter discusses the issues and approaches to evaluation and, most importantly, steps for the consultant, the client, and members of the client system for reflecting and using the learning from the whole process for personal development and organizational learning.

References

Argyris, C. (1993). *Knowledge for Action.* San Francisco: Jossey-Bass.

Beckhard, R., and R. Harris. (1977). *Organizational Transitions: Managing Complex Change.* Reading, MA: Addison-Wesley.

Boehm, D. (1994). *Thought as a System.* London: Routledge.

Boehm, D. (1996). *On Dialogue.* London: Routledge.

Bunker, B., and B. Alban. (1992, December). Editor's introduction to special issue: "Large Group Intervention." *Journal of Applied Behavioral Science, 28,* 4.

Dannemiller-Tyson Associates. (1994). *A Consultant's Guide to Real Time Strategic Change* (2d edition). Ann Arbor, MI: Author.

Jacobs, R. (1994). *Real Time Strategic Change.* San Francisco: Berrett-Koehler Publishers.

Lindfield, M. (1998, June). "Casting Shadows." *Association for the Advancement of Psychosynthesis Journal.*

McCann, J.E., and T.N. Gilmore. (1983, Winter). "Diagnosing Organizational Decision Making Through Responsibility Charting." *Sloan Management Review.*

Owen, H. (1992). *Open Space Technology: A User's Guide.* Potomac, MD: Abbott.

Senge, P.M. (1990). *The Fifth Discipline.* New York: Doubleday.

Senge, P.M., R. Ross, B. Smith, C. Roberts, and A. Kleiner. (1994). *The Fifth Discipline Fieldbook.* New York: Doubleday.

Ulrich, D. (1997). *Human Resource Champions.* Boston: Harvard Business School Press.

Ulrich, D. (1998). *Delivering Results.* Boston: Harvard Business School Press.

Ulrich, D., and D. Lake. (1990). *Organizational Capability: Competing from the Inside Out.* New York: John Wiley & Sons.

Varney, G.H. (1977). *Organization Development for Managers.* Reading, MA: Addison-Wesley.

Waterman, R.H., Jr., J.A. Waterman, and B.A Collard. (1994, July-August). "Toward a Career Resilient Workforce." *Harvard Business Review,* 87–94.

Weisbord, M. (1987). *Productive Workplaces.* San Francisco: Jossey-Bass.

Weisbord, M. (1992). *Discovering Common Ground.* San Francisco: Jossey-Bass.

Chapter 15

Phase Eight: Evaluation and Learning

The evaluation and learning phase is ripe with opportunity to bring closure, to celebrate, to reflect, to learn, and to remind the client system what it has gained. All too often this phase is ignored or given only cursory attention. Evaluation in HRD is confusing and often creates controversy. Many consultants and managers agree that they should conduct an evaluation but time is scant, the data is lacking, or it is too complex. Yet the investment in the development or change initiative demands time, as well as human and financial resources. In any other situation, managers would demand measurement of that investment.

Advantages and Difficulties

Evaluating the results of internal consulting efforts offers a number of benefits:

- increased executive support when top management is confident that consulting interventions are cost effective and valuable to the organization
- lessons from past interventions improves the planning and implementation of future projects
- evaluation during the process of the intervention enables the consultant to make needed midcourse corrections
- feedback from clients and participants enables the consultant to improve his or her own skills
- credibility is enhanced for consulting within the client organization.

Despite these advantages, many barriers can hinder evaluation:

- Evaluation must be planned early in the consulting process to establish baselines, select appropriate metrics, and collect relevant measurements.
- The client may not believe that the benefits of a formal evaluation warrant the cost in time or budget.

- The outcomes of many interventions are not easily measurable.
- Either the client or the consultant may be reluctant to conduct an evaluation if the results are not as successful as hoped.
- In the rapidly changing internal environment, the effect of the intervention is hard to isolate with everything else that is happening.
- The pressure to continue moving on to the next project does not allow time for reflection and learning.

Levels of Evaluation

In any discussion of HRD evaluation, Kirkpatrick's (1959) four-level model is usually cited. Reaction, learning, behavior, results, or organizational effects have become generally accepted components of evaluation. Despite this level of acceptance, more recently the need for evaluation and the model itself have been subject to question (Abernathy 1999). Here we will briefly discuss the value of evaluation for internal consultants at each level, explore alternatives, and conclude with recommendations.

LEVEL 1—REACTION

This is the easiest level of evaluation to apply and gives the internal consultant "customer satisfaction" data from participants in workshops and other group events. A reaction form, often called a "smile sheet," tells the trainer, facilitator, or group leader how the session went in the eyes of the participants. Such information is useful for making midcourse corrections, receiving feedback on facilitation or training skills, and identifying potential problems. Reaction evaluation data can also be solicited verbally at the close of a meeting or individually from particular members following the meeting. Although it is subjective, it is important data for the internal consultant. Negative reactions that remain ignored can undermine the reputation and the credibility of the consultant.

LEVEL 2—LEARNING

In this second level of evaluation, the focus is on what knowledge, skills, or attitudes were learned. We are all familiar with testing used in education and formal certificate programs. Some cynically refer to this level as the one that measures, "How well did you do on the test?"

Internal consultants and their clients, however, seldom need to use testing for change projects except in performance improvement interventions for training new skills or where the job requires tests of driving knowledge or other skills. The steps of performance improvement usually include performance measurement before and after the intervention. Testing can be used in that measurement. In many change projects, new learning is evident through observation: how employees approach their work, how task-force members work as a team to solve problems, or how an executive effectively leads a difficult meeting. Managers and consultants can see the evidence of the learning, which is really the next level of measurement—behavior.

LEVEL 3—BEHAVIOR

Although participants may demonstrate learning in the workplace, an important evaluation measure is the application of the behavior in the work environment. A team-building intervention in which members demonstrate good teamwork in the session is not a measure of teamwork in day-to-day practices of team members at their jobs. Measuring changed behavior in the job setting can be challenging. Finding effective methods that result in independent evaluation or establish a causal relationship between the intervention and the behavior are just two of the difficulties in evaluating behavioral change. Managers, workgroup supervisors, or other team members are usually in the best position to evaluate the results by seeing new behaviors in the workplace.

LEVEL 4—ORGANIZATIONAL EFFECTS

This is the most important level of evaluation. Did the intervention make a difference? Has performance improved? Has the change process affected the bottom line? Evaluation at this level is not only the most important, but it is the most challenging. It requires a long-term focus, identifying measures that have a cause-and-effect relationship, and both hard and soft data.

Hard data consists of quantitative results—documentation of reduced costs, time, or overhead; improved quality or quantity; increased sales or revenue. Soft data is qualitative perceptions regarding the work environment, employee attitudes, employee work habits, or use of skills to solve problems, make decisions, work in teams, and handle conflicts. Hard data is easier to plug into a cost-benefit analysis and documents the client's return-on-investment. Still, isolating the organizational results of the intervention is a challenge. With many changes occurring in both the internal and external environment over the time of the intervention, it is difficult to accurately measure the effect of the intervention. These complexities discourage many consultants and clients from conducting formal evaluation to measure organizational consequences.

Alternatives

One of the difficulties in applying Kirkpatrick's levels of evaluation is a result of the complex, continuous nature of internal-consulting interventions. These four levels work most effectively with finite, short-term projects or classroom training and so may not apply for the many complex, continuous interventions tackled by internal consultants. It is hard to isolate the influence of specific activities, the amount of change or learning, or the outcomes. Current accounting methods only consider the costs in time and money and are unable to adequately measure the costs of low morale or poor teamwork. The intangible benefits of an intervention—employee satisfaction, learning, or ability to change—are harder to measure. The investment in human capital does not appear on the company balance sheet.

Yet, internal consultants are increasingly challenged to justify the business value of consulting interventions. A capital investment of several million dollars would not be approved without justification. To respond to this challenge, many emphasize measuring the bottom-line results through return-on-investment. Still, many critics believe that the current financial measures are inadequate, not only because they fail to measure the investment in intellectual capital, but also because they focus on the past and fail to provide adequate guidance for today and tomorrow. Kaplan and Norton (1992), authors of the balanced-scorecard method, recommend balancing financial measures with customer satisfaction and retention, internal-business processes, and employee learning, development, and readiness for change. Abernathy (1999) also challenged consultants to consider "out-of-the-box" alternatives. She reported that Andersen Consulting Education uses stakeholder expectations in design and evaluation based on the assumption that "managers know what skills and behaviors employees need to do their jobs." Abernathy cites Jack Welch, CEO and chairman at General Electric, who is a believer in developing a "boundaryless learning" culture, and who invests in learning, not evaluation. Return from the investment in developing General Electric's Six Sigma culture comes from both tangible and intangible business results, consumer satisfaction, and career opportunities for employees.

The American Society for Training & Development reports that a sample of 40 publicly traded firms in a broad range of industries provides preliminary evidence that companies that invest heavily in "training" are more successful and profitable. The report used such measures as annualized net sales, gross profit per employee, and ratio of market to book to document the overall value of investment in human capital. Long-term improvement of gross financial measures can also offer evidence of the value of investing in developing the human organization, but it cannot demonstrate a causal relationship.

Recommendations

The best advice for internal consultants is to keep it simple and tie evaluation to the results that clients care about. If the client does not care or is not invested in measuring the outcomes of interventions, it may not be worth the resources to conduct an evaluation. It is important, however, for continued learning and improvement, to ensure that internal consultants do get their own "customer-satisfaction" measurements. The following recommendations can be used in approaching evaluation:

- Discuss with your client how he or she will measure success of the intervention. Good managers know how their units are performing and can make well-informed judgments about what they will consider a measure of success.
- Identify the skills or behaviors that will demonstrate change and how those will be observed or measured. Ask managers to choose two or three critical performance measures that will demonstrate the influence of the intervention on employee behavior.
- Measure what matters. Measuring the behaviors that demonstrate change or contribute to high performance reinforces the intervention.
- Discuss the consequences of the intervention on employee morale and satisfaction. Does your client want a baseline to evaluate improvement? If so, that may influence the choice of tools or methods for collecting data. The same data may be used to analyze the organizational issues and establish a baseline through an employee survey or other methods.
- Approach senior management to consider the balanced-scorecard approach to measure the results of systemwide learning and change.
- Seek out data that is already available on sales performance, operations results, customer satisfaction, or employee retention. It may need to be "cut" or analyzed a little differently for evaluation purposes, but if it is already collected that usually is not too difficult.
- Perhaps the most important consideration is to ensure that the consultant measures "customer satisfaction." Seeking both verbal and written feedback from clients helps the consulting group to continue to improve and to ensure it is meeting client needs.

"Customer Satisfaction" Evaluation

Asking clients to do an evaluation of consulting services at the completion of an intervention, at project milestones, or on an annual basis yields structured feedback that can be summarized and used to report to the internal consultant's boss or senior management. Figure 15-1 provides an example of a consulting-services assessment. In addition to a structured process, internal consultants and their clients can benefit from setting aside time together to evaluate and reflect on the intervention. It can also be an important learning experience for both consultant and client as they discuss such questions as:

- What went well that we would do again?
- What problems did we encounter that we could have prevented?
- What would we do differently?

Figure 15-1. Consulting-services assessment.

For project milestone _____   For end of project_____

Project:

Name: _____   **Date:** _____

Client: _____   **Consultant:** _____

1. What kind of consulting services were performed by the consultant?
   Please check all that apply.

   _____ Management development
   _____ Planning
   _____ Team building
   _____ Problem solving
   _____ Performance improvement
   _____ Coaching
   _____ Employee participation
   _____ Business process improvement
   _____ Organization learning
   _____ Research and needs assessment
   _____ Organization-wide change
   _____ Other_____

2. Has the work performed made a difference for you and your organization?

   Yes _____   No _____   Not Sure_____

3. Did the consultant's services achieve the results expected?

   Yes _____   No _____   Not Sure_____

4. Were commitments made and kept:

   a) By the consultant?

   Yes _____   No _____   Not Sure_____

   b) By you/your organization? ·

   Yes _____   No _____   Not Sure_____

   Were those commitments: (Please check all that apply)

   _____ Reasonable?   _____ Specific
   _____ Achievable?   _____ Understood?
   _____ Important to the business?   _____ Other

5. What can we do to improve our services?

6. Overall, how satisfied are you with the consultant's services?

   1—not at all   2—somewhat   3—fairly   4—more than   5—very

- What insights did I gain about myself?
- What did I do well that I can leverage for the future?
- What issues in myself got in the way?

If I Had to Do It Again

Internal Journal

When I was new to this job, I was bringing in the quality initiative exuberantly. At the same time, we were doing a painful reorganization that was like a divorce in a couple of areas. People saw the two initiatives as being connected even though I said they were different. Now that I have more experience, I would never do that again. The timing was very poor. I understand that now. At the time, the city manager felt that we needed to do something to show that we were taking out the waste and the fat. I relied on his political perception. In looking back, if we had to do the reorganization, I would have separated in time the quality program. Doing them together slowed us down a year or 18 months. If I had been more attuned to how adult learning takes place and answering why we are doing this, it would have helped. It takes time for adults to learn. We need to understand differences in learning styles.

Michael Crnobrna, organizational development coordinator, City of Burnsville, Minnesota

If the client is unavailable or unwilling to participate in such a personal evaluation and reflection, consider taking time with or without other members of the consulting group to evaluate for one's own personal mastery.

School of Hard Knocks

Internal Journal

The one experience I learned the most from in my career was when I got hooked on a particular design that I thought would be neat and leading-edge and would give the results the client needed. But, I got too enamored with the design. As we moved to get buy-in on the design, there was resistance. My boss and I were believers and the client said okay, but he didn't have the enthusiasm. The closer we got, the more resistant he became—not in outward ways but in subversive ways, such as canceling meetings. I ignored it and didn't pay attention. We got to the event, and he undermined it by not setting the stage for it and gave no visible support in front of everyone. It worked, but not as well as it could have and should have. I think it was too high risk for him and I wasn't paying attention.

Laura J. Christenson, director of global organization effectiveness for a pharmaceutical/health-care company

Another measure of customer satisfaction is the feedback from a workshop "smile sheet." Soliciting feedback from the participants in workshops and off-site events ensures that the internal consultant is on target for the needs of the group. Many recommend getting daily reaction sheets or asking for verbal feedback to allow opportunity for midcourse correction. Asking participants to sign their evaluations enables the internal to follow up and address specific negative responses. Figure 15-2 is an example of a reaction evaluation form. Tailor and choose questions to give the specific information needed to determine how well the participants' needs are met by the workshop. Although participants' reactions do not gauge the influence of the intervention in learning, behavior, or organizational change, they are important measures of customer satisfaction. Internal consultants cannot afford to ignore them.

Celebrating Milestones

The closure of a project or the achievement of milestones provides an opportunity to not only evaluate, but also to reflect on the learning and celebrate the contribution of team members and colleagues. A closing celebration lifts the spirits, reinforces important values, and provides a sense of accomplishment and closure for a successful project. Successful celebrations

- have a theme tied to the purpose of the project
- recognize the uniqueness and personal contribution of the team members
- have a festive atmosphere with activities that are fun
- reward hard work, contributions, and accomplishments
- reinforce the values and goals of the project.

Learning

Evaluation is an opportune time to reinforce the value and importance of continuous learning. The process of evaluation supports the learning that occurred in the project by the client, the consultant, and the members of the client system. Because learning gives a competitive advantage, the internal consultant has the responsibility to use every opportunity to emphasize the value and importance of continuous learning. Reinforcing by taking time to reflect, explore, identify, and share learning contributes to both personal mastery and organization learning. Powerful interventions can bring recognition of learning disabilities, such as "functional myopia," which characterizes those who only see things from their own functional position, or the "skilled incompetence" (Argyris 1993) of the highly educated to have open dialogue.

With this recognition of the importance of personal and organizational learning, there is opportunity for the internal consultant to act or recommend alternatives for continuous learning by

Figure 15-2. Training workshop evaluation.

Workshop: _____ Leader: _____

Date:_____

Using the scale below, please circle the number that most accurately represents your response.

1 = To a little or no degree	4 = To a great degree
2 = To a slight degree	5 = To a very great degree.
3 = To a moderate degree	

1. Were the pre-workshop materials useful? N/A 1 2 3 4 5
2. Did the content match the stated objectives? 1 2 3 4 5
3. Was the learning level appropriate for you? 1 2 3 4 5
4. Was the session paced appropriately? 1 2 3 4 5
5. Did you have an opportunity to participate through group discussion, exercises or skill practice? 1 2 3 4 5
6. Were the exercises and skill practices helpful in applying your understanding of the content? 1 2 3 4 5
7. Was the environment conducive to learning? 1 2 3 4 5
8. Did the facilitator:
    Create a nonthreatening atmosphere? 1 2 3 4 5
    Manage group discussion/exercises effectively? 1 2 3 4 5
    Demonstrate knowledge about the subject matter? 1 2 3 4 5
    Provide helpful and constructive suggestions? 1 2 3 4 5
    Encourage participation? 1 2 3 4 5
    Hold your interest and attention? 1 2 3 4 5
9. Was the facilitator effective overall? 1 2 3 4 5
10. Was this session relevant to a real-world performance expected of you back on the job? 1 2 3 4 5
11. Was this session worth your time? 1 2 3 4 5
12. Was this session a success in your opinion? 1 2 3 4 5

Comments or suggestions:

Thanks for your input. Name _____

- promoting the use of dialogue and conversation; listening and exchanging ideas promotes learning at all levels
- modeling, giving, and soliciting personal feedback
- establishing processes and ways of sharing team successes and learning across department or unit boundaries, such as fairs or festivals to tell success stories, conducting 15-minute "mini-versities," or creating vibrant visual-learning environments with process diagrams and output charts

- setting up communities of practice, loosely organized gatherings of like-minded professionals who meet physically or virtually to exchange ideas and learn (Graham, Osgood, & Karren 1998)
- using a common language at all levels of the organization to help create a safe environment and sense of community for shared learning
- creating opportunities for dialogue and examining both organizational successes and problems by asking, "What can we learn here?" and "What can we do differently?"
- applying continuous improvement strategies, such as total quality or business process improvement
- using an internal network or Website to file or publish documents, success stories, new ideas, and practices
- modeling vulnerability as a learner and modeling the behaviors expected from members of the client system
- helping employees find root causes by asking five *why* questions—"And why is that?"
- reinforcing being a novice and learning from action by performing behaviors without being perfect, learning, and repeating, because in fast-paced change, new skills are required even before becoming competent at the old ones
- using systems thinking and supporting others to be systems thinkers
- taking frequent time-outs to reflect and learn from recent actions
- challenging the paradigms and mental models held by members of the client system and offering alternative ways of seeing the situation.

Summing Up and Looking Ahead

In this chapter, we have reviewed the troubling issue of evaluation. The long-established model of evaluation no longer works effectively with complex, fast organization-wide change and learning interventions. Yet the pressure to evaluate the business effects of consulting interventions is building. The traditional accounting approach and current financial measures are inadequate. They emphasize only tangible costs and fail to measure the investment in human capital with the benefits of increasing organizational capability, and they focus on the past rather than provide guidance for the future.

The balanced scorecard or evaluation of client-identified success factors are increasingly recommended options. The best advice for internals is to keep it simple, tie evaluation to client needs, and be sure to measure "customer satisfaction." The client and customer satisfaction evaluation and feedback are critical inputs for the internal consultant's own reflection and learning. Personal mastery and continuing to bring your best self to your work demand the continuous learning process.

The closure of an intervention and the evaluation and learning phase also offer an opportunity to celebrate and recognize others' contributions to the success of the project. Such a celebration not only lifts the spirits, but also reinforces important messages and learning. The reflection of learning at the close of an intervention is yet another opening for the internal consultant to promote continuous learning as clients begin to recognize their learning disabilities. This opportunity may happen sooner in the consulting process, or it may not happen until the next intervention as the consultant cycles back through the consulting process. The internal consultant should be diligent in using opportunities to create a learning environment.

In the next chapter, we will review briefly the opportunities and challenges presented by life "on the inside." The guidelines, advice, and admonishments presented in the preceding 15 chapters are distilled into a "baker's dozen" of rules for the internal consultant.

References

Abernathy, D. (1999, February). "Thinking Outside the Evaluation Box." *Training & Development,* 18–23.

Argyris, C. (1993). *Knowledge for Action.* San Francisco: Jossey-Bass.

Graham, W., D. Osgood, and J. Karren. (1998, May). "A Real-Life Community of Practice." *Training & Development,* 34–38.

Kaplan, R.S., and D.P. Norton. (1992, Jan.–Feb.). "The Balanced Scorecard—Measures that Drive Performance." *Harvard Business Review.*

Kirkpatrick, D. (1959). "Techniques for Evaluating Training Programs." *Journal of American Society of Training Directors, 13*(11).

Chapter 16

The Challenges and Opportunities of Living Inside

Internal consultants live inside their client organization and are invested in its health, viability, and success. They know the business, the organization, and the employees. They know their history and their sensitivities. They know the land mines, the skeletons in the closet, and the attic ghosts. Clients and colleagues become friends. The consultant's competencies and strengths, as well as his or her foibles and weaknesses, become common knowledge. Internal consultants work with their credibility and their reputation at stake with every intervention. If a trust is violated, a confidence broken, or if something does not go well, credibility and reputation can be destroyed quickly.

Living Inside: The Challenges

Internal consultants' intimate knowledge of the organization and the business makes them valuable business partners. Yet, it challenges their role of neutrality and objectivity. As consultants, they must stand at the edge, operate at the margins, and maintain distance. This delicate balance of knowing organizational knowledge and keeping a marginal position at the boundary of the organization defines the paradoxes that confront the internal consultant. Building strong relationships with all levels in the organization is the foundation for internal success; however, internals must also be willing to confront senior executives. Belonging to the organization and finding acceptance helps internal consultants be congruent with their clients; yet, they must be cautious and avoid collusion by not telling senior managers the truth, for example.

Although internal and external consultants are similar in many ways, these paradoxes create conflict and stress for the internal consultant who joins the organization unprepared for these challenges. Both internal and external consultants use their expertise, influence, and personal skills to facilitate a client-requested change without formal authority to implement their recommended actions. Nevertheless, the performance improvement consultants, change management specialists, or OD professionals working inside their client organizations must use their expertise, influence, and personal skills to address more than their client's requests.

Internal consultants must also meet the expectations of their own managers and senior executives, as well. They must navigate around political land mines, please the boss, and join in partnership with other staff functions, such as HR. Internal consultants are often placed on a middle tier of the organization reporting hierarchy through the HR function. They find their status and reporting relationships a barrier to establishing their own competence and credibility. Sometimes their positioning can be a hindrance in establishing a consultant-client relationship with a senior executive who sees the consultant as a subordinate. Many internal consultants struggle with the pressure from senior-level clients to break confidences, take unrealistic projects, or make inappropriate changes.

Living Inside: The Opportunities

Despite the challenges, internal consultants have a unique opportunity to exploit their position inside the organization and many opportunities to have a long-term, significant influence on the organization. They can build strong relationships with clients over time, implement short-term interventions, or tackle smaller pieces of long-term projects simultaneously. Internal consultants' holistic knowledge of the organization enables them to take a systems view and ensure that linkages and processes successfully support the change targets. When they partner with external consultants, they can be a multiplier by disseminating and reinforcing the expertise and cutting-edge concepts, integrating them into the culture of the organization through their day-to-day work. Using their inside knowledge of the business and the organization, they can serve as catalysts for needed change, ensure organizational alignment with the business strategy, prepare employees with skills to cope with forthcoming changes from the tumultuous business environment, and provide candid perspectives as confidential sounding boards for senior executives.

The complexity and challenges of the business environment will expand opportunities for internal consultants to influence business leaders and prepare their client organizations for the unpredictable and turbulent ride ahead. Successful internal consultants must stay abreast of powerful new ideas and tools, introduce them into the organization, and use them to advise their clients and prepare their organizations for enduring success and high performance. This often requires the internal consultant to develop successful partnerships with external consultants who bring credibility with new perspectives and cutting-edge approaches. Although such partnerships are frequently difficult, they can also be of great benefit to the organization with the combined strengths and advantages of both external and internal consultants working together.

Choosing Roles

Internal consultants must choose the emphasis in their roles as expert or process consultants. Many internal consultants must serve in both roles. Today's business environment demands that all internal consultants be experts in change management, know the organization, and understand the business strategy. They may also be experts grounded in HPI or HRD. Many internal consultants bring a systems view of the whole and an intimate understanding of culture and organization dynamics. Many internal consultants believe their value is in contributing an awareness of the energy in the organization and lifting hidden emotions to the surface. They bring a presence that legitimizes addressing the process and feelings of human interaction.

Four factors influence the choices internal consultants make in how they approach their work and in the role they choose. They are the strengths and characteristics of the consultant, the needs of the client, the relationship between the consultant and client, and the characteristics of the organization. Internal consultants must develop the ability to adapt and flexibly move from being a committed partner with a client to being a business driver in an executive meeting to being a change leader for a strategic, process-improvement initiative. They can serve as trusted advisors to senior executives wrestling with critical business decisions and then offer specific expertise to solve tough performance improvement problems. Novice internal consultants may be able to play only one or two of these roles, but as they become experienced mentors and masters of their craft, they often adjust capably from one to another when the situation demands. They interchange these roles easily and successfully.

Building Relationships

The successful work of internal consultants is built on a strong foundation of relationships. As consultants, they must develop authentic partnerships with their clients and make careful judgments regarding the client's resistance, readiness to take the risk of change, need for support, ability to lead the organization through transition, or openness to tough feedback. To achieve the successful outcomes they envision with their clients, they must, because they live inside, also build strong relationships with their bosses, other levels of management, and their peers and colleagues in HR or other staff functions. Building strong relationships requires that internal consultants educate and prepare others to understand and appreciate the role of consultant, take the initiative to understand the others perspectives, be strong and clear, and develop continually their "best selves."

As stewards of the organization and its culture, internal consultants make a choice for service, accountability for results, and responsibility to bring their best selves to work. That commitment means deep self-awareness, integrity with their own physical, emotional, and mental energy, and the discipline of personal mastery (Senge 1990). Personal mastery is a continuous process of learning about oneself—the conscious exploration of the connection of present tension to past negative shadows and movement toward the person we desire to be. Maintaining a grounded and centered presence brings positive energy that offers hope, choice, and transformation. To keep balance, the internal consultant must be committed to managing personal and work boundaries and to practicing self-care. With these commitments, internal consultants can tap into their intuition, their intellect, and their emotions to offer hopeful possibilities and bring positive energy to others who are anxious or discouraged. Internal consultants who learn about self, improve their craft, and stay grounded will bring their best selves to work.

The Consulting Process

The consulting process for the internal consultant is usually a messy, organic process in which the steps are seldom linear, often overlap, or require cycling back to repeat or expand an earlier phase. The consulting process does not begin with entry as it does for external consultants. It begins with the initial contact with the client and is heavily influenced by the consultant's reputation in the organization. That reputation is as valuable as a popular product's brand name and many internal consultants use it to successfully market themselves within the organization. Internal consultants can help position their reputation by setting the stage at the time of hiring and negotiating their charter with their bosses and their most-senior potential clients.

Successful movement through the eight-phase consulting process is influenced continually by the internal consultant's ability to manage relationships and the dynamics of living inside the organization.

A "Baker's Dozen" of Rules for Living Inside and Succeeding

Throughout the book, we have given advice, admonishments, and guidelines. We have used quotations from experienced current and former internal consultants, provided checklists, step-by-step guides, and examples. In an effort to capture the most useful, here is a "baker's dozen" of rules to live by and achieve success inside the organization:

1. Know the business strategy, and identify needs and opportunities for which you can contribute to business results.
2. Learn to manage the paradoxes. Operate at the margins, yet know the organization intimately; build strong relationships but confront with the truth; be congruent with the client organization but do not collude.

3. Build and use the positive energy for change in the organization. Help clients see the "possible," create visions, and articulate their desires for the future to draw others to support and participate in the process.

4. Develop broad support for projects by working with multiple levels of the organization, communicating, educating, modeling, listening, and facilitating.

5. Seek to build relationships with key managers by finding ways to meet small but important needs, serving as a sounding board, or providing them refreshing, candid perspectives.

6. Coach clients to lead change, trust in self-organization, and to communicate often.

7. Seek agreements with clients for the mutual exchange of feedback and the promotion of self-awareness and continuous learning.

8. Develop competence and credibility by keeping agreements, being accountable for results, being authentic in relationships with others.

9. Know the boundaries of your competence; avoid going out on "skinny branches."

10. Develop the ability to initiate and build strong partnerships.

11. Be a systems thinker; identify and support linkages and interconnections.

12. Recognize and accept the client's readiness to take the risks of change.

And, perhaps the greatest secret to success:

13. Improve continuously the internal-consulting craft, practice personal mastery as a life-long journey, and stay grounded.

The internal consultant who uses these rules will find success and rewards. Consultants have an exciting, challenging opportunity when they live inside their client organization for several years. Meeting the challenges of applying their craft as internal consultants brings rewards and gifts: increased self-awareness and personal learning, the pleasure and reward of seeing clients and colleagues learn and grow, and the opportunity to leave a legacy of organizational vitality and performance.

Reference

Senge, P.M. (1990). *The Fifth Discipline.* New York: Doubleday.

An Inventory
for Internal Consultants

Directions: Consider the expectations and demands of your current position and your future career goals. Read through the list and rate the items as follows:

3—Doing well
2—Doing okay
1—Needs improvement.

Some activities may be important to you but are not listed here. Write these on the blank lines. Go back over the whole list and circle the numbers of the *three or four* items that you would most like to improve.

Relationships:

Listen and understand client's point of point _____
Support and not judge my client _____
Help explore alternatives without pushing solutions _____
Clarify role—expert or process _____
Establish rapport easily _____
Comfortable with ambiguity _____
Develop a balanced partnership with my client _____
Commitment to client's success _____
Credibility and trust _____
Confront unpleasant issues with my client _____
Am sensitive to my client's feelings _____
Help client see his or her own issues _____
Comfortable in letting the client know who I am _____
Give sensitive feedback in way it can be heard _____
Appropriately discuss feelings _____
Choose the right time to discuss bad news _____
Give the client recognition and positive feedback _____
Inspire client's confidence in my ability _____
Draw out "hidden" information or feelings _____
Actively listen and clarify my understanding _____

Provide safe environment for client to express feelings   _____

Ask questions that provoke further thought   _____

Help client see and value own competence   _____

See the client realistically   _____

Maintain relationships with prior clients   _____

Position myself when entering new organization   _____

Business and Organization:

Understand how the business works   _____

Understand the business goals and strategies   _____

Connect client's need to business strategy or goals   _____

Understand the customers' needs   _____

Understand the financial drivers of the business   _____

Understand the competition and the industry   _____

Know the key people in the organization   _____

Have an established network of support at all levels   _____

Know the organizational culture (norms, values, and so forth)   _____

In touch with employee morale and current issues.   _____

Approach intervention/project with spirit of inquiry   _____

Ask open-ended questions to gain needed information   _____

Use systems thinking to understand organizational dynamics   _____

Work collaboratively with peers in other departments   _____

Change:

Know my beliefs and model for change   _____

Help my client understand change   _____

Sensitive to client's readiness for change   _____

Focus on the goals and outcomes to build positive energy   _____

Avoid focusing on problems   _____

Recognize and use resistance appropriately   _____

Help the client create vision of desired future   _____

Coach clients to lead change   _____

Help members of the client system adjust to change   _____

Help clients pay attention to what they want   _____

Willing to go slower to go faster   _____

Know the change drivers in our business   _____

Take a systems view in planning and implementing change   _____

Agreement:

Understand the issue/need before saying yes   _____

Clear about my competence and approach   _____

Check out assumptions and expectations   _____

Negotiate differences for mutual satisfaction   _____

Seek balance of ownership for project   _____

Explain my theoretical foundation and biases   _____

Know the client's wants and goals   _____

Determine how decisions will be made   _____

Accept the client's limits and restrictions   _____

Say no if not strategic   _____

Clarify issues with primary and secondary clients   _____

Find other resources to meet client's needs   _____

Refuse projects when I lack the competence   _____

Assess "relevance and fit" with client needs   _____

Review agreement regularly with client   _____

Check out client's capacity to give attention to project   _____

Address conflicts with agreement promptly   _____

Willing to end project with client's decision   _____

Set realistic goals and timelines for the project   _____

Seek needed resources to support project   _____

Information and Assessment:

Have the technical skills required   _____

Ask for resources to supplement my skills as needed   _____

Use a framework to analyze the data/information   _____

Identify patterns and themes in the data/information   _____

Identify underlying structures or causes of problems   _____

Use information gathering to involve the client system   _____

Summarize information and analysis clearly and succinctly   _____

Gain an "independent view" of issues   _____

Feedback:

Prepare my client to hear difficult information   _____

Aware of sensitivities and concerns in my client   _____

Surface and address resistance   _____

Use effective feedback skills   _____

Prepare for data feedback presentation   _____

Use a practical rather than a conceptual approach   _____

Consider concerns of multiple clients in presentation   _____

Present data from client's point of view   _____

Remind client of goals, outcomes, and desired future   _____

Acknowledge positive factors and strengths   _____

Use reframing to present opportunities   _____

Offer alternatives to address the problems   _____

Present the advantages/disadvantages or cost/benefits   _____

Willing to go with the client's choice   _____

Targets, Strategies, Implementation:

Clarify client's goals and outcomes   _____

Seek alignment with client's desired future   _____

Break down the project into small pieces   _____

Obtain necessary support for the project   _____

Involve those affected by the project   _____

Plan and manage projects   _____

Identify systems and processes to change   _____

Transfer skills and knowledge to client system   _____

Have knowledge base and skills needed for this phase   _____

Involve other functions or specialties as needed   _____

Use a variety of interventions   _____

Make formal presentations   _____

Involve facilitation groups at any level   _____

Understand the dynamics of groups   _____

Comfortable with unpredictable changes   _____

Communicate with all the stakeholders   _____

Evaluation and Learning:

Provide alternative methods to evaluate   _____

Help client see quantitative and qualitative results   _____

Seek client participation in evaluation   _____

Build in time for client learning and reflection   _____

Solicit feedback from the client and others   _____

Take time to reflect on my own learning   _____

Acknowledge both successes and failures   _____

Find ways to celebrate   _____

Best Self:

Work easily with authority figures   _____

Let others take the glory   _____

Can say no without guilt or fear   _____

Manage my fear of rejection   _____

Accept responsibility for failures or goof-ups   _____

Understand my stewardship role   _____

Turn off my issues; listen to client   _____

Resist pointing fingers or blaming   _____

Limit tendency to "toot my own horn" too much   _____

Stay grounded and centered when under pressure   _____

Work has meaning and purpose   _____

Know my boundaries and limitations   _____

Promise only what I can deliver   _____

Work with people I do not particularly like   _____
Work through my shadow and other personal issues   _____
Invest in both personal and professional development   _____
Practice emotional and energetic integrity   _____
Confident in my skills and ability   _____
Practice discipline of personal mastery   _____
Recognize my signals of anxiety and tension   _____
Change unproductive or ineffective beliefs   _____
Clear personal and professional values   _____
Practice self care   _____

Other:

_____   _____
_____   _____
_____   _____
_____   _____

Safely Processing Your Shadow*

What are we so afraid of in that part of ourselves we deny? The shadow is the part of ourselves that we judge as unacceptable. We empower it through denying it. Yet, we brought it with us so that it could be healed, and it can only be healed if we give it expression. But, if we are so afraid of it we will never give it expression.

Everything in the universe is composed of energy, and energy needs to move. Therefore, if you will not allow your shadow to move by giving it expression, it will move of its own accord. When it does, at the very least, it embarrasses us thoroughly or, worse, causes problems in our lives. The trick is to give it safe expression. As you give it safe expression, it will reveal to you what it needs to be healed. When you give your shadow room to move safely, with harm to none, you are responsibly bringing this part of you back into the light.

To process your shadow, start by asking yourself the following questions:
- What part of my personality, thoughts, desires, or behaviors do I try to keep secret from others or even myself?
- Why am I so ashamed or terrified of other people knowing about this?
- Can I accept this part of me in the context of bringing it into this life so that it can be healed?
- If I gave that part of myself a voice, what would it say?
- How can I give expression to this part of myself so that it can move safely?

Here are some ideas for safely moving your shadow:
- After doing the grounding and centering technique (see appendix 3) and wrapping your energy field with three layers of blue flame, visualize in meditation that you allow your shadow side to run rampant. Stay conscious with your visualization, watch what the shadow does, and see how it feels to do those things. Be willing to receive an insight from your shadow regarding what it gets from this experience and what is driving it. Often it will show you unprocessed feelings and wounds from the past.
- Alone, or with a friend or group of trusted friends, allow the part of yourself you judge and suppress freedom to move. For example, if you hate the part of yourself that

---

*Provided by Ashmore, Essential Partnerships; former internal consultant with Charles Schwab Corporation.

is judgmental, then allow yourself to judge everything until it runs out of steam. Then ask yourself, "What does this part of me need?" You'll be surprised at how entertaining this activity can be. It can lighten things up considerably especially if you collapse into laughter after running the act for a while.

• Write a story with your shadow as the main character. Give your shadow the room to be, do, or say anything it wants and notice how it makes you feel. Be willing to let it feel good; it probably feels great to the shadow to finally have freedom to move. Let it show you which part of yourself needs healing.

Grounding and Centering: A Practical Technique Used by the Author*

What Does It Mean to be Grounded?

A person who is grounded is one who is strong and powerful, who cannot easily be knocked off balance, and who is clear, present, and aware. With this strong presence, balance, and clarity, we can use the full range of our human capacity to think, to move, to express feelings, and to access our higher wisdom. We can maintain balance and presence no matter what comes our way. It contrasts with being ungrounded, which is like standing with your two feet held tightly together and your knees locked. In this position, you are very vulnerable to losing your balance and keeling over.

The Grounding Process

This grounding process is a practical, solid foundation to meet the challenges we face in our daily work with clients. The following techniques can be practiced in the privacy of your office or your home.

1. Find a comfortable position. Loosen your belt and move around a bit until you are sitting and comfortably relaxed. Place your feet firmly on the floor about a foot apart with your knees resting comfortably above your feet. Place your hands at your side with palms toward your thighs and gently close your eyes.

2. Breathe a little more fully and allow yourself to relax. Notice how your body feels. Notice any spots of tension and breathe into them. You may hold tension in your shoulders, the back of your neck, your knees, or your jaw. Continue breathing fully, breathing into the spots of tension and letting them go. Find the balance of relaxed awareness so you won't drift off to sleep.

3. Shift your attention to the base of your spine. Visualize a grounding cord attached to the base of your spine. You may visualize the cord as the root of a tree or a strong steel cable—whatever works for you. With your awareness on this cord, inhale deeply. Then exhale fully (through your open mouth) into this grounding cord that extends

---

*Adapted from material developed by Mitani d'Antien, spiritual teacher and coach.

deep into the center of the earth. Once again, inhale deeply and exhale again, making your grounding cord denser and stronger. With your breath, exhale two similar cords from the base of your spine through your legs and feet into the center of the earth.

4.   Now shift your breath to a bellows breath, a deep breath in through your nose and short exhalation through your mouth with a forceful "ahaa." Visualize the warm earth energy flowing up through the grounding cords in your legs with each breath. Be sure to bring up the earth energy through the two cords in your legs and not through the central grounding cord. Take six to eight of these breaths. Pause to allow the earth energy to fill every cell in your body. Take a moment to compare how you feel now with how you felt when you started the exercise. Open your eyes gently, feeling refreshed and recharged.

When you are first learning the grounding process, it is helpful to practice it slowly every day. When I started I would begin and end my day with this exercise. As I became more familiar with the process, I could also use it frequently during the day to reestablish my grounding with a deep breath. I reground myself, not only when a stressful event threatens my balance, but also any time I need clarity and focus or to release negative energy I pick up from the environment around me. Once this energetic circuitry is established, the central grounding cord serves as a drainpipe to send negative energy down and away. The three grounding cords give you balance like a dynamic, three-legged stool that has flexibility and mobility, allowing you to smoothly move and flex with the swirling currents around you.

The Centering Process

After you have established the grounding circuitry described previously, you can add the centering process to your practice. Centering is a way of protecting yourself from the negative energy around you.

The centering process encircles you with a protective blue flame much like the blue ozone layer that encircles and protects planet earth. The ozone layer allows the healthy rays of the sun needed for growth and warmth to reach the earth and filters out the damaging radioactive rays. The blue flame in the centering process serves the same purpose: It allows in warmth, caring, and supportive energy from those around you and protects you from damaging, negative energy.

After you have completed the grounding process and before you open your eyes, follow these steps to complete your centering:

1.   About 15 inches above your head imagine a small flicker of blue flame, much like a pilot light on a gas burner. Inhale deeply and, as you exhale, imagine bringing a swath of blue flame from above your head all the way down the front, 15 inches under your feet and up your back.

2.   Then breathe a swath down the sides and seal it all around to ensure that you are completely surrounded by your own protective blue ozone layer.

3.   Take a moment to feel your grounding into the earth and the safe protection of your blue flame.

4.   Bend over and place your hands on the floor, drop your head between your knees, gently shake it from side to side, take a deep breath, and let go of any excess energy you may have taken in. You may feel a tingling or some heat. Let that pass and then slowly sit up and gently open your eyes feeling safe, refreshed, and energized.

Although to some this technique may seem either silly or scary, I have found the centering process very valuable. It gives me my own "ozone layer," a protective shield against energetic contamination as frustrations, fears, and anxieties mount during turbulent organizational change.

Sample Agreement Memoranda

Sample Memorandum for a Short-Term Project

Date:
To: Client
From: Consultant

Re: Team off-site event

I enjoyed our meeting this morning, and I am pleased to be working with you again to plan the off-site event for your new team. As we discussed, I plan to interview the members of your team for approximately an hour to gather their perspectives on the team, their expectations of you, their hopes for the next year, and any barriers that are potential impediments to accomplishing their goals. We agreed that you would inform the team of the date, your objectives, and that I would be contacting each of them for the interview. Please also reassure them that the information they share will be treated confidentially. I will also review that principle with them.

I understand that your objectives for this off-site event are:

- to build closer working relationships among members of the team and with you
- to clarify expectations with you as their new manager
- to build a collective view of future goals and what it will take to achieve them.

I expect to complete my interviews by the middle of next week. As we agreed, I will then set up an appointment with you to review the data and to begin to plan the agenda for the meeting. We agreed that I would work with your administrative assistant to finalize the logistics and to copy any materials I may need.

If you have any questions or want to discuss any issues before our next meeting, please give me a call. I look forward to working together.

Sample Memorandum for a Long-Term or Complex Project

Date:
To: Client
From: Consultant

Re: Change project

I am pleased to begin the change project with your department. Because this project is long term and involves several potential systems and processes, we agreed that we would start with observation and selected interviews of members of your organization. Based on the data from my observation and the interviews, we will develop a plan. I understand that, as you expressed, you feel uncertain as to how to proceed. After the data is collected and reviewed, I am confident that we can work as partners to identify the first steps and develop a plan with goals, timelines, and needed resources.

My understanding of your goal is to develop a high-performing department that achieves performance levels above the industry norms. This will require changing management style, the culture, organization structure, skill levels, and work processes. We agreed that this a long-term process of probably more than a year. I suggested and you concurred that we break this initiative into smaller projects, which are more manageable and will produce results more quickly.

My commitment is to keep the information and data I collect confidential to your organization and the employees interviewed will be assured of anonymity. We agreed that I would work with your managers to establish time for observation and identify a sampling of 10 to 15 frontline employees for my interviews of approximately an hour each. I plan to meet with the managers next Monday morning. I expect to complete my observation and interviews by the 15th. I will call you to set an appointment to review the data and my recommendations. We will then plan joint meetings with the managers and the employees.

If you have any questions before then, please let me know.

Organization Development Contract*

Leadership and Team Development

[name], Consultant

This is a contract for OD work between [name], president and CEO, and [name], consultant, for ongoing OD consultation.

The first portion of the contract is for development work between the CEO and the director of engineering, and for data feedback to the senior staff group, and for a three-day, off-site event. This work will be completed by [date].

PURPOSE OF THE WORK:
Facilitate and enhance organization effectiveness at [name of company] by working with the executive staff team to develop their leadership.

DESIRED OUTCOMES:
All members of the senior staff are

- behaving as a cohesive management team, demonstrating congruent leadership behavior
- consistently sharing responsibility for the success of the company with one another and with the senior management team as a whole
- achieving a common sense of values that allows them to work together effectively and efficiently
- demonstrating their ability and willingness to learn from their peers and organization contributors and to consistently model a learning mentality.

ROLES:
- *Consultants:* Provide the OD technologies and processes, guidance, and support to help the sponsor and senior staff members become a leadership team, which uses and models learning in its everyday operations with each other and within each senior staff member's organization.

---

*Provided by Marilyn E. Blair, TeamWork; former internal consultant with 3Com Corporation.

- *Sponsor [name] and senior staff members:* Hold the OD consultation work as a major priority in daily operations. Be open to learning, applying, and choosing new models and technologies for organization effectiveness and change. Practice the behaviors of a team-based organization as they are learned.

RESPONSIBILITIES OF CONSULTANT(S):

- Hold confidentiality of sources as a sacred trust.
- Show up on time for scheduled events and be fully present.
- Ask standardized questions of those interviewed and continually gather as much data as possible to understand the current state of the organization.
- Identify which dynamics at play within the senior staff group support organization change and which prevent change from occurring.
- Present data to the senior staff and achieve concordance regarding the data assessment and the consultants' plan to move forward.
- Furnish state-of-the-art and cutting-edge change and leadership theory and technologies to the systems senior staff.
- Make appropriate interventions and manage the process of development in consultation with members of the senior staff.
- Gather and provide ongoing data at agreed-upon intervals.
- Help senior staff evaluate their progress and reset expectations when necessary.
- Give personal feedback to the sponsor and to each member of the senior staff with regard to their individual development progress.
- Provide feedback to the senior staff group regarding their individual and group behaviors as observed by the consultants.

RESPONSIBILITIES OF SPONSOR AND SENIOR STAFF:

- Directly and indirectly give full support and endorsement to the OD efforts by clear actions and statements that demonstrate the importance of the project to colleagues and contributors within all work groups.
- Commit to being fully present at all development activities. For example, clear schedule of possible conflicts, show up on time, and eliminate all external distractions and interruptions including telephone calls.
- Complete related OD activities in a timely fashion.
- Consistently communicate with the consultants on matters that affect the consultation and keep them in the feedback loops.

THEORY BASE FOR THE WORK:

- Action research—Kurt Lewin et al.
- Leadership development—Ronald Heifetz
- Action science—Chris Argyris
- Total quality—W. Edwards Deming
- Learning organizations—Peter Senge et al.

PROCESS:

- Work with the CEO/president and the director of development to reestablish a positive working relationship that will help the senior staff work together more effectively, as well as the two individuals involved.
- Provide data feedback and diagnosis based on the interviews of the CEO and senior staff as a group (courtesy feedback to CEO immediately prior to group).
- Conduct a three-day, off-site event with the senior staff members, which includes work in decision making, communication, leadership (including authority), meeting management, and team development. The general purpose of the event is to (1) develop more self-awareness within the group, (2) build a strong relationship base between participants, (3) awaken the desire in the group for practicing strong leadership in the organization.

EVALUATION AND FOLLOW-UP:

The sponsor and the consultant agree that, if the work is deemed successful, the sponsor will include in this contract two follow-up periods for evaluation. The first will be three months from the end of the contract and the second three months later, or six months from the end of the contract. Each follow-up will consist of interviews with the senior staff, as well as a diagonal-slice focus group. The feedback will be synthesized and fed back to the senior staff. A course correction plan will be developed between the consultants and the senior staff.

AGREED to this [date] day of [month], [year]

_____

[name], President

_____

[name], Consultant

Conducting the Courtesy Feedback Meeting and the Feedback Meeting

Step One: Review Agreement

COURTESY MEETING
Take time to review the agreements made with the client regarding the actions you would take and the processes for collecting data and delivering negative feedback or bad news. Identify any deviations from those agreements and confirm the client's understanding of the reasons for those deviations. *Anticipated Time: 2–3 minutes.*

GROUP MEETING
Highlight the agreement with the client about the project and the process used to collect information. *Anticipated Time: 2–3 minutes.*

Step Two: Review the Planned Agenda for the Meeting

Letting people know the process of the meeting and the topics to be discussed helps them to be more active and effective participants and helps you more effectively manage the meeting. *Anticipated Time: 2–3 minutes.*

Step Three: Review Ground Rules to be Used During the Meeting

GROUP MEETING
Ground rules are helpful to ensure that members have common expectations about participation and interaction during the meeting. See chapter 12 for some sample ground rules. *Anticipated Time: 2–3 minutes.*

Step Four: Present the Model or Constructs Used to Analyze the Information/Data

Giving a brief overview of the model used in the analysis or assessment will help the clients understand and interpret the data for themselves. *Anticipated Time: 5–10 minutes.*

Step Five: Present the Information/Data

Distribute a written handout for both the courtesy meeting and the group meeting. Many consultants also like to use flipcharts or overhead projection to present the data for the group meeting so that members are focused on a common visual aid. This is not the time to do any interpretation or point out particular results. Hand out or post the data and tell the client to take some time to review it. *Anticipated Time: 3–5 minutes.*

Step Six: Client Review and Discussion of Information and Data

It is useful to give the client or the group members a framework for their review to identify "good-news items," which identify positive qualities, "question items" that need clarity or explanation, "concern items" that need some further discussion or attention, and "disagree items" that initially the client is unwilling to accept. Allow the client or group members time to express their reactions, explore the meaning, and move toward acceptance if not in agreement with the data. *Anticipated Time: 20–60 minutes depending on the extent and nature of the data and the number of group members.*

Step Seven: Offer Consultant Observations and Interpretation

After the clients have reviewed the data and discussed their reactions, they are ready to hear the consultant's perspective and interpretation of the data. Using the model introduced at the beginning of the meeting, the consultant describes the opportunity the client and the organization have to move toward their desired future and recommends changes in the organization and in their personal behavior to achieve their future goals. *Anticipated Time: 10–15 minutes.*

Step Eight: Dialogue and Decision

COURTESY MEETING

In the meeting with the individual client, the dialogue should lead to a decision about the client's willingness to make personal behavior changes and commitment to lead the organization through a change process. With those commitments, the consultant and client can partner to plan the meeting with organizational members.

GROUP MEETING

As the consultant facilitates the group dialogue in response to the consultant observations or recommendations, group members may return to concerns and questions about the data. The consultant's goal is to give members enough time to understand and accept the observations and recommendations, and, at the same time, move the group members toward a commitment and a group decision to initiate a change initiative. See accompanying text box for a clever metaphorical approach to presenting the consultant's observations. *Anticipated Time: 20–60 minutes depending on the acceptance of the recommendations and the degree of consensus in the group.*

Step Nine: Test and Confirm Agreement

It is helpful to test to see if the client or any group members have any final concerns or questions and to restate the agreement. *Anticipated Time: 55 minutes depending on final questions.*

Step Ten: Identify Next Steps

Before closing the meeting, be sure everyone is clear about next steps and who will be involved in those actions. *Anticipated Time: 5–10 minutes depending on the next steps, the complexity of scheduling, and the number who are involved.*

Step Eleven: Give Acknowledgment and Support

It is hoped that the consultant has taken opportunity throughout the meeting to acknowledge members for their participation, positive approach, vision, ideas, and commitment. At the close of the meeting, reinforce that acknowledgment, provide encouragement, and offer your support for the exciting and challenging change journey ahead. *Anticipated Time: 3–4 minutes.*

Although these above steps are presented as one meeting with the client manager and one meeting with the members of the organization, often either feedback process requires more than one meeting to adequately explore the data, discussion and interpret the data, and reach agreement on recommendations. Appropriate meeting breaks could occur after Step 6, Step 7, or Step 8.

A Portrait of XXX Incorporated
February 1998

During the months of November and December, we conducted data collection interviews with the members of the management group of the organization.

As we sifted through the interview data, a metaphor arose. We hope that the metaphor that came to us is also a useful tool to you as we try to come to a common understanding of the present reality that is XXX Incorporated.

Our observation is that, in several ways, XXX Incorporated functions like a feudal system. As we know, feudalism was a system of social organization that once dominated what is now known as Europe. Europe was made up of many fiefdoms, each dominated by a lord whose castles dotted the hills. Like the hills of present-day Italy or Mont Saint Michel on the coast of France, these were girded with housing for the lord's court, clergy, and soldiers and were surrounded by the houses of the serfs. Feudalism was marked by economic and political wars for scarce land and resources. Kings wielded limited power and functioned mainly with the permission of the lords. Let's spell out this metaphor in the form of a story.

Once upon a time, in the not too distant past, several fiefdoms came to dominate the land. In each fiefdom, a lord held control of the land, the people, and the resources. The people in each fiefdom looked to their lord to provide security and protection from invaders and from other lords who fought with them over resources and power.

The lords live an uneasy peace. They are dependent on each other for needed resources and ultimately provide each other with enough resources so that all of them fare well and make the lives of those in their fiefdom acceptable. Often, however, they are in conflict over resources, assumptions, and perspectives. Trust does not come easily.

The lords meet in council to facilitate the exchange of resources and iron out differences. They sometimes arrive at agreements, agree on solutions, and take common action. Sometimes they shout their demands, call names, blame and judge each other, and so fall short of agreement.

When on occasion they do arrive at agreements in council, they cannot trust that the agreements will continue over time. Their scribes do not always record the terms of the agreements. Sometimes a lord may not buy into the decisions that are made, but holds his silence rather than create conflict in the council. Upon returning to his fiefdom, he forgets the agreement or disregards it as that which he did not truly support. His noncompliance is not enforced and when it is, he fights the lord who tries to enforce it.

The power in the land is mainly held by two of the lords. One is the original lord of the land. He invited the other into the land when he needed help maintaining his growing and struggling kingdom. They are like brothers, and each has abilities and resources upon which the other depends. Together they control the land and the other lords: the one, because he is king, and the other because he is knowledgeable as a weasel and fearsome as a bear.

The two fall in and out of favor with each other. Their common history is marked by cycles of peace and war. The other lords are fearful lest they be perceived as taking sides. They see the two shouting at each other using terms like sabotage and ruthless, over-controlling and indecisive. The lords know that if the other lord does not like a kingly decision, he will simply not abide it and may even withhold his resources to prevent it from coming to fruition.

The land of the fiefdoms is not poor, but neither is it prosperous. The latent civil war that erupts periodically depletes the storeroom. All the people manage to maintain a minimum of security. Each person swears fealty to one of the lords and receives his protection. In exchange, all have work and pay, manageable (if not flexible) work hours, defined responsibilities, and much freedom to do as they wish, for few laws are enforced. The workload is limited because each is expected to take on only some responsibilities of one fiefdom and not for the whole of the land. Some people occasionally leave the fiefdoms for more challenging, if less secure, work.

The prosperity of the land and the people are mainly the concern of the king. The far-away kings who put this king on his throne do not appear to the people as very concerned with the ongoing state of the fiefdoms. The lords-in-council speak for their fiefdoms, but rarely discuss the good of the land.

The lords have carried on in this way for many years. But now, new opportunities are arising— new and vast markets for their goods and services. They know that they are not able to thrive in these markets without a larger delivery structure. In private conversations among themselves, the lords whisper about pledging allegiance to a more powerful kingdom that will enhance their capacity to produce and distribute. They wonder how they can make the fiefdoms attractive for inclusion in the new and powerful kingdom. The lords worry that the new king may reject one or more of them. They worry that the new king may see that the land has not been as productive as it could be and that their council has not been able to sustain agreements and create strategic directions for the good of the land.

A new day is dawning in the land. The old ways of feudalism are giving way to new and different forms. The lords know that they need one another's resources to succeed and that, as a group, they need to collaborate with larger kingdoms to enrich themselves. The lords and the king meet in council. They ask, "How can we prepare ourselves for the challenge?"

Marilyn E. Blair, TeamWork; former internal consultant with 3Com Corporation.

Alignment Checklist

VISION, GOALS, AND OUTCOMES

My client and I have

- ☐ developed a common vision for the desired future
- ☐ made an agreement about desired outcomes and results
- ☐ set goals for our work together
- ☐ written a provocative proposition.

RELATIONSHIPS

My client and I have

- ☐ established a working partnership
- ☐ developed trust and credibility
- ☐ made an agreement to give and receive feedback
- ☐ agreed that I will provide coaching
- ☐ set a clear agreement regarding levels of confidentiality
- ☐ identified key stakeholders.

ORGANIZATION AND STAKEHOLDER INVOLVEMENT

My client and I have

- ☐ confirmed support and agreement from appropriate senior management
- ☐ clarified the role of my client's boss or other senior managers
- ☐ agreed on participation of members in the department, unit, or function
- ☐ clarified roles of other stakeholders, such as HR or other departments
- ☐ identified the role of customers or vendors.

SCHEDULE AND TIMELINES

My client and I have

- ☐ agreed to a schedule with milestones and completion dates
- ☐ scheduled critical meetings or off-site events
- ☐ identified key decision points
- ☐ developed alternative or contingency plans.

ROLES AND RESPONSIBILITIES

My client and I have

- [ ] developed a mutual understanding of both our roles
- [ ] agreed on the usage and role of outside consulting resources
- [ ] set clear expectations of design, project, or transition teams
- [ ] agreed on arrangements for administrative, logistic, and clerical support.

COMMUNICATION

My client and I have

- [ ] determined how we will communicate and keep each other current
- [ ] developed key messages and symbols needed to communicate the vision and purpose of the change process
- [ ] decided who will be primary communicator to project, design, or transition teams
- [ ] agreed who needs to be kept informed of our progress
- [ ] identified vehicles, such as newsletters or critical meetings, to reinforce key messages.

DECISION MAKING

My client and I have agreed on

- [ ] who has what level of decision-making authority
- [ ] how decisions related to this intervention or project will be made
- [ ] who will be involved in key decisions
- [ ] how differences will be resolved.

ADDITIONAL INFORMATION OR KNOWLEDGE

My client and I have

- [ ] discussed what further information I need about the business or the organization
- [ ] agreed on how additional information will be gathered
- [ ] identified areas about which my client needs further education or knowledge
- [ ] determined who in the organization needs to receive further information.

SYSTEMS PERSPECTIVE

My client and I have

- [ ] discussed the wider implications of this project
- [ ] clarified the connection to other initiatives in the organization
- [ ] agreed on extrinsic and intrinsic rewards for members who support the change process
- [ ] agreed about organizational systems and structures that need to change to support this effort
- [ ] shared our views on the effect of organizational politics.

CHANGE AND INTERVENTION

My client and I have

- [ ] agreed on how change will be managed in the organization
- [ ] discussed the importance of transition for members of the organization
- [ ] agreed on how the change process will proceed
- [ ] discussed and selected intervention approaches to accomplish the desired outcomes or to create the desired future.

COSTS AND BUDGETS

My client and I have

- [ ] clarified who has budget approval for this project
- [ ] agreed on the cost parameters
- [ ] discussed the anticipated expenses for learning materials, travel, off-site expenses, and we have determined how those expenses will be covered
- [ ] reviewed procedures for charge-backs and identified budget codes.

EVALUATION

My client and I have

- [ ] determined the measures of success or change
- [ ] agreed on the method for evaluating this project
- [ ] identified data to be used in establishing a baseline.

LEARNING

My client and I have

- [ ] a shared understanding of the importance of learning
- [ ] agreed to set aside time periodically and at the project's close to exchange
- [ ] committed to feedback and reflection on what we have learned
- [ ] planned to create processes and structures for organizational learning.

POTENTIAL PROBLEMS

My client and I have

- [ ] identified potential problem areas and how the project could get derailed
- [ ] developed preventive actions and alternatives.

Charter for the Human Resources Transition Team*

This document is the charter to the transition team from the director of HR. Its function is to clarify the

- purpose
- desired outcome
- authority delegated to the transition manager
- expectations of the members of the team and the consultant
- timeframe for completion of the work.

Purpose

It is my intention that the HR department shall become a team-based organization in which all staff members are behaving according to our explicit working-values statement and our commitment of intentions for providing client services. A team-based organization is defined as one for which the daily operations and the special projects of the department are accomplished by designated teams who hold full responsibility for accomplishing the defined outcomes.

Desired Outcome

All members of the HR staff, including the manager, have agreed to a structural model for teaming (developed by the transition team and adopted by the director of HR and staff members); implementation plans are clearly defined and underway.

Authority Delegated to the Transition Manager

She may act on my behalf during my absences from the Berkeley site in all matters that pertain to the transition.

---

*Provided by Marilyn E. Blair, TeamWork; former internal consultant with 3Com Corporation.

Expectations of the Members of the Transition Team (TT) and the Consultant

Team members shall

- represent [name of business], policies, and procedures equitably in leading the HR department in the transition from a functionally organized group to a team-based organization
- serve as participating members of the TT representing the perspective of the HR department as a whole, remembering that our company responsibility is to provide high-quality HR services to the people of the corporation who work at the Berkeley site
- attend all TT meetings and participate in setting forth ideas and giving attention to the ideas others set forth in the work of the TT
- work to reach consensus on proposals within the TT so that those brought from the TT to the director of HR and the staff members represent the collaborative work of the TT
- provide and receive timely feedback to and from the OD consultant and collaboratively work through any difficulties that arise within the TT during the course of the consultation.

The OD consultant shall

- serve as the OD consultant to the director of HR, the TT members, and staff members in the transition of HR from a functionally based department to a team-based organization
- provide the participants with state-of-the-art and cutting-edge information and processes about team-based organizations
- help the TT members make decisions about which team model to propose to the director and staff based on previous organization-consulting experiences
- provide and receive timely feedback to and from all department participants and collaboratively work through any difficulties that arise during the course of the planning and implementing of the team-based HR department.

Timeframe for Completion of the Work

By the end of June, 1997, the HR department will have established a team-based organization. During the six months' work of the TT, the TT and OD consultant will keep me regularly apprised of their process, timeline expectations, and resource needs. It is my intention to fully support the work of the TT, and I ask team members to let me know as soon as they know about resource needs other than consultant fees.

It is my expectation that any questions by TT members about the organization's policies or procedures will be discussed with me immediately prior to any formal decisions implemented by the TT.

Team-Building Designs*

One-Day Design

TIME	ACTIVITY/TOPIC
15 min	Warm-up exercise for breaking the ice and getting to know each other better
15 min	What kind of team are we? Discussion of interdependence
60 min	Herrmann Brain Dominance Instrument (Available from Herrmann International, Lake Lure, NC, 28746) Review of the model and the mentality preferences of the group
30 min	Communication: How do we communicate?
30 min	Team development —Post four stages of group development: forming, storming, norming, performing —Using six factors of team development: commitment, purpose, involvement, trust, communication, how we work, conduct a living/moving survey by asking people to stand by group development stage for each factor
60 min	Lunch
90 min	"Value-added" presentations —Individuals prepare presentation on "What I bring or contribute best" and "How am I underused?" Group feedback Individual confirmation
90 min	Needs exchange —"What I need more of from you is …" —"What I want less of from you is…" —"Please do not change…"
30 min	Standard setting —How will we work in the future?
10 min	Closure

---

*Provided by Jim McKnight, OD consultant, California Federal Bank.

Six-Meeting Design

DURATION	TIMING	TOPIC
Meeting I		
4 hr	At your convenience	Review of survey data
		Defining a "team"
		Criteria for teams
		Review of Herrmann Brain Dominance Instrument and communication implications
		Homework: a quality team
Meeting II		
4 hr	2–3 weeks later	How we work
		What makes a quality team?
		Criteria for team membership
		Team membership obligations
		Factors that influence team effectiveness
		Homework: team player survey "Value I bring to the team"
Meeting III		
3 hr	2–3 weeks later	Review of team player survey and implications for team
		Review of "Value I bring" exercise
		Exercise: "What I need you to know about my work and how I work"
		Homework: positive feedback
Meeting IV		
3 hr	2–3 weeks later	Trust
		Treating each other as "prime customer"
		Giving and receiving feedback
		Helping each other to learn (part 1)
		Homework: helping each other to learn (part 2)
Meeting V		
3 hr	2–3 weeks later	Helping each other to learn (part 2)
		Unfinished business
Meeting VI		
3.5 hr	2–3 weeks later	Conflict-resolution workshop

Model for Conflict Management in Teams*

Objectives

- Share with each other individual perceptions of the conflict.
- Produce agreed-upon, working goal statements.
- Contract as to how and when it will be done.

Process

- *Step 1, Individual analysis:* Each person writes what the conflict is about on a piece of chart paper.
- *Step 2, Share individual analysis with everyone:* This is a process of comparing and contrasting perceptions, a process that surfaces differences and encourages understanding of them. The facilitator helps the group devise a single list from the many.
- *Step 3, Parties separate and note their insights on individual analysis sheets:* Look for core or crucial issues and reconceptualize the conflict in writing.
- *Step 4, Joint session to share reconceptualizations:* Everyone shares his or her reframing of the conflict. The facilitator helps the group recognize where agreement exists and where there are still differences. The group needs to come to agreement on the reconceptualization before moving on to the next step.
- *Step 5, Construction of the working goal statements:* At this point, most likely, there will be more than one crucial issue, thus there will need to be more than one goal statement. Divide the group into smaller groups so that groups can work simultaneously on goal statements.

Examples of working goal statements
- We want *X* to stop making impossible promises to our customers.
- We want extra help so we can produce our deliverables to our customers on time.

---

*Provided by Marilyn E. Blair, TeamWork; former internal consultant with 3Com Corporation.

Criteria for goal statements

- *Clear:* stated in plain, simple, distinct, intelligible language
- *Specific:* stated in particular, precise, definite terms
- *Attainable:* goals should be valuable, agreeable, profitable, and advantageous to the organization
- *Depersonalized:* where possible. Stated in words that address the problem rather than the parties involved. Remember, beat up on the problem or issue, not on the individual!

- *Step 6, Share goal statements:* Decide which ones the group wants to problem solve. The facilitator, when recording the goal statements, categorizes them as being related to individual factors, interactional factors, or organizational conditions.

After completing the above steps, look for similarities and build agreed-upon goal statement(s).

- *Step 7, Contract:* Answer the questions about priority (order of working the identified goal statements) and time (how much and when).

At the next meeting use an interactive, problem-solving process. The steps could be

- generate options
- judge options
- test the options for suitability and acceptability
- negotiate differences and agree on solutions
- formulate action plans
- implement action plans
- evaluate the effort.

Role-Clarification Meeting*

The goals of a role-clarification meeting are to
- develop a clear understanding of the team purpose, functions, and processes
- understand clearly team members' roles and responsibilities and how each member can best contribute to the team effort
- identify the strengths and needs of the team and establish a plan for improvement.

Pre-work assignment (to be completed before the meeting)

Possible questions include the following (choose questions based on data collected earlier):

- What do you believe the team expects of you? (What is your official role or function?)
- What do you *actually do* for the team? (Make note of any discrepancies between your official role and what you actually do.)
- What specific difficulties or concerns are you having in working with other team members?
- What do you need to know about other team members or their jobs that would help you perform your role or function on the team?
- What do you believe others should know about you or your role that would help them perform their work?
- What changes in the organization, assignments, or activities do you believe would improve the functioning of the team?
- How have you contributed to the team success or lack of success?
- What do you believe are the team strengths?
- What do you believe are the team limitations or development needs?
- What are the major milestones, problems, and concerns that the team should discuss and resolve?
- What initiatives do you need to take personally that you have been putting off?
- In working with this team, where do you believe your knowledge and talents are being underused?
- In working with this team, where do you believe your knowledge and talents are being overused?

Process

Ask members to share their responses by going around the group one question at a time, discuss the issues, and come to any needed agreements.

---

*Provided by Jim Harley, director, organization development, Westinghouse Electric Company.

New Manager Assimilation Process*

Goals

This process is designed to be used when a group has a new manager. It speeds up the inevitable transition time, which allows for effective leadership. This process requires facilitation by a neutral third party. The purpose of the exercise is to discuss openly

- mutual expectations
- ways that the group can be a resource to the manager
- the manager's operating style
- concerns of the group.

Logistics

The manager invites all team members to the meeting.

Time required: Three hours
Equipment: Flipchart and easel stand

Agenda

10 min   Opening: Manager communicates purpose and structure of meeting. Facilitator reviews agenda and explains process.

45 min   Team brainstorms questions, expectations, and critical advice for the manager.
Manager, in a separate room, lists his or her expectations, operating style, and concerns.

15 min   Break: Allow manager to see flipcharts and prepare response.

---

*Provided by Jan M. Schmuckler, Consultation; former internal consultant with high-technology industry.

1 hr, 45 min   Flipchart items are presented by person who brought up item or by facilitator and manager responds.

Order of discussion:

- Team questions, such as
  Do you plan to reorganize?
  Do you hold one-on-one meetings?
  What changes do you plan to make?
- Team expectations, such as
  We expect you to support us.
  We expect you to hold staff meetings
  at least every two weeks.
- Manager's expectations
  I don't like to be surprised by bad news.
- Manager's operating style
  My style of managing is: I don't want to be
  copied on every problem, etc.
- Manager's concerns

5 min   Closure: Manager thanks group for their candor and advice.

Two-Year Process Improvement Process*

Outline

- description (excerpt below)
- structure (excerpt below)
- roles and responsibilities (excerpt below)
- design of team outcomes (excerpt below)
- communication process
- decision-making process
- resources needed
- estimated budget
- timeline
- design of team guidelines
- training curriculum for design teams
- glossary

Description (excerpt)

We will use a steering committee to provide direction and focus for the redesign efforts. Design teams will be selected and directed to clarify a project's scope, parameters, and goals, and to gain alignment from the steering team. Roles, communication, and decision making are described further in this document.

Baselines and Measurements

Baselines will be established at the front end of the project within the education, definition, and analysis phase. Project consultants will assist the design teams in establishing the criteria and baseline. Baselines will serve as

- measurements for the existing process to help establish improvement goals and targets
- data points for redesign

---

*Provided by Helm Lehmann, author; former OD manager, REI.

- benchmarks against which to measure design efforts and improvements internally and externally for best practices
- measurements will also serve as evaluation tools to gauge post-implementation effectiveness of design team effort. Post-implementation measurements will also serve as baselines for subsequent, ongoing, continuous process-improvement efforts.

Responsibilities and Roles

Steering committee:
- establish mission for design teams
- define focus and scope of redesign efforts
- supply necessary resources
- remove barriers and obstacles
- encourage and reward design-team efforts and contributions to the business goals
- be keepers of the vision and promote change efforts throughout organization
- provide one-on-one guidance to design team leaders
- promote partnerships between team leaders and project consultants.

Project consultants:
- provide guidelines to steering committee and design teams through a formal framework and process for redesign efforts
- establish the plan, do, check, act (PDCA) cycle as the theoretical, continuous process-improvement underpinning for the redesign efforts
- establish effective and productive working relationships with steering committee and design team leaders
- assist team leaders with formation of design teams and be available to consult as needed
- provide or outsource consultation services to project participants as needed
- develop and implement redesign curriculum, methodology, and tools
- assist design teams in formulation of baseline measurements and criteria
- serve as facilitators for design teams and steering committee meetings.

Team leaders:
- select design team members and establish team, customer, and stakeholder roles
- establish team ground rules, mission, and scope of project
- establish process mission, vision, and scope
- lead, direct, and guide design team efforts
- lead, direct, and guide team meetings: agenda, content, deliverables
- be responsible for overall performance of the design team, including implementation and evaluation
- be the information conduit, providing timely progress reports to project champions and steering committee, as well as communications link to design team, customers, stakeholders, and project consultants
- establish working partnerships with project consultants to help achieve project goals

- work with project consultants before and after team meetings to continually improve team effectiveness, efficiency, and productivity
- identify resource needs (people, budget, materials, time, machines, knowledge, skills) to project champions, steering committee, and project consultants as appropriate
- work with project consultants to formulate baseline measurements and criteria
- carry out the redesign process and attain project goals.

Design teams:
- support the leadership of the team leader
- define and analyze the process, including mapping, establishing baselines, and assessing the effectiveness and efficiency
- redesign the process: propose modifications, changes, and implementation plans
- serve as members of implementation team(s)
- be evaluated according to contributions to the overall effectiveness of the team in attaining its goals.

Implementation teams:
- implement process improvements including technical (e.g., management information systems) and social (e.g., HR/work redesign) components
- evaluate process improvements
- launch continuous process-improvement efforts.

Project Outcomes

The consultants see their work as consisting of five phases:
1. planning
2. education, definition, and analysis
3. redesign
4. implementation
5. evaluation/continuous improvement.

Phases 1 and 2 will encompass 80 percent of our start-up efforts and will be the focus for six months. The outcomes for each phase are outlined in table 1.

The roles of consultants will be consultant, educator, trainer, and facilitator. Consultant objectives are to provide the necessary methodology, tools, and ongoing support to help design teams be as efficient, effective, and successful as possible in their work.

Table 1. Outcomes for five phases of consultant projects.

Project phase	Date (projected)	Outcomes	PDCA Cycle
Planning		• Agreement on charter, framework, baseline methodology, design knowledge, and skills curriculum • Assembly of design teams • Begin strategic partnership with team leaders • Assess current projects with associated team leaders	Plan
Education, definition, and analysis		• Teams understand redesign principals, are able to map their process, collect and assess customers' needs, analyze the process and internal/external challenges • Structured site visits conducted	Plan
Redesign		• Proposed process modifications and changes (systems, structure, skills, etc.) to the extent appropriate • Organizational effect assessed • Congruence with organizational goals • Strategies for implementation	Plan
Implementation		• Fail-safe strategies (pilots, early warning systems) • Implementation plans • Evaluation plans	Do
Evaluation		• Evaluation of redesign efforts underway with modifications and continuous process-improvement steps taken	Check Act

Example Plan and Agenda for Restructuring and Cross-Functional Teamwork Consultation*

Here is the draft plan and agenda for the July 17 working session with the XYZ executive management and administrative-support staff. I have incorporated the input from the retreat notes and the meeting on May 12 and would like you to review the agenda and plan to see if they reflect your expectations. After we have discussed and you have finalized them, I can work with AB to get the session agenda and the related materials for pre-work sent out a week before the meeting.

Plan for Working Session

PURPOSE
The purpose of this session is to think through and have an implementation plan for how this group will involve and enlist participation and support from the middle management and supervisory staff across the agency toward the agency restructuring underway and to work collaboratively and intradepartmentally, across functions.

WORKING ASSUMPTIONS
- Continue to build on the teamwork process already underway.
- Acknowledge that this is a new approach and way of working for everyone involved, including this group.
- Work with the information generated from the retreat, from the agency director's meetings with all agency staff, from the various teams and groups working at the departmental level.
- Work with a basic planning model of generating, understanding, sorting, and categorizing of information, analysis, action plan, and evaluation.
- Model the change in behavior and thinking that you are expecting from your staff; get direct involvement of the directors in actually delivering the orientations and running the meeting session with all of them playing roles.

---

*Provided by Perviz Randeria, organization and management development consultant; former internal consultant with city government.

It is important that you have collectively identified and defined which items are relevant for the collaborative team process and have a shared understanding before you follow up with the actual design of the team development process for the next level.

QUESTIONS TO CONSIDER
- What are the critical issues and agendas that your department is working with for the year and what are the expected outcomes of those?
- Where are the performance plans for the department directors and where are those discussed? This would be a good way to narrow down the arenas for collaboration as separated from the direct functional leadership of the department.
- What is the critical work underway that lends itself to collaborative planning and implementation? What are the existing projects that would be opportunities for involving staff across the agency? (Refer to the team handbook and handout from other development projects.)
- How are the department directors already working to demonstrate collaboration across agencies, and what are the issues that are department specific that need to be considered as we design the plan?
- Is there a shared understanding of various team efforts underway that is already moving toward the collaborative, cross-functional model, and what are the benchmarks to check against?
- How do you clearly define and see your change management role and responsibilities as separate from the department-directing responsibilities?
- Are you seeing this group as a reviewing-recommendations body? Is the group facilitating the implementation hurdles of the teams and working groups?
- For the process training of staff teams, are you considering using other resources?
- Do you have to be clear and "charter" a team or group and then shepherd it through to the particular outcomes that the team has to deliver? Can you be a member rather than a leader for the team?

Draft Agenda for Working Session

1. Overview of purpose and outcomes
2. Facilitator role
3. Ground rules/agreements review
4. Information sharing (written responses to pre-work questions)
5. Discussion, clarification, shared understanding
6. Common themes and working through to agreement
7. Actual design of implementation plan
8. Evaluation and next steps

Creating a Vision Process*

Pre-work

Send out reading homework to prepare participants on what a vision statement is and is not.

Session 1
GUIDING PHILOSOPHY
- Recap the chronological history of the organization with a couple of old timers. Present verbally with a handout.
- Identify the core values and beliefs people saw/felt/knew throughout the evolution of the company or unit.
- Identify the present core values and beliefs: "What values and beliefs do we actually hold in our gut today?"

Session 2
PURPOSE STATEMENT
- *Develop a purpose statement:* a one- or two-sentence statement that quickly and clearly conveys how the organization fills basic human needs. Good purpose statements capture the soul of the organization and are considered to be motivating, not differentiating. One leading question here is, "What would the world lose if our company ceased to exist?"

Session 3
ENVIRONMENTAL SCAN
This session requires homework by several individuals, each of whom makes a presentation to the group on one of the following:

- *Macro-environment:* demographic changes, technological, economic, and political factors
- *Industry environment:* structure of the industry, how financed, changes in the degree of governmental regulation, typical products offered by the industry, typical industry marketing strategies and techniques
- *Competitive environment:* competitor profiles, market-segmentation patterns, research and development trends, emergence of new competitors

*Provided by Marilyn E. Blair, TeamWork; former internal consultant with 3Com Corporation.

- *Customer environment:* customer complaints and compliments, return rates, warranty costs, customer needs and concerns
- *Internal environment:* appropriateness of the organization's structure, lessons to be learned from the organization history, climate and culture, distinctive competencies

A group discussion will follow each scan-section presentation.

Session 4

TANGIBLE IMAGE

- Develop the mission statement: "a clear and compelling goal that serves to unify an organization's efforts. An effective mission must stretch and challenge the organization, yet be achievable; focuses the efforts of the organization on a specific goal; needs to be bold, exciting, and emotionally charged. It is crisp, clear, engaging—reaches out and grabs people in the gut. People 'get it' right away; it requires little or no explanation. A good mission is risky, falling in the gray area where reason says, 'This is unreasonable,' and intuition says, '. . . but we believe that we can do it nonetheless.' It is a 'big, hairy, audacious goal'" (Collins & Porras 1994).
- Review four approaches to setting the VISION: targeting, common enemy, role model, and internal transformation.
- Divide the group into small groups of five or six and take the first pass at a mission statement—1.5 hours.
- Groups return and present to the whole. At this point, the consultant is looking for unanimity or threads of commonality to help the group sense and see what might be the mission statement.

Session 5

MISSION STATEMENT, CONTINUED

If possible, conduct this session no more than three or four days after the last session.

- Share random thoughts, images, dreams during from last few days.
- Divide the group into two groups; each group writes a mission statement—30 minutes.
- Reconvene in whole group. Review two statements.
- Work with full group to reach agreement.
- Develop a vivid description: a vibrant, engaging, and specific description of what it will be like when the mission is achieved. It should provoke emotion and generate excitement, transform the mission from words into pictures, and bring it to life. Begin in small groups and bring back work to the whole.

Session 6

SIGN-OFF AND COMMUNICATION PLAN

- Review and signing off on the completed vision.
- Work out the communication plan, make assignments, and set timeframes.

Reference

Collins, J.C., and J.I. Porras. (1994). *Build to Last.* New York: HarperCollins.

For Further Reading

In addition to the many resources listed in the reference notes throughout the chapters of the book, here are some additional recommended resources for internal consultants. This is not an exhaustive list as there are many good resources available. These suggestions are drawn from recently published books the author and other internal consultants have found useful.

Block, P. (1987). *The Empowered Manager*. San Francisco: Jossey-Bass.

Briskin, A. (1996). *The Stirring of Soul in the Workplace*. San Francisco: Jossey-Bass.

Champy, J. (1995). *Reengineering Management: The Mandate for New Leadership*. New York: Harper Business.

Daniels, W.R. (1995). *Breakthrough Performance: Managing for Speed and Flexibility*. Mill Valley, CA: ACT Publishing.

Goleman, D. (1998). *Working with Emotional Intelligence*. New York: Bantam Books.

Hesselbein, F., M. Goldsmith, and R. Beckhard, editors. (1997). *The Organization of the Future*. San Francisco: Jossey-Bass.

Kilmann, R.H. (1989). *Managing Beyond the Quick Fix: A Completely Integrated Program for Creating and Maintaining Organizational Success*. San Francisco: Jossey-Bass.

Lipnack, J., and J. Stamps. (1997). *Virtual Teams: Reaching Across Space, Time and Organizations with Technology*. New York: John Wiley & Sons.

McLagen, P., and C. Nel. (1995). *The Age of Participation*. San Francisco: Berrett-Koehler Publishers.

Oshry, B. (1995). *Seeing Systems: Unlocking the Mysteries of Organizational Life*. San Francisco: Berrett-Koehler Publishers.

Robinson, D.G., and J.C. Robinson, contributor. (1995). *Performance Consulting: Moving Beyond Training*. San Francisco: Berrett-Koehler Publishers.

Rummler, G.A., and A.P. Brache. (1991). *Improving Performance: How to Manage the White Space on the Organization Chart*. San Francisco: Jossey-Bass.

Schein, E.H. (1992). *Organizational Culture and Leadership* (2d edition). San Francisco: Jossey-Bass.

Tannen, D. (1994). *Talking from 9 to 5: How Women's and Men's Conversational Styles Affect Who Gets Heard, Who Gets Credit, and What Gets Done at Work*. New York: William Morrow.

Terry, R.W. (1993). *Authentic Leadership: Courage in Action*. San Francisco: Jossey-Bass.

Tichy, N.M. (1983). *Managing Strategic Change: Technical, Political, and Cultural Dynamics*. New York: McGraw-Hill.

Ulrich, D., editor. (1998). *Delivering Results*. Cambridge, MA: Harvard Business Review.

Wellins, R.S., W.C. Byham, and G.R. Dixon. (1995). *Inside Teams: How 20 World Class Organizations Are Winning Through Teamwork*. San Francisco: Jossey-Bass.

About the Author

As a consultant to organizations and senior leaders, Bev Scott brings clarity, focus, integrity, and a sense of purpose to her work. She has over 25 years of experience in a full range of organizational and management development services, including organization change efforts, management-development systems and programs, and guidance of management teams. Her goal is to promote organizational effectiveness and employee satisfaction through the use of team building, problem solving, skill building, leadership development, employee involvement, and survey feedback. In her current practice, Bev Scott Consulting, her work focuses on leadership development, executive coaching, large system change, and development of internal consultants.

Bev has used her consulting experience in the private, public, and volunteer sectors. She served for 15 years as the director of organization and management development for McKesson Corporation. Before joining McKesson, she was a development consultant for Bendix Corporation. She was also a senior consultant for Consulting Associates and a partner in Change—both Michigan-based consulting firms specializing in HRD.

Bev wrote with Ronald Kregoski *Quality Circles,* an extensive "how-to" manual published in 1982. She has collaborated on assertiveness skill manuals and published articles in trade journals on change and employee involvement. She served as editor of *Vision/Action,* the professional journal for the Bay Area Organization Development Network for five years.

She is active in the Organization Development Network at the local and national levels. She is serving currently as the chair-elect of the Network's national board of trustees. She was program co-chair for the 1985 national conference held in San Francisco and was a member of the program committee for the 1997 national conference in Scottsdale, Arizona. She has presented her work at the national conferences of the Organization Development Network and the American Society for Training & Development. She has served as a speaker and facilitator for many professional association meetings.

Bev is listed in *Who's Who in the World, Who's Who of American Women, International Who's Who of Professional and Business Women,* and *Most Admired Men and Women of the Year.* She has master's degrees in sociology and HRD and has completed doctoral coursework at the University of Michigan.

Bev lives and works in San Francisco. When she is not consulting to organizations, she enjoys gardening, the theater, walking, hiking, and traveling with her partner. She can be reached through her Website at www.bevscott.com.